NATIONALISM AND IDENTITY

ABOUT THE AUTHOR

Stefano Harney is a graduate of Harvard University, New York University and the University of Cambridge, where he received his Ph.D. He has taught cultural studies, the sociology of culture and post-colonial literature and literary theory in the West Indies and at the University of Cambridge. Having worked as an education and cultural policy consultant, he is currently an Assistant Professor of Social Sciences at Pace University in New York. He has published in numerous scholarly journals, including *Journal of American Studies*, *Journal of Ethno-Development*, *Journal of Commonwealth Literature* and *European Journal for Intercultural Studies*.

NATIONALISM AND IDENTITY

*Culture and the Imagination
in a Caribbean Diaspora*

STEFANO HARNEY

UNIVERSITY OF THE WEST INDIES
Kingston

ZED BOOKS
London & New Jersey

Nationalism and Identity was first published in 1996 by
Zed Books Ltd, 7 Cynthia Street, London N1 9JF, UK, and
165 First Avenue, Atlantic Highlands, New Jersey 07716, USA

and in the West Indies by the University of the West Indies,
1 Aqueduct Flats, Mona, Kingston 7, Jamaica.

Zed Books gratefully acknowledges that earlier versions of chapters of
this book appeared in the following journals: Chapter 1: *Commonwealth*
(vol. 13, no. 2, 1991); Chapter 2: *World Literature Written in English* (Spring
1993); Chapter 3: *Journal of Commonwealth Literature* (vol. 25, no. 1, 1990);
Chapter 4: *European Journal for Intercultural Studies* (Spring 1994); Chapter
5: *Journal of West Indian Literature* (vol. 6, no. 1, 1993); Chapter 7: *Journal
of Ethno-Development* (Spring 1990).

Typeset in Monotype Baskerville by Lucy Morton, London SE12
Printed and bound in the United Kingdom
by Redwood Books, Trowbridge, Wiltshire.

A catalogue record for this book is available from the British Library
US CIP data is available from the Library of Congress

Zed ISBN 1 85649 375 X (Hb)
ISBN 1 85649 376 8 (Pb)

University of the West Indies ISBN 976 640 016 4

Cataloguing in Publication Data (Jamaica)
Harney, Stefano
Nationalism and identity : culture and the imagination in a
Caribbean diaspora / Stefano Harney.
p. cm.
Includes bibliographical references
ISBN 976 640 016 4
1. Nationalism and literature – Trinidad and Tobago. 2. Nationalism
and literature – Caribbean, English-speaking. 3. Ethnicity in literature
– Trinidad and Tobago. 4. Trinidad and Tobago, literature – History
and criticism. 5. Postmodernism (literature) – Trinidad and
Tobago. I. Title.
PR 9272.H37 1995   813–dc20

Contents

Acknowledgements

I would like to thank the staff of the West Indiana Collection at the University of the West Indies, St Augustine, Trinidad, for their kindness and help. My thanks also to my cousins, Edlyn and Emma MacIntosh, and to Carl Thorpe, for all their support. I would like to thank Dr Susan Benson, my supervisor at Cambridge, and Professor Martin Kilson and Dr Jagdish Gundara, who inspired me to finish. My editor at Zed Books, Carol-Anne Bois, also supported me with long-distance advice. This book is dedicated to the memories of my father, Professor Robert F. Harney, and my father-in-law, Norris P. Joseph. They never met, but they meet in this book.

And to Alice.

SH

In the early 1960s, during the gripping years that saw the birth of the independent state of Trinidad and Tobago, the great Marxist thinker C.L.R. James threw himself into an endless series of talks and public lectures upon his return to his native land. At the Port of Spain public library on a humid afternoon, or under a corrugated roof of a union hall in Pointe-a-Pierre, James strove to define a nation for its people, to give them back their history, and to give them what he called a future in the present. 'The good life', James told his audience, 'is that community between the individual and the state; the sense that he belongs to the state and the state belongs to him ... the citizen's alive when he feels that he himself in his own national community is overcoming difficulty.'[1] In those heady days, and in the difficult years to come, James would add this important provision: 'the nation we are building needs also the supreme artist'.[2]

The nation of Trinidad and Tobago has not always – either before or after its independence – been a community of individual and state; and despite the talent and faith of its people it has not been a national community in which citizens are always able to overcome difficulties. But Trinidad and Tobago *has* had supreme artists. And those artists, as James would have been quick to point out, have risen from the artistic genius of the people, and become urgent examples of that genius. The project of nationhood and an abiding peoplehood has been difficult for Trinidad and Tobago. But the supreme artists, products and directors of this difficult project – writers, poets, calypsonians, carnival mas-makers (carnival costume designers) – represent the advancement of that Jamesian ideal, that harmonious community of individual and state.

In their concern for national community, in their testing of individual vision in community, in their writing of the national text and reading of the national discourse, the artists and writers of Trinidad provide the student of Caribbean nation-states with supreme material for analysis – and a supreme conundrum. Their texts become the effort in language of making a nation: direct descendants of those humid afternoons in the public libraries and those countless rain-beaten nights in the South during which the great Trinidadian dreamers of nationhood – C.L.R. James, Adrian Rienzi, Uriah Butler, or Eric Williams – stood before excited or indifferent crowds and for a moment, in the heavy heat or the heavy dark, saw a people.

Trinidad and Tobago is a nation of only 1.2 million people; but, in addition to a vibrant culture of calypso and soca music, mas-making and religious celebration, political and labour debate, it holds a wealth of novelists well beyond its share. From international stars like V.S. Naipaul and Derek Walcott (St Lucian by birth) to local organic intellectuals like Merle Hodge and Earl Lovelace, the two islands have been imagined and re-imagined as communities in dozens of novels over the last forty years. This study looks to harness those imaginations in the service of a discussion and analysis of the process of nation-building in a Caribbean nation-state; and to understand the complexities of personal identity, race, belonging, and peoplehood in a modern multicultural New World nation.

As a sociology of literature, and an exercise in cultural studies, this book emphasizes the societal and historical content of literary texts. As the Martiniquan Frantz Fanon wrote, 'culture abhors simplification', and it may be that the weaknesses of literary texts as raw material for general social analysis – their indeterminacy and their individuality – are in fact strengths in the pursuit of the concepts of nationhood and peoplehood, concepts that often defy hard data and reasoned argument, as some of the studies on nationalism cited in this work will attest. Indeed, it might even be argued that literary texts have a unique advantage in the interrogation of the nation. As Jacques Derrida has phrased it,

while literature shares a certain power and a certain destiny with
jurisdiction, with the juridico-political production of institutional foundations, the constitutions of States, fundamental legislation, and even
the law, it can also exceed them, interrogate them, fictionalize them:
with nothing, or almost nothing, in view, of course, and by producing
events whose reality or duration is never assured, but which by that
very fact are more thought-provoking.[3]

Reading the Nation

To help with the reading of national identity and belonging in
these texts, I will draw on different sources of thought and study.
I hope in their combination to produce something new, something
that can approximate the strange alchemy of post-colonial nationalism in the Caribbean: part economics, part politics, part ethnic
ghosts and visions, part daily practice. At the same time, their
combinations point to weaknesses in each, point to partly ob-
structed views of nationalism and identity in the Caribbean. The
case studies of writers utilize these sources of thought and study,
but also interrogate them, and I introduce these sources with the
understanding that they will be taken up critically in the studies.

I will conclude this introduction by providing a first reading of
the socio-historical context of Trinidadian nationhood, giving an
explanation for the selection of Trinidadian writers and texts, before
moving on to specific case studies of literature and nationalism.

I am pursuing what I will term habitable texts of identity for
the Trinidadian writer, and the Trinidadian citizen. These habitable texts are often contained in the written text, but not contained
by that writing. Gayatri Spivak has suggested that 'the text [in]
the sense we use it, is not just books. It refers to the possibility
that every socio-political, psycho-sexual phenomenon is organized
by, woven by many, many strands that are discontinuous, that come
from way off, that carry their histories within them, and that are
not within our control. We are inserted in them.' She concludes
that 'we have no alternative but to involve ourselves and mire
ourselves in what we are calling the textuality of the socius. The
real task here is to displace and undo that killing opposition between the text narrowly conceived as the verbal text and activism
narrowly conceived as some sort of mindless engagement.'[4] The

real task of this book is to uncover habitable texts that do link the words of a novel to a way of living and being in the world in Trinidad, and in its diaspora.

A good deal has been written about the creative literature of the Caribbean. What came to be known as the West Indian Renaissance in the English-speaking Caribbean and its metropoles (chiefly London at that time) was nurtured and heralded by both West Indian and metropolitan critics of the same generation in the 1950s and the 1960s. As young Trinidadian novelists like V.S. Naipaul and Samuel Selvon came to the attention of British readers, critics like Kenneth Ramchand, Edward Baugh, G.R. Coulthard and Louis James began a process of analysing and championing the new literature. The critical writing tended to restrict itself to a mixture of formal textual analysis and social analysis. It was committed, intelligent writing, focused on a region, a people, and the aspirations of a new national literature that many of them saw as integral to the high aspirations of the English-speaking Caribbean and its struggle for independence and identity. Such optimism in the late 1950s and early 1960s regarding Caribbean, or at least English-speaking West Indian, nationalism was reasonable in the years around the granting of independence to many of the colonial West Indian islands. The brief life of the West Indian Federation – a nascent nation-state incorporating most of the Eastern Caribbean and Jamaica – contributed to this sense of regional awakening. Yet in this study many of the younger writers, like Earl Lovelace or Willi Chen, write against the disintegration of this critical vision, against a political nationalism – pan-Caribbean or otherwise. Indeed, refuge in a more cultural nationalism – less state-bound, less political – leads to a second generation of critics and writers free to dream of a wider Caribbean nationalism based only on culture. Without the constraints of political pan-Caribbeanism, a younger generation of scholars like Marjorie Thorpe and Frank Birbalsingh retain a way of looking at symbols and events in the novel to divine the past and future of the Caribbean. The map of the region has grown beyond the boundaries of language, to encompass the French- and Spanish-speaking Caribbean; but more importantly it has become increasingly cultural, and perhaps fictional.[5] This study will test the reality of pan-Caribbean identity against the reality of the nation-state.

Post-Colonial Theory

In recent years the novels and poems of Trinidad and the Caribbean have been subjected to a new kind of literary criticism. This criticism revolves less around a nation, a region, or even a culture, and more around a set of theories, viewing novels written by Trinidadians as part of a larger discourse on post-colonialism, the centre versus the periphery, Europe and the other, language as a contested terrain of Third-World versus industrialized powers. I will call this body of work 'high theory'. The critics involved in these recodings and redefinitions do not adhere to a single politics or even a single strain of literary theory. But, for my purposes, they can be grouped by their common concern for a 'world-systems theory' of new literatures, rather than an interest in the socio-historical struggles of individual nation-states like Trinidad. Their work is nonetheless valuable to my study, as much for what it does not grant Trinidad and its writers as for the invitation it offers to those writers to join a worldwide movement. The subfield of high theory, post-colonial literary theory, has enjoyed a boom in the last few years. Leaving aside the number of literary journals that encourage this theoretical trend, at least half a dozen collections of essays have been published in the last three years alone. The most sophisticated of these is *Nation and Narration*, edited by Homi K. Bhabha. Bhabha's own essay on the importance of migrants in redefining what he calls the 'nation-space' will be useful to this study, and I will try to draw out the some of the unexplored consequences of migration for nation-building in the nation-space of the sending country,[6] but Bhabha's book represents only a small fraction of what is a virtual industry in this criticism.[7] Bhabha's writings and the work of Fredric Jameson on post-colonialism will be explored in the chapter on Earl Lovelace's writing, and much of the remaining high theory will be scrutinized in the chapter on Naipaul.[8] As welcome as the attention must be to Caribbean writers, in this book I suggest that it amounts to a neo-colonial exploitation in post-colonial theory.

Competing for attention in the new commerce of post-colonial literary theory is the growing body of work specifically focused on Caribbean women writers.[9] These works insist on a concrete, historical analysis of women of colour in the Caribbean, and they implicitly reject any theory that obscures that specificity or alienates ordinary working women from literature or criticism. In many ways, although there are elements of Julia Kristeva and Michel Foucault running through some of these essays and introductory texts, these works continue the tradition in the Caribbean of locally based, committed social criticism of literature, and the mission of publicizing that literature and its social commentary. In the chapter on Valerie Belgrave, I concentrate on the habitable text of gender that so many Caribbean women, and a few men, take as their project.

Theories of Nationalism

Anthony D. Smith has written that 'nation-building describes succinctly what Third World elites are trying to do. If anything nation-building is the basic Third World ideology and project.'[10] Literary critic Tim Brennan extends the centrality of nation-building to the imagination of the artist, writing that 'from the late 1940s, with a Europe weakened by war and decolonisation in full swing, the empowering image for many Third World intellectuals has been the nation.'[11] Theorists on nationalism and ethnic relations agree that the idea of the nation and the task of nation-building has been at the centre of the discourse in most Third World nations for the last forty years at least, but they agree on little else. I believe that the Trinidadian writers in this study reveal specific historical conditions that allow us to test a number of the theories on nationalism and ethnic relations, especially those put forward by European scholars. The complexity of the nationalist discourse in multicultural, multiracial Third World and New World nations like Trinidad and Tobago will challenge the flexibility of the best of these theories. The novelists of Trinidad face the same challenge in imagining their nation. I will analyse the efforts of these novelists to envision their nation in light of the efforts of many theorists, including Anthony D. Smith, Eric Hobsbawm, Benedict Anderson, M.G. Smith, Donald Horowitz, Anthony Giddens and Ernest Gellner. But I will do so without prior commitment to any of the arguments about blood and belonging that are currently enjoying a surge in popularity. This disclaimer is important because I do not want the reader to suppose that the use of novelists, of culture and art, points to a bias on my part (or that of these writers) for the affective arguments of nationalism. On the contrary, I believe that the novelists of the Caribbean, as this study will show, are more conscious of the pull of the political and economic organizing forces of nationalism than many scholars in the field. At the same time, they are more ambivalent about the nation itself, be it created for production or springing from the ancient songs of the heart.

In 1985, Ian Smart wrote a study called *Central American Writers of West Indian Origin: A New Hispanic Literature*, in which he identified yet another strand in the diaspora of Caribbean culture and writing.[12] The book records the historical movement of Caribbean labour to Central and South American capital. Smart illustrates the danger of confusing terms like 'nation', 'nation-state' and 'peoplehood'. Theorists speak of interactive ethnicities, of changing boundaries, but the Caribbean diaspora, dispersed around the globe but often looking home in its imagination, presents a formidable task of understanding the limits and meanings of terms like 'the Caribbean people' or 'the Trinidadian nation'. The theorists of nationalism and post-colonial literary theorists rarely match the writers featured in this study in their understanding of the diasporic, tentative nature of the nation, nor in their attention to the ethnogenesis and repluralization that diaspora implies. Richard Jenkins has noted that 'much that is of interest has been written recently on nationalism, some of it by anthropologists, [e.g. Anderson, 1983; Breuilly, 1982; Gellner, 1983; Lewis, 1983] but there is little doubt that more remains to be done, particularly with respect to the emergent nation-states of the ex-colonial Third World.'[13] I have undertaken to fill a small part of that gap, but I found the brilliant imagined nations of Third World novelists already waiting there.

Caribbean Studies

Stuart Hall has written recently in *New Left Review* that 'identity is not in the past to be found, but in the future to be constructed.'[14] He adds that he does not believe that the people of the Caribbean should abandon their project of recovering the past; but he also cautions that old identities should not be taken literally, but rather used 'as the different musics out of which a Caribbean sound might someday come.' The best sociology, history and anthropology of the Caribbean involves this kind of construction.[15]

Indeed the novelists in the study start from a distinct advantage in this respect. They are highly conscious of their construction, as are we. But in the social sciences, or in what I am calling Caribbean Studies, the construction is not always apparent, or apparently admitted. Whether we are speaking of Dr Eric Williams and his historical studies, or of Lloyd Brathwaite and M.G. Smith in sociology, novelists are important guides to uncovering the false naturalness of the subject in the social sciences. Dr Eric Williams, first prime minister of an independent Trinidad, was also the pre-eminent historian of his new nation. *From Columbus to Castro* and *Capitalism and Slavery* are scholarly bench-marks that do not hide the nationalist leader in Williams.[16] In the former work he calls for a psychological revolution, having devoted five hundred pages to the often grim history of the region, – five hundred pages of emplotment, as Hayden White would say. The insightful sociology of Lloyd Brathwaite and M.G. Smith, combined with more recent race-related studies like those of John La Guerre, and those that fill the recent volume *India in the Caribbean*, are also emplotments.[17] Nor can the few anthropological essays that also exist, particularly that by Stephen Glazier on urban street culture, and that by Michael Lieber on religion in a rural town in Trinidad, escape this charge.[18] Even the most recent contribution to the field of Caribbean Studies relevant to this study, *Trinidad Ethnicity*, edited by Kelvin Yelvington, seeks a truth about identity and whether it can best be discovered by native or foreign scholars, in a way that neglects the constructed nature of the social sciences.[19] Writers like V.S. Naipaul throw cold water on this approach. Somebody, whether Shango Priest, Oxford-educated poet, or British Petroleum, is out there imagining identity, not making truth. And as writers like Naipaul are quick to point out about their nation, that somebody is usually virtually everybody.

In David Maughan-Brown's *Land, Freedom, and Fiction: History and Ideology in Kenya*, the author concludes his study of Kenyan novels by stating that 'the literary cannot properly be understood in isolation from the political and my analysis of the fiction of the Mau Mau should ... have justified my contention that the literary is ... an ideal site for research into the operations of ideological interpellation.'[20] I look to the novels of Trinidad to be a similarly appropriate site for studying the constructions of nationalism and peoplehood in the Caribbean.

Readings of Trinidad

This introduction must also say something about the 'land' of Trinidad and Tobago, and I intend that term to convey both its physical and mythological meaning. In a sense, this entire study and the writings of each of the artists considered are obsessed with this description of the islands of Trinidad and Tobago. I approach any description of the place as Italo Calvino approached the description of his city, Venice. He has admitted that his masterful book *Invisible Cities*, with its myriad tales of fabled cities told to Kubla Khan by Marco Polo, is nothing more (or less) than an attempt to capture his own city, Venice, in all its appearances and imaginations.[21] Recognizing that, for a study like this one, there is no Venice, no Trinidad, except in the telling, it would be worthwhile to keep in mind some of the most famous attempts to imagine these invisible islands.

Dr Eric Williams, trained as an economic historian, and called on to be an independence leader, saw his Trinidad from this perspective – a place of restricted and unfair economic development where at the time of his birth in 1911 there was 'cocoa the reigning queen, sugar the ex-king, oil the future emperor' and the 'crown colony legislature fostered and promoted British interests at the expense of Trinidadian. It did this either positively, as in its vigorous support of the sugar and oil industries, or negatively, as in its subordination of the cocoa industry or its passive indifference or active hostility to the small farmer.'[22] But even the Doc's Trinidad was not made fully visible by these economic and political relations and he suggests another Trinidad, a visceral and carnal one. The first chapter of his autobiography takes 1911, the year of his birth, as a starting point for the opening survey of Trinidad's economic history. He writes barely seven pages on that history at the opening of the book. He does not introduce himself or explain the significance of the date 1911 until the second chapter (and then only in passing). And suddenly, on the seventh page, another Trinidad emerges on the site of the first Trinidad of colonial tax collection and capital accumulation among the poor. 'West Indian society has inherited a tradition of immorality from the slave system', writes Williams, and he continues:

> the Portuguese rumshop keeper or the Chinese shopkeeper with his black partner was as familiar and notorious in Port-of-Spain as the sun at noonday ... the Trinidad calypso has immortalised the efficiency of the permutations and the fecundity of the combinations which swelled the island's illegitimacy statistics and bequeathed to later generations that exasperating colour complex which became for so long one of the most powerful centrifugal forces in the life of the island.[23]

Another Trinidad emerges: not a land described by cocoa and sugar production, but a land that cannot be entered with old concepts of colour and race, a land that must be imagined as a 'fecundity of combinations' that the world has not seen.

I draw on these competing attempts by Eric Williams to envision Trinidad because Williams was concerned with building a nation. For this task he needed a people and he needed an independent economy.[24] He imagined Trinidad accordingly and he inscribed his invisible islands with these needs. This tension between the idea of a nation as an independent, unfettered political whole, and the idea of a nation as a people is one that challenges the writers and scholars in this study. Some are inspired by the fecundity of the people, others bewildered by it, and still others deny the notion of peoplehood as nation, seeking the nation instead in history and politics. But beneath all these imagined Trinidads lies the tension between the nation as peoplehood and the nation as state. It is the particular genius of many of these writers that this tension is itself undermined, in the manner of a Derridean difference, by the profusion of images and visions that are neither wholly of people nor of state.

V.S. Naipaul has never seen the nation as his home. His search for community, and for meaning in his Caribbean post-colonial existence, has been no less exacting however. Asked to describe Trinidad, he dwelled on neither economics nor complexions but plunged into the early Spanish colonial history of the islands, imagining a place of cruelty and beauty, seeking a psychological explanation for the nation he finds so inadequate. His invisible islands live and die never knowing the islands of Eric Williams. But he gives us another reading of Trinidad, and one that does not entirely escape, as Naipaul himself has not, the search for the nation. In his history of Trinidad, *The Loss of El Dorado*,[25] the bitter brilliance comes from decentring the ideas of nation as either a primordial or evolving sense of peoplehood, or as a necessary arrangement of capital and labour, with a kind of psychological interrogation that is too rational to be accused of seeking the national psyche and too heartfelt to be reduced to a materialist reading.

For Naipaul, the attempt to envision his invisible Trinidad involves a search of the records. He looks to the early settlement and use of the islands as a base for a Spanish search for El Dorado; and later he concentrates on the British attempt to inspire revolution in Spanish Latin America, again from Port of Spain. What is so haunting about Naipaul's search for the invisible Trinidad is that, even though envisioned, it remains for him invisible; imagined again and again, it remains, unimaginable, much like the historically correct story that obsesses him of Luisa Calderon, the slave girl tortured to death by the English governor and his cronies. For Naipaul, Trinidad exists without historical fact; the evidence of life stories, and all attempts to describe the place, flicker in the powerlessness and marginality of its past. Of the Spanish opportunity to create an early written history of the island, he writes:

> of all these journeys little remains. The conquistador who found nothing had nothing to report. Believing in wonders, he had no gift of wonder.... To the conquistador, where there were no wonders there was nothing. A place was then its name alone, and landscape was land, difficult or easy ... the spareness of much Spanish narrative is a Spanish deficiency. Untouched by imagination or intellect, great actions become mere activity.[26]

Naipaul is no kinder to the English who take over administration of the islands two hundred years later. 'In the Spanish–French– African city of planters, launch-captains, soldiers, slaves, whores, keepers of grog-shops and retail shops selling salt, tobacco and dried meat for peons, the early English immigrants had been new and startlingly', wrote Naipaul of the new British administration of an essentially non-British culture at the turn of the nineteenth century. 'They dominated naturally. This liveliness – the threat of letters to London lawyers and newspapers, the affirmation of rights and freedoms – was a carry-over from the metropolis.' But Naipaul believes that even this brief stir of intellectual liveliness was undone by the immorality and absence in the islands' history.

> In the slave society, where self-fulfilment came so easily, this liveliness began to be perverted and then to fade, and the English saw their preeminence, more simply, as a type of racial magic.... The English in Trinidad became like the French. The quality of controversy declined, and the stature of men. What was left was a colony.[27]

Naipaul has been sharply criticized for finding no joy in the wealth of African- and Catholic-inspired festivals and arts in Trinidadian history. But for Naipaul, that history, passed down in oral and performance culture, remains as invisible and enslaved to the viciousness and marginality of the colony's history as the torpor and dullness of European intellectual activity there. Naipaul imagines the history of Trinidad as a psychological absence in the mind of the nation. I will try to show in a later chapter how this reading does not escape the discourse on nationalism, but for now I present it simply as another Trinidad living among many.

There are more conventional histories of Trinidad that try to envision these islands, and in so doing give us new readings of the nation. Radical historian James Millette attempts an interesting union of Trinidad's diverse peoples with its sad history of dictatorial colonial administration. He notes that Trinidad owes much of its diverse European tradition to the mass influx of a planter class from French West Indian islands, following a cedula, published in 1783 by the Spanish Crown, that invited Catholic immigrants to help populate Trinidad. 'The security and scope which Trinidad offered to non-white property owners was unrivalled', writes Millette explaining the results of this cedula, the immigration of thousands of coloured and even black landowners and often slave-owners.[28] But this diversity and this tolerance were to condemn Trinidad in the eyes of its new master, Britain. British colonial policy favoured limited assembly power for colonies with land-holders able to vote and sit in a parliament. As Millette observed, from 1810 up until Williams's birth and beyond to the labour agitation of the 1930s, Britain would deny this unique, mixed colony representation for fear of encouraging racial and religious equality.[29] And the French Republican fires that would smoulder periodically through its history only strengthened British resolve to deny representative government.

From Millette's reading of the colonial history of people and land, we could turn to historian Bridget Brereton's reading of another invisible Trinidad, another submerged nation. 'Large numbers were involved in Indian (indentured) immigration to Trinidad: over the whole period, 1845–1917, a total of 143,939 people came to the island', writes Brereton of the latest of a long string of immigrants to Trinidad, following on the heels of 2,500 Chinese and hundreds of Madeiran Portuguese to the fields of Trinidad's plantations, still haunted by the ghost of slavery. Brereton suggests that

> the Indians entered what was an essentially hostile environment, and the host society became even less sympathetic as time went on and it became clear that they would be a permanent element in the population. Planters, officials, upper-class whites, educated coloured and black Creoles and the black working class all, to different degrees and for different reasons, reacted unsympathetically to the arrival of the Indians.[30]

Thus Brereton emplots a history of the Trinidadian nation centred around the arrival of groups and their interaction, an attractive emplotment for any study of the emergence of peoplehood on these islands.

But there is another method of imagining Trinidad, again germane to this study, and that is to inscribe the history of the nation's creative imagination. Brereton shifts to this method in her final chapter, 'Free At Last'. Brereton notes that 'political decolonization (1962) was accompanied by a remarkable cultural renaissance, an upsurge of popular creativity that developed a new cultural identity which was Creole and national in orientation.'[31] She identifies pioneering dancer Beryl McBurnie in this cultural vision of Trinidad as one of the leading figures in this renaissance in Trinidad (and the West Indies as a whole) ... who began research on West Indian folk dances in the late 1930s and opened, in 1948, the first Little Carib Theatre in a shack situated in her own backyard in Woodbrook, a middle-class suburb in Port-of-Spain. Here she organized and presented folk dances based on Trinidad and Tobago's rich multi-cultural heritage, jeopardizing her standing in the city's coloured middle class (to which she belonged by birth) by her active participation in African dances and her co-operation with young dancers of all ethnic backgrounds.

McBurnie has herself written of her influences in this new national dance; she remembers that 'on V.J. Day, the Chinese Association held high in the street a lovely dragon, the symbol of their famous dragon dance'. This dance is mixed in memory for her with the 'Muslim dance of the kissing moons', with the sad sound of the Portuguese fado she hears echoing in calypsos, with parang guitar music from Venezuela, and with what she calls, 'the naughty dances brought by the French'.[32] Like many of the writers in this study, McBurnie's text resonates, as Gayatri Spivak might say, with Brereton's scholarly text.

Brereton's solid history of Trinidad is a history of groups, which turns to a contemporary history of culture by the book's end. It could be said that it moves from groups to nation, from the importation of cultures to the making of culture. It is at the level of national culture that we might sample one more historical vision of Trinidad. Michael Anthony is one of Trinidad's most talented novelists, and one of the subjects of Chapter 1 of this book, but he is also a popular local historian. His book *Glimpses of Trinidad and Tobago* takes up where Brereton leaves off, taking us on a cultural tour through the history of modern Trinidad. In one chapter Anthony interviews the elderly calypsonian Lord Beginner. 'They didn't think much of us', says Lord Beginner of the calypsonian around the time of the First World War. 'Now calypso is looked upon as an art. Which it is. But in those days not so. You couldn't get into the newspapers even if you made a somersault. They didn't like us and that's that.'[33] Anthony and Lord Beginner create a portrait of a nation struggling to emerge and express itself culturally; Trinidad as the history of artists speaking of Trinidad. But what all these histories give us, whether they be economic, political, cultural or social, is a sense of the futility of trying to describe the land of Trinidad in a satisfactory manner. It is even more difficult to describe the nation submerged in that land.

The political sociologist Ivar Oxaal attempts a transparent description for the setting of his study, *Black Intellectuals and the Dilemmas of Race and Class in Trinidad*. He calls his descriptive chapter 'A Sociologist's Baedeker to Trinidad and Tobago'. 'Despite the existence of first-class roads throughout contemporary Trinidad', writes Oxaal in 1967, 'the island today, as always, turns its back on the Atlantic and is developing chiefly along the western coast facing the Gulf of Paria. The most important functional areas, and correspondingly, the areas of greatest population density, are located within a richly endowed north-south crescent which runs from the northwestern to southwestern tips of the island.' Oxaal continues:

> these areas, from top to bottom, contain the former U.S. naval base at Chaguaramas Bay, with its excellent deep-water harbour, two major storage areas from which bauxite from Guyana and Surinam is trans-shipped; Port-of-Spain, the administrative and commercial capital; the sugar belt, which extends from just south of the capital's suburbs and on south past the town of San Fernando; the oil refineries and oil-producing region, which begins just to the north of San Fernando and extends down into the southwestern peninsula and out into the Gulf of Paria.

And Oxaal completes the picture with the suggestion that 'if one visits the North Post wireless station on the hilly northern shore above the suburbs of Port-of-Spain, one can easily discern the silver glitter of the Texaco storage tanks at Point-a-Pierre.' From Point-a-Pierre it is easy to see the Venezuelan mainland.[34] Again, the intertextuality of this passage is enlightening. Oxaal, the sociologist, moves out of sociology, and is moved to a traveller's description, very much like Naipaul's in tone, reminding the reader, as Naipaul often does, of the intimacy, the closeness, the public visibility that becomes so claustrophobic for Naipaul.

Finally C.L.R. James reminds us of the role of sport in the West Indies and in the imagining of a nation called Trinidad and Tobago. 'What do they know of cricket who only cricket know?', he begins in a famous phrase.

> West Indians crowding to Tests bring with them the whole past history and future hopes of the islands. English people, for example, have a

conception of themselves breathed from birth. Drake and mighty Nelson, the few who did so much for so many, the success of parliamentary democracy, those and such as those constitute a national tradition. Underdeveloped countries have to go back centuries to rebuild one. We of the West Indies have none at all, none that we know of. To such people the three W's, Ram and Val wrecking English batting, help to fill a huge gap in their consciousness and in their needs.[35]

Trinidad Imagined

What emerges from these invisible Trinidads? Two islands, discovered by Columbus, colonized ineffectively for two hundred years by the Spanish, decimating the Arawak and Carib aboriginals, planted by French-speaking whites, coloureds and blacks, worked first by enslaved blacks, then Chinese, Portuguese and East Indians. A nation first of cocoa, then sugar, then oil, where union agitation in the 1930s was diffused and independence achieved gradually, led by a coloured middle class. Black Power riots in 1970 marked a shift toward nationalization and also entailed the second major attempt, after the union agitation of the 1930s, to unite African and Indian citizens, who represent, respectively, roughly 40 per cent and 40–45 per cent of the population (with large mixed elements) of 1.2 million. And finally, the oil bust in the 1980s, mass migration to Canada and the United States, and a new diaspora in Toronto, Brooklyn and Miami watching with disbelief an attempted coup in 1990. And finally, an emergent nation, bursting with music, sport, dance, religion, literature and carnival. A people engaged every day, not only going back, as James has said, centuries to rebuild a consciousness, but going forward into the mystery of a new identity. It is into this land and into this search that the writers of this study are born. They spend more time and more energy in the quest than most of their fellow citizens, and if we hope to make visible a Trinidadian nation, to see the challenges, contradictions and triumphs of that nation, we must turn to their imaginations.

These writers and their texts will serve in this study as the basis for a discussion of nationalism in Trinidad and Tobago. I will try to extend their observations and to merge them. But I do not want to pretend that Trinidadian writers write solely about the

Trinidadian nation, nor that the idea of the nation stops at the border of legal nation-states. Without opening a debate in this introduction about the proper unit of study for a national literature – language, region, ethnic group, or nation – I would like to set these writers within the context of the development and flowering of Caribbean literature in this century.

Readings of the Caribbean

Recently Roberto Marquez has spoken of 'a uniquely Caribbean genesis' and confirmed that 'Caribbean literature has obviously reached [its] moment of maturity and conscious self-perception', and asserted that this literature 'argues the presence of a Caribbean ethos – and aesthetic – whose elements cohere beyond the limiting colonial, specifically national, or strictly linguistic [boundaries]'. Marquez argues that this Caribbean ethos 'has its antecedents: it represents only the most recent phase in a centuries-long process of cultural and literary evolution.'[36] Rex Nettleford's lectures are still more ambitious. They praise an array of common Caribbean cultural forms, including literature, music, dance and religion. At an inaugural address at the tenth anniversary of independence in St Lucia, Nettleford stressed that,

> what is important is the Caribbean product from the process of cross-fertilization over time, since it is this that will cut across old imperial boundaries which still attempt to hyphenate the region into Anglo-This, Franco-That or Hispanic-the other, etc.... The ideal is to be able to find definitions of the region largely in terms of its inner logic and cultural consistencies.[37]

These recent visions of the Caribbean as a single region, sharing a single historical condition, a single creative ethos – being, in fact, a national community with a sense of peoplehood – represent the new thinking on identity by intellectuals and artists in Caribbean nation-states and protectorates. It is not so much that such regional identities have never been postulated before – José Martí thought of the Caribbean as one nation, and so later did C.L.R. James – but rather that the evidence of artistic commonality has become, for this generation of intellectuals, overwhelming.

I believe this distinction is important in a study of nationalism. The evidence of a common historical predicament has always been there for political visionaries to see. But a new cultural proof, a new proof of peoplehood, has emerged in the second half of the twentieth century which has emboldened many to speak of a Caribbean nation. Literature, together with song, dance, religion and sport, provided a new kind of evidence. But this latest level of confidence in Caribbean peoplehood should not obscure the history of the discourse on nationalism in the Caribbean and the way in which its gradual development has affected the literary history of the region; nor, this study suggests, should this latest level of confidence in a pan-Caribbean peoplehood obscure the deep political and ethno-class schisms that still mark the region. And yet the evidence of parallel and common states of literary imagination across the Caribbean is today compelling, and the idea of a pan-Caribbean ethos and aesthetic now dominates the discourse.

Until recently, the task for English-speaking literary critics has been the assertion only of a 'West Indian identity' in literature and culture – that is, a common identity among English-speaking people of the Caribbean. As recently as 1987, the critic and poet David Dabydeen, together with Nana Wilson-Tagoe, wrote that 'it is still possible to talk in general terms of a West Indian literature of English expression. A common history of colonisation, displacement, slavery, indenture, emancipation, and nationalism has shaped most West Indian environments, creating a unity of experience that can be identified as particularly West Indian.'[38] Dabydeen would be aware of Caribbean literature in other languages, but his choice of a West Indian, English-speaking nation can be seen partly as a practical matter – he is writing here for a British audience, and partly as a stage in the growth in confidence of nationalist thought in the region. (It will be worth coming back to a superior poet like Dabydeen to consider the schism of ethnicity in all of these progressive definitions of peoplehood.) What is perhaps liberating about Dabydeen's and Wilson-Tagoe's West Indian identity is that it comes from a sense of what Nettleford called cultural consistencies, rather than from any arrangement of sovereignty or independence, unlike a generation before when either British colonialism or the short-lived West Indian Federation provided an external logic for the grouping.

In 1980, the critic Bruce King appealed to exactly this history in a similar decision to mark the borders of Caribbean peoplehood according to language and imperial past. 'To discuss Caribbean writing in English as if it were a national literature may seem unusual', writes King. 'The West Indian Federation collapsed in 1962 and the region now consists of small nations and some remaining political dependencies of Britain. While national traditions are observable, unfortunately no one country has yet produced a sufficient number of major writers to speak of its own literature.' And then King adds a second reason for speaking of a West Indian literary identity: 'Because of the similarities between the various islands, their common history, and the fact that the emergence of West Indian literature occurred during the period when hopes of federation were prevalent, many writers see themselves as belonging more to the region than to a specific country.'[39] King gives two distinct reasons for supporting an English-speaking, West Indian definition of identity. The first is that the individual Caribbean nation-states have not produced sufficient numbers of writers to enable us to speak of separate literatures; and the second is that the writers of the 'West Indian Renaissance' of the 1950s and 1960s saw themselves as West Indians. Of course, this study will try to call into question the first of these reasons; and the second is a simplification of the identity of most of the Caribbean writers of the 1950s and 1960s. As we shall see, many of them would answer Yes to the question of West Indian identity, but they might simultaneously answer Yes to questions of wider Caribbean identity, black/African identity, East Indian identity, creole identity, South American identity, and so on. The most we could say of West Indian identity for these writers is that it probably figures high in what Robert Magocsi has called the 'hierarchy of multiple loyalties'.[40] Nonetheless King's configuration of national identity is a significant and representative stage in the growth of a regional Caribbean imagination.

Imperialism in the Caribbean has ensured that there has always been some sense of connection between islands held under a common thrall and language. But by the 1930s in the English-speaking and French-speaking Caribbean, and as early as the turn of the century in the Spanish-speaking Caribbean, an island-specific nationalist literature working from local conditions and predicaments began to emerge. The protagonists were often aware of stirrings on neighbouring islands of the same language, but the movements drew strength from their local situations, often more in contact with European metropoles and their literary and political currents than with other Caribbean islands. J. Michael Dash's superb study, *Literature and Ideology in Haiti*, indicates the extent to which islands were divided by more than water. He recounts the strident opposition to the basic tenets of the Negritude movement by Haitian writers Réné Depêstre and Jacques-Stephen Alexis at the First Congress of Negro Writers and Artists in Paris in 1956. Part of a nation independent since 1804, and schooled in the French Marxist tradition, they rejected Martiniquan Aime Cesaire's notion that culture was organic and not a system of conditional reflexes. As Dash points out, a proud tradition of independent culture and productive creolized African arts in Haiti led these writers to reject the view of Black Caribbean history as sterile and uncreative, and to mock the notion of a return to Africa to find an ahistorical Black cultural ideal.[41] Ironically the lesson of the Haitian Marxist argument about culture would be extended to the world five years later in the first edition of *The Wretched of the Earth*, by a Martiniquan medical doctor named Frantz Fanon.[42]

The Spanish-speaking Caribbean, under the influence of Bolívar and Martí, struggled not with its African past in the first half of this century, but more often against it. And yet, the search for national identity in Cuba, the Dominican Republic and Puerto Rico in the first decades of this century struggled with many of the same themes that dominated the English-speaking Caribbean. Their literary history reflects the social tensions of a more considerable population identifying itself as of European descent. A recent comparative study of the 'ciudad letrada', the city or society of writers/intellectuals, in Puerto Rico and Cuba provides a much needed map of the Hispanic national discourse. The author, Arcadio Diaz-Quinones, traces the evolution of an exclusive nationalism in both islands. The Cuban writer Ramiro Guerra y Sanchez imagines a Cuban nation of small, landowning farmers of European descent (an oddly Jeffersonian phrasing), and warns that if Cuba moves fully to a plantation economy (and imports more black labour) it will 'renounce its history, its present, and its ideals. Either Barbados or Canada.' Barbados and Haiti are elsewhere described by Guerra as 'two horrible dungeons'.[43] The author also quotes the Puerto Rican sociologist/historian Pedreira agonizing over the mixed ancestry of his people in an even more telling moment of deformed nationalism.

> In instances of historical transcendence, when the martial rhythms of European blood flower in our gestures, we are capable of the greatest undertakings and most courageous heroism. But when the gesture comes soaked in waves of African blood, we remain indecisive, as if dumb-founded before the coloured beads or intimidated by the cinematic vision of witches and ghosts.[44]

The author struggles with the problem of national identity in Cuba, but he sounds more like the visiting racist imperial historian James Anthony Froude upon his visit to the English-speaking Caribbean in the 1880s than like his counterparts in the nationalist movement in Trinidad of the 1930s, some of whom were 'French creoles' and Portuguese.

When contemporary critics and pan-Caribbeanists speak of a regional struggle, a regional history, and a regional literature, it is worth recalling these schisms of race and political ideology, and therefore insisting on a concrete historical analysis of these islands now incorporated into a pan-Caribbean vision. And yet, even that analysis must be subject to competing readings. The racially obsessive nationalism of Cuba's Guerra must coexist in the national discourse with the effort of poet Nicholas Guillen to valorize Black Cuba, and with Fidel Castro's bold assertion that Cuba is an Afro-Latin nation, something that is anathema in the ethno-class-specific Cuban diaspora. Gustavo Perez Firmat represents the synthetic progress of these readings in Cuban peoplehood. Referring both to Barbadian poet Edward Brathwaite's idea of a 'nation language' and to Guillen's poetry, Firmat identifies a 'critical criollism' as against the 'primitive criollism' (of Pedreira and Guerra), insisting that critical criollism is the 'problematic, critical assessment of the possibilities of nativism in an island without natives ... Cuban criollism is rootless, unearthy, movable, translational rather than foundational.'[45] This sense of a translational, transforming, consuming criollism will resurface as a strength of Trinidadian national culture, both as creative style and as resistance to imposed cultural patterns.

Reading Literary History

The beginnings of a national literature in Trinidad and Tobago in the 1930s were not without the kind of racial and ideological inconsistencies that undermine smooth narratives of Caribbean commonality. The group that formed in Trinidad around two successive small literary magazines, *The Trinidad* and *The Beacon*, included C.L.R. James, a Black Trinidadian, Portuguese Trinidadians like Alfred Mendes and Albert Gomes, and a light-skinned creole named Ralph De Boissiere. Their imaginations, as Reinhard Sander points out in his book on this 'Trinidad awakening' were fired by a socialist ideal of recording the heroic lives of ordinary working people – in Trinidad, the people of the barrack yards.[46] James, Mendes and De Boissiere would all write novels inspired by this social(ist) realism. But it is worth noting that their interracial nature and their strong socialist tendencies made them sceptical of some other Caribbean national awakenings, particularly the Garveyism of Jamaica. The divisions were also internal, and James was quick to point out that he left Trinidad for England shortly after this awakening because his prospects as a Black intellectual were so limited on the island, and that any criticism of his leaving, by Albert Gomes for instance, confused the rhetoric of racial harmony with the reality.[47]

Despite these schisms the new writers of Trinidad were united in their celebration of the local, of the creolized, of the culture of the Black and East Indian working class and peasant class, and of the struggle for national dignity and independence from England. They were not without predecessors or allies. The pioneering Trinidadian scholar J.J. Thomas produced a *tour de force* of local language and culture in response to British imperial historian James Anthony Froude's negrophobic analysis of the West Indies. Thomas's work *Froudacity* already had much of the characteristic strategy that writers like James and Naipaul would employ sixty years later: a thorough mastery of European and Classical culture turned on Europe like a stolen weapon, and loaded with a dynamic local culture and speech.[48] The Beacon Group, as they came to be called, also had the figures of Captain Cipriani and Uriah Butler to inspire them. Cipriani, a French Creole, fought a lonely battle for self-government in Trinidad after World War I – lonely because the few Black Trinidadians conscious of the debate were thoroughly disenfranchised and silenced. He would finally find allies in the late 1920s and 1930s in the interracial (Black and East Indian) oil and sugar workers' unions. Just as quickly, labour leaders like Uriah Butler and Adrian Rienzi would shove aside the moderate Cipriani – but not before Cipriani's rhetoric of self-government infected the Beacon Group, and James in particular, who wrote a biography of Cipriani which was at once a manifesto for independence. The Butler Labour Riots of 1937, which spread throughout the English-speaking Caribbean and rocked the colonial office, resulted in the Moyne Commission being set up to look into the question of self-government, and the official mechanism of nationhood was begun.

The Second World War interrupted some of this national awakening but spurred on other parts of it, as Black Caribbean RAF pilots got a taste of the world outside of the Caribbean, and some of the elusive freedoms it promised. After the war, a new generation of writers from Trinidad, Guyana, Jamaica and Barbados began to emerge and quickly sought the attention, excitement and support they perceived in the metropole, following in the footsteps of James, Jamaica's Claude McKay, Dominica's Jean Rhys and others before the war. Among the most talented and famous of this West Indian renaissance generation were V.S. Naipaul, Samuel Selvon and Michael Anthony from Trinidad; George Lamming and poet Edward Brathwaite from Barbados; Roger Mais, Vic Reid and Andrew Salkey from Jamaica; and Wilson Harris and Edgar Mittelholzer from Guyana. Most of these writers ended up in London in the 1950s, introduced to each other by catalytic literary figures like John Figueroa from Jamaica, or Barbadian Frank Collymore, or Trinidadian John La Rose. This concentration of young writers in London, together with the first waves of labour from the Caribbean to Britain, oddly enough augmented nationalism back home. West Indians in London came to know each other and recognize common traits in an alien and often hostile city. They developed a regional sense of identity, and the disappointments of the metropole and the blossoming of the anti-colonial movement emboldened some to return to the Caribbean to create a more perfect nation. Some returned only in imagination, and some of them are included in this study. Others either never left or returned for creative strength. Some of them make up the rest of this study.

Why, then, a study at the level of the nation-state? A number of reasons can be given. The most mechanical one is that the nation-state, as so many of the analysts of nationalism will admit, is a central fact of modern life, and no other form of socio-political organization in the Caribbean appears likely in the near future. A more political reason, as I believe will become evident from the complexity of Trinidadian nationalism that emerges in this study, is that the Caribbean nation-state is an appropriate unit of examination for a study of the literary and political vagaries of nationalism and peoplehood in the modern Caribbean; and on this evidence, both the overwhelming wealth of literature, and the depth of political achievement and variety of social relations in each Caribbean nation-state will be validated. Third, this study is not strictly about a nation-state in the old sense of the term, but about a national diaspora. And finally, as David Lowenthal observed, 'insularity is a basic fact of West Indian life ... it is at the island level that West Indians mainly identify.'[49] Such a statement must be qualified, of course, by acknowledging diasporic ethnogenesis, and by paying attention to the multiple ethnic identities and loyalties in the Caribbean. Moreover, I hope the decision to create a case study at the nation-state level will not discount real and imaginary pan-Caribbean connections. I am more certain that the writers dealt with here will put to rest any talk of insufficient talent for a study at the level of the nation-state. I have selected nine writers who imagine Trinidad and the Caribbean in a variety of original and interesting ways, all of them novelists (though in the case of James, I concentrate on his essays and lectures). For reasons of economy I have omitted several worthy novelists, including Ismith Khan, whose novels of Obeah, an African-derived constellation of religious beliefs, coming from a Trinidadian of East Indian descent, are an obvious example of the fascinating admixture of people and culture.[50] Derek Walcott, the best-known playwright of the English-speaking Caribbean, was born in St Lucia, an island with an independent artistic heritage; and so, despite his work with the Little Carib Theatre in Trinidad and his widespread fame, he is not examined in this study. Perhaps, most importantly, the huge wealth of popular poets, the calypsonians, do not receive direct attention. They deserve their own study. No really thoughtful study of contemporary calypso exists, though Gordon Rohlehr's work on calypsos of the 1930s deserves attention.[51] Similarly, the festivals of Trinidad, Carnival, Hosay, the Parang of Christmas, are considered largely in the context of the literary texts that represent them. Much work on the public theatre of these festivals in Trinidad still needs to be done. Abner Cohen's work in the context of Britain's Notting Hill Carnival, and Errol Hill's work, *Trinidad Carnival: Mandate for a National Theatre*, are a good start, however.[52] One of the writers in this study, Michael Anthony, has also written an illustrated popular history of Trinidad carnival.[53] Some combination of Cohen and Hill, together with the work of Augosto Boal, would be necessary to gauge the dominant impact on identity and politics of the carnival theatre arts in the Trinidadian diaspora today.[54] Cohen's work interacts with this book in another way too. His faith in the contested territory of cultural resistance, together with his insistence on the 'microsociological' examination of the cultural forms of that resistance, are an important assumption of this book, particularly in the context of the diasporic communities.

The writers that form the centres of my chapters are Earl Lovelace, Michael Anthony, Samuel Selvon, Valerie Belgrave, V.S. Naipaul, Willi Chen, Neil Bissoondath, and C.L.R. James.[55] These writers have all taken it as their task to imagine Trinidad, to make it visible to its people. The task is not without great obstacles. Eric Hobsbawm has recently questioned whether nationalism is even an appropriate term for the process of identity formation in postcolonial, multi-ethnic states. He sees little similarity between the creation of the Trinidadian nation and the great national upheavals and realignments of Europe in the previous century.[56] He suggests that the attention nationalism is receiving from historians is a sign of its demise. Partha Chatterjee, in his oft-cited book on Third World nationalism, condemns the process of nation-formation as part of the ideological subjugation of formerly colonial peoples.[57]

And the forces of international capital, together with the World Bank, the continued flow of labour out to capital, and the emergence of an American trading bloc, divide and confuse Trinidadian loyalties and imaginations. But the nation-state of Trinidad and Tobago remains a fact of international life. And, to paraphrase Naipaul, as Europe continues to prove itself incapable of a multiracial ethos and America disintegrates into neighbourhood turf wars, the closing of accounts on this side of the middle passage may yet hold some surprises.

Lastly, this study needs a brief note on terminology. I have used the adjectival terms 'Afro-Trinidadian' and 'Indo-Trinidadian', but I have used the nouns, 'African Trinidadian' and 'Indian Trinidadian' to denote the descendants of slaves and the descendants of indentured labourers from India, respectively. Often, these terms do not suffice to represent the mixed descent of over 30 per cent of Trinidadians, and I have tried to qualify these terms where possible. While I have tried to use the adjective 'Caribbean' rather than 'West Indian' in most instances, sometimes for consistency with quoted texts, I have used the latter term. In any case, there is little agreed usage for the two terms, except that sometimes 'West Indian' is used to delimit the English-speaking Caribbean. Finally, I have often abbreviated 'Trinidad and Tobago' to simply 'Trinidad'.

I now turn to the readings of Trinidad by specific writers. The study starts with an examination of the tensions between the writerly imagination and the nationalist concern with the making of a people. Novelists Earl Lovelace and Michael Anthony both undermine that nationalist concern, perhaps unconsciously, Lovelace with his insistence on individual creativity and renewal, and Anthony with his insistence on an already existent peoplehood. Both consequently offer alternative readings of the nation. In Chapter 2, Valerie Belgrave hears the siren song of the nationalist discourse, but the women of her novel suffer the price of a nationalism obsessed with peoplehood and blind to class and gender. In Chapter 3, Willi Chen displaces all readings of the nation with his texts of carnival identity, taking on and discarding images of nation and peoplehood with a reveller's abandon. In Chapter 4, Samuel Selvon presents us with the complication of the diaspora and the 'mother country'. But his faith in creolization as Caribbean nationalism forces a new reading of both Trinidad and England. Chapter 5 takes another look at the diaspora, this time in the newer ethnie of Toronto. Bissoondath's work tests the limits of the writer and the nation in his rebellion from Trinidadian identity. His uncle, V.S. Naipaul, is the subject of Chapter 6. His anti-nationalist posture is used to test the political dangers and pitfalls of the nationalist discourse. Finally, in Chapter 7, C.L.R. James's lectures and essays suggest a way toward a harmony between the literary imagination and the national stage of history; indeed, James suggests a way toward a harmony of every citizen and the nation.

Notes

1. C.L.R. James, *The Artist in the Caribbean*, Mona, Jamaica: Open Lecture Series, University of the West Indies, 1965, p. 6.
2. Ibid., p. 15.
3. Derek Attridge, 'An Interview with Jacques Derrida', in J. Derrida, *Acts of Literature*, New York: Routledge, 1992, p. 72.
4. Gayatri Spivak, *The Post-Colonial Critic: Interviews, Strategies, and Dialogues*, New York: Routledge, 1990, p. 120.
5. Roberto Marquez, 'Nation, Nationalism, and Ideology', in Franklin W. Knight and Colin A. Palmer, eds., *The Modern Caribbean*, Chapel Hill, N.C.: University of North Carolina Press, 1989.
6. Homi K. Bhabha, ed., *Nation and Narration*, London: Routledge, 1990, and particularly the essay 'Dissemi-nation: Time, Narrative, and the Margins of the Modern Nation', pp. 291–320.
7. Ian Adam and Helen Tiffin, eds., *Past the Last Post*, Hemel Hempstead: Harvester Wheatsheaf, 1991; Bill Ashcroft, Gareth Griffiths, and Helen Tiffin, eds., *The Empire Writes Back*, London: Routledge, 1989; Stephen Slemon and Helen Tiffin, eds., *After Europe*, Sydney: Dangaroo Press, 1989.
8. Fredric Jameson, 'Third World Literature in the Era of Multinational Capitalism', *Social Text*, vol. 15, no. 1, 1986, pp. 65–80.
9. Selwyn R. Cudjoe, ed., *Caribbean Women Writers*, Wellesley, Mass.: Calaloux Publications, 1990; R. Espinet, ed., *Creation Fire*, Toronto: Sister Vision, 1990; P. Mordecai and B. Wilson, eds., *Her True-True Name*, London: Heinemann, 1989.
10. Anthony D. Smith, *State and Nation in the Third World*, New York: St Martin's Press, 1983, p. 232.
11. Tim Brennan, 'Cosmopolitans and Celebrities', *Race and Class*, vol.

31, no. 1, 1989, p. 1.

12. Ian Smart, *Central American Writers of West Indian Origin: A New Hispanic Literature*, Washington, DC: Three Continents, 1985.

13. Richard Jenkins, 'Social Anthropological Models of Inter-Ethnic Relations', in J. Rex and D. Mason, *Theories of Race and Ethnic Relations*, Cambridge: Cambridge University Press, 1986, p. 185.

14. Stuart Hall, 'Negotiating Caribbean Identities', *New Left Review* January–February 1995, pp. 3–14.

15. Ivar Oxaal, *Black Intellectuals and the Dilemmas of Race and Class in Trinidad*, Cambridge, Mass.: Schenkman, 1982; Clive Thomas, *The Poor and the Powerless: Economic Policy and Change in the Caribbean*, London: Latin American Bureau, 1988; Manning Marable, *African and Caribbean Politics*, London: Verso, 1987.

16. Eric Williams, *From Columbus to Castro*, London: Andre Deutsch, 1970, and *Capitalism and Slavery*, London: Andre Deutsch, 1964.

17. John La Guerre, *Calcutta to Caroni: The East Indians of Trinidad*, Port of Spain, Trinidad and New York: Longman Caribbean, 1974; David Dabydeen and Brinsley Samaroo, eds., *India in the Caribbean*, London: Hansib, 1987.

18. Stephen D. Glazier, *Marchin' the Pilgrims Home: Leadership and Decision-making in an Afro-Caribbean Faith*, London: Greenwood Press, 1983. Michael Lieber, *Street Liming: Afro-American Culture in Urban Trinidad*, Boston: G.K. Hall, 1981.

19. Kelvin Yelvington, ed., *Trinidad Ethnicity*, Centre for Caribbean Studies at the University of Warwick Series, Knoxville: University of Tennessee Press, 1993.

20. David Maughan-Brown, *Land, Freedom, and Fiction: History and Ideology in Kenya*, London: Zed Books, 1985, p. 260.

21. Italo Calvino, *Invisible Cities*, New York: Harcourt Brace Jovanovich, 1972.

22. Eric Williams, *Inward Hunger: The Education of a Prime Minister*, London: Andre Deutsch, 1969, pp. 13–14.

23. Ibid., p. 18

24. Ibid., p. 338.

25. V.S. Naipaul, *The Loss of El Dorado*, London: Andre Deutsch, 1969.

26. Ibid., p. 11.

27. Ibid., p. 316.

28. James Millette, *Society and Politics in Colonial Trinidad*, London: Zed Books, 1985, p. 17.

29. Ibid., p 265.

30. Bridget Brereton, *A History of Modern Trinidad 1783–1962*, London: Heinemann, 1981, p. 110.

31. Ibid., p. 223.

32. Beryl McBurnie, 'West Indian Dance', in A. Salkey, ed., *Caribbean*

Essays, London: Evans Brothers, 1973, pp. 98–9.

33. Michael Anthony, *Glimpses of Trinidad and Tobago*, Port of Spain: Columbus Publishers, 1974, p. 63.

34. Ivar Oxaal, *Black Intellectuals and the Dilemma of Race and Class in Trinidad*, Cambridge, Mass.: Schenkman, 1982, pp. 7–8.

35. C.L.R. James, *Beyond a Boundary*, London: Pantheon, 1983, p. 225.

36. Roberto Marquez, 'Nationalism, Nation, and Ideology: Trends in the Emergence of a Caribbean Literature', in Knight and Palmer, eds., *The Modern Caribbean*, p. 295.

37. Rex Nettleford, 'The Caribbean Imperative and the Fight Against Folksy Exoticist Tastes', *Caribbean Affairs*, vol. 2, no. 2, 1990, p. 29.

38. David Dabydeen and Nana Wilson-Tagoe, 'Selected Themes in West Indian Literature: An Annotated Bibliography', *Third World Quarterly*, vol. 9, no. 3, July 1987, p. 927.

39. Bruce King, *The New Literatures in English: Cultural Nationalism in a Changing World*, London: Macmillan, 1980.

40. Paul Robert Magocsi, 'The Ukrainian National Revival: A New Analytical Framework', *Canadian Review of Studies in Nationalism*, vol. 26, no. 1–2, 1989, p. 57.

41. J. Michael Dash, *Literature and Ideology in Haiti, 1915–1961*, Brunswick, New Jersey: Barnes and Noble, 1981, pp. 174–85.

42. Frantz Fanon, *The Wretched of the Earth*, Hammondsworth: Penguin, 1970.

43. Arcadio Diaz Quinones, 'The Hispanic-Caribbean National Discourse: Antonio S. Pedreira and Ramiro Guerra y Sanchez', in *Intellectuals in the Caribbean*, Warwick: University of Warwick, forthcoming, pp. 23–4.

44. Ibid., p. 18.

45. Gustavo Perez Firmat, *The Cuban Condition: Translation and Identity in Modern Cuban Literature*, Cambridge: Cambridge University Press, 1989, pp. 7–8.

46. Reinhard Sander, *The Trinidad Awakening: West Indian Literature of the 1930s*, New York: Greenwood Press, 1988.

47. Like many Afro- and Indo-Trinidadian migrants to the metropoles, it took migration to London for Gomes, a well-known Portuguese Trinidadian independence figure, to see the paradox of colour stratification in the Caribbean. 'I was accepted as a white person in Trinidad. For all practical purposes, I am coloured in England', he wrote in an essay, 'I Am an Immigrant', in Andrew Salkey, ed., *Caribbean Essays*, London: Evans Brothers, 1973, p. 53.

48. J.J. Thomas, *Froudacity: West Indian Fables Explained* [c.1889], London: New Beacon Books, 1969; James Anthony Froude, *The English in the West Indies*, London: Longman, Green, 1888.

49. David Lowenthal, *West Indian Societies*, London: Oxford University Press, 1972, p. 14.

50. See, for instance, Ismith Khan, *The Jumbie Bird*, London: Longman, 1985.

51. Gordon Rohlehr, 'Images of Men and Women in the 1930s Calypsos', in P. Mohammed and C. Shephard, eds., *Gender in Caribbean Development*, St Augustine, Trinidad: University of the West Indies, 1988.

52. For Cohen, see particularly 'A Polyethnic London Carnival as Contested Cultural Performance', *Ethnic and Racial Studies*, vol. 5, no. 1, 1982, pp. 23–41; and 'Drama and Politics in the Development of a London Carnival', *Man*, vol. 15, no. 1, 1980, pp. 65–87. Errol Hill's book, *Trinidad Carnival: Mandate for a National Theatre*, Austin: University of Texas Press, 1972, could now be usefully updated and expanded as Trinidad carnival and its overseas spores have grown and changed.

53. Michael Anthony, *Parade of Carnivals of Trinidad: 1839–1989*, Port of Spain, Trinidad: Circle Press, 1989.

54. Augosto Boal, *Theatre of the Oppressed*, London: Pluto, 1979. Boal's work, although concerned with radical theatre techniques, shows the heavy influence of shifting indentities and hierarchies of South American and Caribbean carnivals.

55. Biographical and bibliographical data from these writers is cited from the very useful book; Daryl Cumber Dance, ed., *Fifty Caribbean Writers*, New York: Greenwood Press, 1986.

56. Eric Hobsbawm, *Nations and Nationalism since 1780*, Cambridge: Cambridge University Press, 1990, p. 160.

57. Partha Chatterjee, *Nationalist Thought and the Colonial World: A Derivative Discourse*, Tokyo and London: United Nations University and Zed Books, 1986.

CHAPTER I

Beyond Nationalism:
Literary Nation-building in the Work of
Earl Lovelace and Michael Anthony

In 1986 the influential American literary critic Fredric Jameson published an article entitled 'Third World Literature in the Era of Multinational Capitalism',[1] in which he argued that in Third World literature, and particularly in the novel, the private and public spheres of existence have not been split, as they have been in developed societies, by post-industrial capitalism. Consequently, writers in the Third World always produce novels that are 'national allegories' in which the growth and self-realization of the narrative reproduce those of the nation. Despite the postmodernist discourse of the article, Jameson's point is not entirely new. Kenneth Ramchand certainly appreciated the Caribbean novels of childhood for their allegorical value in his study, *The West Indian Novel and Its Background*,[2] some thirty years ago. Ramchand wrote about an older generation of Caribbean novelists who used the theme of growing up in the West Indies as a way to talk about decolonization in the West Indies. In this first chapter I want to discuss two younger, contemporary writers; Earl Lovelace and Michael Anthony. Just as decolonization has proved to be a far more complicated project than early theories predicted, so the project of linking the imagination to the nation has also proved to be a thorny issue. Both Lovelace and Anthony represent this new ambivalence toward the nation and its literary companion the national allegory. If they do not wholly reject the connection between their nation and their craft, they do interrogate that connection with fluid energy. Jameson's theory insists that writing in a developing country, and a post-colonial one, will necessarily lead to these national allego-ries. Indeed, Jameson seems to be arguing that because the world economic order also informs literary production, the post-colonial writer can only reproduce allegories of his/her nation's becoming, can only construct narrative traditions for that new nation. In other words, the obsession with nation, its history, its imagination, its relation to peoplehood and ethnicity, cannot be escaped in the post-colonial world. One does not have to agree entirely with Fredric Jameson's somewhat dated dependency theory of capitalism to see in the literature of Trinidad and Tobago readings, re-readings and misreadings of a national text of identity. But in a new era of neo-colonialism, the dedication to, or obsession with, the linked production of literature and nationalism has grown more complex than Jameson's formula.

In his study of the origin and spread of nationalism, *Imagined Communities*, Benedict Anderson notes that 'nation-ness is the most universally legitimate value in the political life of our time.'[3] And, he states, both Marxists, who thought it should wither away, and liberals, who have befriended it, are at a loss to understand its political and psychological power. But the value of nationalism to the imagination might not be the same as its value to a state apparatus or to commerce. This is so even as some theorists of nationalism are discovering the imagination. Two recent surveys of the literature on nationalism by two of its major theorists re-confirm its persistence in the world and the continuing inadequacy of academic explanations for the phenomenon. Anthony D. Smith recalls most of the recent principal theorists of nationalism, among them Benedict Anderson, Ernest Gellner, Tom Nairn and Eric Hobsbawm, noting that all connect the rise of nationalism with modernization. Smith denies that 'the invention of mass-national traditions is an inevitable consequence of the divisions generated by modern capitalism.'[4] Instead, Smith wants to locate the nation in what he calls a historical sequence of cultural forms of identity. Smith's move away from determinist explanations to residual and primordial forms of nationalism in culture would mandate a con-sideration of such cultural productions as the novel, and his view lends support to Jameson's attention to the novel in nationalism and nationalism in the novel. Similarly, in 'A Critique of Recent Trends in the Analysis of Ethnonationalism', William Douglass

insists that, to develop an understanding of the power of nationalism, theorists, must balance what he calls their instrumentalist
view of nations as malleable constructs (created by different forms
of alienation) with more attention to the primordialism in national
thinking. He insists that 'if we are to progress beyond our current
rather mechanistic and uninspired models we must be prepared to
address the elements of affect and altruism germane to particular
nationalistic traditions.'[5] Both Smith and Douglass, reacting to the
tenacity and intensity of nationalism as it extends into the next
century, suggest that investigation of the phenomenon must include
a history of the psychological, emotional and spiritual grip it exerts,
to complement existing studies of the political and economic
reasons for the spread of nationalism. The literary imagination is
both a logical and a highly articulate place to attempt this syn-
thesis of historical and affective nationalism. But while the two
writers in this chapter can illuminate nationalism, it is unclear
whether the discourse on nationalism, in academe or in Trinidad,
can fully illuminate these writers and their texts. The unmistakable
conversation between writer and nation does produce sparks to set
alight conceptions of nationalism and peoplehood, but with these
contemporary writers, caught in a web of neo-colonialism, the
sparks serve to shed light on the chaos too.

It is difficult to say whether C.L.R. James's comment about
Earl Lovelace and Michael Anthony reflects not just a Jamesian
but also a Jamesonian belief in the project of literary nationalism,
or whether it is simply the enigmatic James trying to make room
for his countrymen in his internationalism. In an interview in
1972 James said that

> [the] peculiar thing I find about Michael Anthony and Earl Lovelace
> is that they are not literary in that sense at all. They are persons who
> learnt the English language, read some books, listened to some preach-
> ers, read in the newspapers and practised writing. They are native and
> national in a sense that the previous generation (Lamming, Naipaul,
> Harris) is not.[6]

Elsewhere, James has elaborate praise for such writers as Lamming
and Harris, and even for the committed anti-nationalist, Naipaul.
But, as with his cricket writing, James's public lectures on West
Indian literature demonstrate an awareness of the restriction that

nationalism places on the writer, and of the tension between allegory and chaos in the nationalist imagination of the contemporary Caribbean writer. 'Artistic production is essentially individual
and the artistic individual, is above all, unpredictable.' Perhaps as
a very flexible Marxist, James understood that nationalism could
not be explained solely by invoking alienation and the functional
needs of capital. For James, as indeed we shall see for Lovelace
and Anthony, his two conscripts, every human project, including
that of liberation, required what nationalism had: an existence
both historically determined and primordially felt. 'The nation we
are building needs also the supreme artist', said James. Whether,
for James, this nation is literally the Trinidad nation-state in contemporary form or a nation of all men is unclear. James did
consider the nation-state a temporary but important step in the
struggle for world liberation. He notes: 'In my view the great
artist is the product of long and deeply rooted national tradition....
He appears at a moment of transition in national life ... but the
universal artist is universal because he is above all national.'[7] One
can guess that for James, Lovelace and Anthony are thus important as both products and inventors of the national stage in human history, which for Trinidad marks a level of liberation and
psychological renewal on the path beyond nationalism. Out of
this nationalism comes the universal artist summoning the common community of mankind. Similar confidence in the necessity
of national artists in the unfinished struggle for liberation in Third
World Marxism can be found in the writings of Frantz Fanon and
Amilcar Cabral. What is significant for our purposes is that even
James, committed as he was to individual creativity and an end to
the bourgeois nation-state, summoned the national writer, and
found him in Earl Lovelace and Michael Anthony in Trinidad.

Dilemmas of Literary Nationalism

It is Earl Lovelace himself who voices the dilemma that faces
theorists of nationalism and national writers alike. In an interview
in 1977, two years before the publication of his seminal novel *The
Dragon Can't Dance*, but with the book already written, he said, 'the
writer is not another citizen. I don't think the writer is another

citizen. I would want to feel that the writer is a most important citizen in a state.' But, Lovelace concludes, 'they don't want to hear you. They just want to know they have a writer.'[8] It is unclear whether 'they' are the state's elites or its whole citizenry, but the tension between the boundaries and the substance of nationalism, between a mechanistic insistence on nationalism and an epistemology of nationalism itself, is not just the concern of theorists like Anthony Smith, but also, as Lovelace implies, of national literatures and national novelists. Lovelace understands both the pull of nationalism and its manipulation – both products of nationalism's stubborn resistance to explanation and interpretation. And in Trinidad the national literature is subject not just to theoretical debates about the nature of nationalism; as a discourse in the fray of a particular nationalism, it is also subject to the specific vagaries, inconsistencies and passions of Trinidad's national discourse. One consequence of the descent into the specifics of a nationalism is the need to define history, culture and peoplehood along the boundaries of the modern nation-state. And another is to subject the idea of the strict historical nationalism of the juridical nation-state to the passion of affective nationalism, and to treat affective nationalism as materially based.

One reason Anthony and Lovelace are what James called native and national is that, unlike Naipaul or Lamming, they are not West Indian or Caribbean writers as much as they are national writers – in their case, Trinidadians. A look at their tighter definition of community – tighter than many of the other writers in this study – as well as the more general task of reading their national allegories, should start with attention to the discourse of nationalism in the nation-state of Trinidad and Tobago.

Class Struggle and Anti-Colonial Struggle

Though the goal of an, independent national community in Trinidad may have its roots in Eric Williams's anti-colonialist, pre-independence rhetoric, the discourse on community, on common political interest, first reached the level of mass appeal in the hopeful and turbulent era of labour in the 1930s. Malcolm Cross has noted, after interviewing Indo-Trinidadian labour leader

Adrian Rienzi just before his death, that the discourse of trade unions, labour leaders and labour journalism was one of community, of coming together as one people.[9] Membership in this community was not based on citizenship or on race, but on class. Whether or not, with the coming of independence and the creation of a nation-state, this working-class community would have added the cloth of nationalism to its ideology is a matter of speculation. Williams and his Afro-Trinidadian bureaucratic class replaced the disintegrating labour movement in the 1950s and 1960s with a nationalist anti-colonialism that had very little to say about class politics; and, as David Horowitz notes, until the fall of the PNM in 1986, 'party politics remained the same: Creole majority, Indian minority.'[10] Thus, with the collapse of the labour movement (frustrated by the colonial office and local elites), Trinidad's nationalist discourse was characterized both by a lack of class politics and by an overdetermined politics of race. To be sure, the discourse of class is not entirely absent from Trinidad national life, and strong trade unionism is an important and sophisticated part of the political landscape. But the cooptation of nationalism by a multi-class elite has had consequences for labour politics, with no party truly representing the unions. As Colin Clarke notes, 'the impact that the trade unions have attempted to have has not been through collaboration with the established parties – especially the party forming the government.'[11] Forced into adversarial roles by race-based parties, the unions have traditionally been vulnerable to anti-nationalist charges from the left and the right, conflating race and nationalism to counter the unions. Advocates of a Trinidadian nationalism, as opposed to advocates of a Trinidadian nation, came to see and to use the problem of race and the project of peoplehood, rather than class or post-colonialism, as the main obstacle to a fully imagined community. Needless to say, in the wrong hands nationalism became racism.

But for most social scientists, writers, and even politicians, after the initial years of independence, the project of nationalism continued to inform their discourse, as a kind of precondition of both political and economic development in Trinidad. For instance, in his *Race and Nationalism in Trinidad and Tobago*, Selwyn Ryan concludes that his aim is 'to describe the political and constitutional evolution of Trinidad and Tobago and to identify and analyze the factors which have impeded the development of a disciplined and united nationalist movement with a socially relevant development programme.'[12] Selwyn Ryan, who remains a prominent figure today, straddling the academic and political spheres of Trinidadian society, clearly believes that a united nationalist movement must be in place in order to begin a socially relevant development programme. Writing about Indo-Trinidadians, John La Guerre insists that

> there is little point in trying to be more Indian than the Indian from India as the Negro intellectual tried not so long ago to be more African than the African. For culture is not a god. It is a set of rules and a way of life that enables its adherents to exist within a national community.[13]

Again, a national community is presented as the logical referent for behaviour. Most recently, the Trinidadian football team's match against the United States on 19 November 1989 for a place in the World Cup finals was greeted by journalists and intellectuals as an opportunity for forging national unity and instilling national feeling in a nation thought to be wanting. The discourse of nationalism was as ever-present as the red shirts of the team's fans, but it was not just the team's losing that stifled the discourse that Sunday. Unity against the American enemy could only postpone questions of the attachment of all citizens to one imagined community. 'Kaisoca soccer' could more easily define itself in opposition to the plodding soccer of the American team than it could define itself for all Trinidadians. But, beyond the salience of the national discourse in the daily life of the nation, there is also the hegemonic metadiscourse of race that determines the nationalist discourse. The quest for racial harmony, growing as it does from a lack of racial unity in the initial national independence movement, becomes the hidden text of all discourse on nationalism. Visitors to the island state will quickly encounter platitudes about the nation's multi-ethnic character. Trinidadians are quick to say they are 'one big pilau' – a dish of sweetened rice with any number of meats and vegetables mixed in to it. (Interestingly, this expression is more telling still, since the Chinese, Spanish, Africans and Indians all claim they brought the recipe to the island.) Race and peoplehood always become problematized. Nationalism becomes no more than racial unity, emptied of history, class or common social goals.[14] It is in this campaign for nationalism that Earl Lovelace and Michael Anthony enlist. And in the process of trying to understand the writer's role in nationalism, Anthony and Lovelace call into question not just the literary activism of Jameson's theory of national allegories, but also the dominant discourse of Trinidadian nationalism itself.

Although the idea of nationalism and the writer's role in constructing it are evident throughout the work of both these writers, the later, more mature novels of each are the most fully inscribed with problems of nationalism and nation-building. Anthony's *Green Days by the River* and Lovelace's *The Dragon Can't Dance* are also good texts with which to test Jameson's theory of national allegory because both lend themselves readily to allegorical readings. Anthony's novel was published in 1967 and Lovelace's twelve years later.[15] They are very different responses to the call to nationalism and very different readings of the discourse of nationalism and the metadiscourse of race that informs it; they nevertheless present similar problems of literary nation-building.

The Struggle for the Trinidadian

In an interview in 1971, Michael Anthony was asked about his audience. He replied: 'I am writing to the Trinidadian ... to this imaginary person who is next to you, who is very sympathetic and knows what you are talking about; and he is going to be Trinidadian.'[16] Anthony's response is at once a reaction against West Indian writing written for the metropoles and an assertion of national imagination. He contends that those who know 'what you are talking about' are going to be Trinidadians – that is, those who share your imagination, those who are part of your community of imagination. Anthony, then, wants to suggest that his nation is bound by socio-political fact – those who will know; but it is also a nation held together by common feeling – those who both know and are sympathetic. *Green Days by the River* is a novel written for Trinidad, as part of the national discourse. But whether it is part of a nationalist discourse – that is, a call to greater national feeling and construction – is another matter for investigation. What is immediately clear from the story is that it lends itself both to the specifics of Trinidadian experience and to a reading of national allegory – allegory not only of Trinidadians who know and are sympathetic, but of any people who know and are sympathetic.

The novel tells the story of a boy of fifteen named Shellie. He has recently moved into a small rural community in Trinidad, from another such community by the sea. As is usually the case with Anthony, the language of the novel is simply constructed and the voice of the narrative is that of Shellie, displaying the consciousness of a fifteen-year-old boy. Shellie lives in Pierre Hill with his hard-working mother and ailing father. He has a close and playful relationship with his dying father. As the novel unfolds, Shellie meets the local kids by pelting cashews with them. He encounters a 'doogla' (mixed African and Indian – also spelled 'dougla'; from the Hindi word for a bastard, but carrying less of that negative connotation in Trinidad today[17]) girl named Rosalie Ghidaree, but he assumes she is more interested in one of the local Afro-Trinidadian boys than in him. Her mother is an African Trinidadian and her father is a powerful Indo-Trinidadian man, both physically and symbolically. Mr Ghidaree, sensing the poverty of Shellie's family, takes him to his farm lands in the woods, where Shellie spends long days working crops, eating sweet sapodillas, befriending Ghidaree's huge dogs, and marvelling at the strength and confidence of his adopted father. Eventually Shellie has an unwritten sexual encounter with Rosalie just before the arrival of his new girlfriend, an African Trinidadian from another town. Ghidaree learns of the encounter and sets his dogs on Shellie. Shellie is savaged by the dogs but recovers, with a remorseful and now tender Mr Ghidaree by his bed. Shellie's father dies, and the novel ends with Shellie telling Ghidaree that he is nervous about doing the right thing during the upcoming Hindu wedding ceremony in which he is now pledged to marry Rosalie. Ghidaree laughs at Shellie's nervousness, and tells him not to worry. Shellie thinks: 'I felt very close to him and fond of him. I knew if he said the engagement would go well it would go well' (p. 191).

The desultory nature of Anthony's style of narrative, never more masterful than in this novel, has caused some critics to dismiss the author.[18] To the nationalist critic, Anthony gives a reading neither of Caribbean history, nor of racial conflict, nor of anti-colonial

struggle. Here he differs from more famous Caribbean writers like
George Lamming of Barbados, or Roger Mais of Jamaica. One
critic has claimed that the narratives 'reflect Anthony's dis-
inclination or inability to coax the lion of contemporary history
into lying down with the lamb of his private world of enchantment'.[19] But here it is worth recalling both James and Lovelace.
James considered Anthony to be native and national, and Lovelace
said that 'they' don't want to hear you, just know they have you.
What in the light of these statements is most remarkable about
Anthony's narrative is the utter confidence, the sure sense of place
and voice, that inhabits the text. Unlike the combative or conflicting
voices of Lamming or Mais, the outside world does not intrude
because it is just that – outside. Now there is a nation drawn both
by international law and by the confidence of those who live together in its imagined community. This is not to say that conflict
does not exist, but that the history of Pierre Hill is its own. The
project of nationalism for Anthony takes the form, in allegory, of
a coming to terms with what already exists as community and
nation in Trinidad. Fredric Jameson might be unhappy with the
autonomy of Anthony's national community, its coherence and
certain step; but for Anthony, Pierre Hill does not require an anti-
colonialist discourse to achieve a sense of itself. And in allegory,
the nation of Pierre Hill presents interesting problems for the discourse on nationalism and the metadiscourse on race in Trinidad.

Whether or not Anthony conforms to nationalist expectations,
his work is nonetheless viewed as a text within the discourse on
nationalism, as the critical response indicates.[20] Anthony suggests
that his work does have something to say about peoplehood. 'My
real preoccupation is not to aggravate the problem but to try to
do whatever I can to bridge the racial gap', asserts the writer.[21]
Yet even without the author's consent, as some critical disaffection
attests, the text enters the discourse of nationalism precisely
because that discourse is dominant and seeks out the national
writer. Willingly or unwillingly, Anthony's text does therefore
present the dominant discourse on nationalism with a study in
peoplehood. Both Africans and Indians in Pierre Hill, with
Africans apparently the dominant population, share a common
local culture. Ghidaree moves easily in the town, integrated, and
further integrated by his marriage to an African. Neither Shellie

nor any other African boy seems concerned with Rosalie's Indian heritage, and even the hint of racial fetishism implied in the term 'doogla girl' is not carried very far. Several subversions of stereotypes are also at work in Anthony's construction of community. Despite clichés of Indian chastity and African permissiveness, Shellie is seduced by Rosalie and cannot seduce Joan. (Whether there is a proto-feminist aspect to Rosalie is unclear – in a nation that often prides itself on sexually forceful and liberated women. It has been suggested that both indenture and slavery had significant effects on the patriarchy of African and Indian cultures. Rhoda Reddock has written that attempts to reinstate a patriarchy 'either in a supposedly traditional African form or in a Western nuclear form have never been completely successful'.[22]) Also, it is the Indian, Ghidaree, who displays the most connection with the land (and not just the sugar cane worked by indentured Indian labour) of Pierre Hill, understanding its indigenous flora and fauna and placing himself firmly in the soil of Trinidad, more firmly than the African Trinidadians who claim two hundred more years of residence. But, despite these subversions, what is most obvious in the allegory is cultural compromise, sometimes at some sacrifice. The symbol of compromise grows from the single figure of Rosalie as a product of Indian–African love, to the entire dilemma of Shellie – his painful journey towards acceptance of his new Indian father and his mixed wife. Almost none of this, because it is allegory, is presented in racial or national terms in the narrative. But at the point of utmost responsibility for Shellie and by extension for the nation, the point is bluntly put. And, again, Anthony acknowledges as much, saying: 'I, of course, know the stereotyped views of each other that the Indians and Africans have. The Indians feeling that, and knowing, and perhaps they are right, that the Negro boys do not like to marry.'[23] Shellie must take responsibility for his action with Rosalie and marry her, as the nation must take responsibility for its history and forge a marriage of culture. Shellie's nervousness over the Hindu ceremony then becomes a symbol of the encounter with the new, and Ghidaree's assurance a faith in the results of a new culture built on compromise and sacrifice of the old.

It is perhaps easier to examine the place where Michael Anthony meets Fredric Jameson, and his own nationalist intelligentsia. His text is not part of a dialectical struggle with post-colonial power. Nor is it a 'minority discourse' in which a minority uses a majority language to deterritorialize the received sense of people, as Deleuze and Guattari have characterized some writing strategies, such as that of Jews in Middle Europe or African Americans in the United States.[24] Nor, even, is it a call to unify into a single nation many diverse communities. Rather, what Anthony's national allegory does is deterritorialize the nationalist discourse of Trinidad itself. By presenting the allegory of race in the nation as a bittersweet but natural process, Anthony displaces the metadiscourse on race that fuels the discourse on nationalism. In other words, Anthony makes the issue of racial harmony in nationalism seem inevitable, tender, and full of hope. He thereby forces the nationalist discourse away from the issue of racial harmony by observing its success, leaving Trinidadian nationalism without its major weapon, the meta-discourse on race. Anthony disarms Trinidadian nationalism by forcing it to consider that the problems facing the nation-state are not caused by race; nor will they be solved by a smooth people-hood. (African-on-African violence is far more widespread during Jamaican elections than African-on-Indian violence ever has been in Trinidad, for instance.[25]) Michael Anthony's text is surely part of the national discourse, possibly even a national allegory, but it is not part of the dominant discourse on nationalism. Pierre Hill is, as James would say, the product of a truly national writer, and, as such, transcends Trinidadian nationalism to become a universal text beyond the manipulation of nationalists.

The Independent Imagination
in the Independent Nation

In a very different way, Earl Lovelace's text also defies nationalist attempts to read it as an allegory of a nation's search for itself. But with Lovelace, his very desire to enlist the artist in the struggle for national identity ultimately makes his text unfit for duty. Lovelace's novel concentrates both overtly and in allegory on the roles of art and artist in the making of community. It takes the evolution of a communal artistic expression, carnival, from its colonial days in the 1950s to its new form in the late 1960s and early 1970s. As one critic put it,

The yard on Calvary Hill is experiencing the social transition which must be made from imperial dependency to a new era. The old order is represented not only by vestiges of its discredited value system, but by the rapidly changing character of the new nation's famous Carnival celebrations.[26]

The novel features several major characters, among them two artist figures: Aldrick, the Dragonmaker and main character, and Philo, the Calypsonian. Lovelace's novel is a rich and complex one. But it can be best understood by what it has to say about the history of art and culture in Trinidad. It is both a literal history and a national allegory of the major popular art forms in Trinidad – costume-making, steelband and calypso. At first the novel might appear to be an account of the emasculation of carnival, from its rough roots in the poor hills around Port of Spain, where playing mas, stick fighting, or beating pan were not only methods of expression but a substitute for real empowerment, to its middle-class, and nationalist, cooptation by corporate sponsorship, tourism and consumerism. Such a narrative history, and accompanying allegory, would suit Jameson's national allegory well since the novel tells the small story of a single yard of characters while also telling a larger history of nation and culture. Such a narrative would also suit politicians and intellectuals seeking to forge a greater union in Trinidad, or feeling the need for more invented traditions. Certainly art forms such as steelband and calypso would enjoy more respect, and perhaps commercial success, if the novel could help establish what Anthony Giddens has described as a 'time–space distantiation'. That is, their relative newness, and precarious-ness in a small post-colonial island, could be grounded in 'the legitimation of tradition,' and gain authority from the appearance of having deep and unquestionable roots in the heart of Trini-dadian indigenous culture.[27] Perhaps even Lovelace wanted to write a history of national culture. But on closer examination he has not, or at least not one that can help reduce national culture to the signs and invention necessary to the nationalist trade.

The 1990 carnival in Trinidad featured a mas band created by Peter Minshall called Tantana. Drawing on old Trinidad folk tales, Minshall created two huge puppets as king and queen of his band, Tantan and Saga Boy, who delighted carnival crowds by magni-fying the grinding dance of a carnival reveller tenfold. Carlisle

Chang, a visual artist in Trinidad, said afterwards of Minshall's marvellous show that it was a 'landmark in our Art history and development, and shows clearly that artists/creative people should consciously be a part of the turnaround of our economy'.[28] The idea of the artist as national leader also fills Lovelace's text, both as meditation on his own role as a writer, and as central drama in the figure of Aldrick, the Dragonmaker. But there is a point in the text where the artist – both Aldrick and Lovelace – comes to realize that the duty of the artist, and by extension every man or woman who tries to think and create, is first and always to individual vision and creative impulse. And a nation, particularly one charged with a post-colonial dominant discourse on the making of itself, cannot always be served by complete individual assertion of identity and freedom to revoke that identity at any time. Nationalism in Trinidad is too fragile, too inflexible, to assimilate and use Lovelace's text because, beneath the narrative of steel-band, urban yard ethics, race relations and carnival, there is a deep rejection of group identity in Lovelace's novel. Along with the badjohns and stick fights of the 1950s, Lovelace discards group culture, communal expression, the national arts. How else to explain Aldrick's decision to quit playing the dragon at carnival, or Philo's sellout to commercial calypso, or the general break-down of the culture of the yard, or Lovelace's retelling of the 1970 Black Power revolution as farce? These forms of common cultural expression among urban African Trinidadians are not replaced by any new forms of national culture that are judged worthwhile by Aldrick or the author. Instead, Aldrick goes forth with a new belief in individualism, leaving behind past imagined communities like the yard or carnival. In the end Aldrick thinks each man 'has responsibility for his own living, had responsibility for the world he lived in, and had to claim himself and grow and grow and grow' (p. 204). Aldrick escapes the past rather than inventing it. To underscore the estrangement of the past, at the end of the novel the calypsonian Philo plays his old records and goes back to his old mistress in the yard for the sad touch of the past.

But the most telling evidence of Lovelace's assertion of individual identity over either an old or a new group identity comes in Aldrick's relationship to the Indian Trinidadian, Pariag, who wanted to be part of the hill but was never accepted and finally became a shopkeeper there, economically attached but socially distanced. This relationship caused critic Kenneth Ramchand some difficulty in his favourable interpretation of Lovelace's novel. Aldrick believes to the end that there is nothing to explain to Pariag about his isolation, and that every man has to work out his identity for himself. This causes Ramchand to insist that 'the truth of the novel is that Aldrick does have things to explain to Pariag, and is now able to do so.'[29] But Lovelace must insist that the individual cannot be bound by a perceived national need for cultural understanding, that Pariag does not represent Indians in Trinidad and Aldrick Africans in Trinidad. Aldrick will not be known by his yard, or his carnival, or his state, but by his individual creativity. His stance seems confirmed by the scene directly after this decision in which Pariag and his wife reach a new level of tenderness and understanding. They cannot wait for group or gender resolution to seek themselves. Lovelace achieves, like Anthony by different means, a deterritorialization of the dominant discourse on nationalism, insisting that it is not a prior condition, in any form, for self-fulfilment and achievement of individual identity. He goes beyond the displacement of the meta-discourse on race in Trinidadian nationalism to a displacement of nationalism itself as a means of self-realization and definition. C.L.R. James would see Lovelace as a product of a break in a nation's history, at the birth of post-colonial nationhood and all its disruptions of identity and ethics, but James would see Lovelace the national and native writer as an artist who recognized the universal truth of the sovereignty of individual identity and creativity, challenging the very nation-state that produced him.

But James is also right to call these writers national and native because of the confines of the national discourse they work within. In this way, too, Lovelace and Anthony differ from V.S. Naipaul and Neil Bissoondath, other Trinidadian novelists considered in this study, who often try to escape the nation, rather than working through it – as I will try to show in subsequent chapters. But the growth of Trinidad as a separate nation-state, however uncertain its imagined community and invented traditions, has forced most of these writers to deal with specifics of history and culture as they have evolved in Trinidad. No other

Caribbean nation has at its core steel band, calypso and carnival (though some smaller Eastern Caribbean islands now share these traditions). These are Trinidadian cultural phenomena. Neither Jamaica, nor Cuba, nor Barbados would claim these phenomena as their own. No other country is as truly multiracial and integrated in the Caribbean, except Guyana. The other English-speaking Caribbean nations are essentially African-majority islands where multiracial society means socio-political peace, or pragmatic accommodation, with small European, Syrian and Chinese elites (and sometimes a small Indian shopkeeping class). One of the watchwords used by separatist Hindu leaders in Trinidad is 'dooglarization'. They warn that dooglarization is secret government policy. It represents an unfortunate escalation in the metadiscourse on race within nationalism. But it is also a fear that could only exist in Trinidad among the Caribbean islands, particularly since Guyana is too polarized even to entertain such rhetoric. (The Africanization of post-revolutionary Cuba is the closest parallel, but one that the émigré community has not yet begun to fathom, and one sure to cause suffering and intolerance in any future 'reconciliation'.)

Lovelace and Anthony write in a nation-state that by legalistic reasoning alone is already realized as an imagined nation, if we qualify that term in this instance by saying that Trinidad has been politically imagined and confirmed. But the task of understanding or developing a more primordial and historical nationalism in Trinidad to legitimize the state as nation, while it may be the goal of intellectuals and politicians in Trinidad, is too limited even for the sympathetic writer. Lovelace and Anthony cannot be contained by Fredric Jameson's national allegory. Their texts move from individual to nation, and then beyond to an unfettered individual whose national identity is universal. They may be the kind of organic intellectuals that both Antonio Gramsci and Frantz Fanon dreamt of, intellectuals who live among the people and take a new wisdom from the people. And yet like James, Fanon and Gramsci are prepared to see the nation only as passage. Lovelace and Anthony may have identified in their texts, primordial or affective strains in the people of Trinidad, but it is unlikely that those strains will shore up the official nationalism of the state. Lovelace and Anthony challenge the hegemony of the nationalist metadiscourse in Trinidad, dismissing the privileging of race and opening up the question of individual will and creativity inside the nation, which in turn introduces the idea of the nation as a state to be transcended. Their imaginations move through the state of nation, past Jameson, past the nationalist politician, drawing strength from local and national culture but moving ultimately beyond it. Caribbean writers have often been eager to define national identities, and Caribbean politicians have often been eager to enlist them. (Eric Williams asked V.S. Naipaul to help him imagine the Caribbean and the result was the notorious book *The Middle Passage*[30] – hardly a confidence-builder for a nation-builder.) But the lesson of the imagined Trinidads of Lovelace and Anthony may be that neither Fredric Jameson nor Eric Williams will get the national allegory, or the nation-state, they anticipated.

While a reading of Anthony and Lovelace does indicate the oversimplicity of Jameson's national-allegory theory, such a reading also confirms the importance of ethnicity and nationalism in the imagination of the writer, and in the search for a habitable text of personal and common identity. If Benedict Anderson confirms for us that nationalism is a ubiquitous and stubborn fact of modern or postmodern life, and Smith and Douglass confirm that the definition and understanding of this phenomenon is still largely contested, then Lovelace and Anthony perhaps use the creative act, the unfettered imagination, to pry open the debate between primordial, affective visions of nationalism, or of ethnicity (depending on the referents and disciplines in the debate), and the instrumentalist, circumstantialist vision of nationalism. On the one hand, Anthony's novel contains images of a primordial nation, in the forest, in farming, in the timelessness of small community life. On the other hand, the novel registers subtle cultural and social changes brought on by the pressures of social forces, suggesting a more instrumentalist approach to nationhood. Lovelace's novel similarly contains obvious affection for the images of an indigenous, primordial culture of the hill, steel band, calypso, the scorn for property and material goods, and yet the Dragonmaker, in the end, rejects these immutable values and cultural practices, sensing the need to change and remake his imagination outside of these practices.

The Practice of Peoplehood

Clearly these novelists are working in a world of more dimensions than mere structure and agency; clearly there are elements of the personality in them and in their characters that struggle with a primordial sense of ethnicity, or culture, or nationhood. They are not mere agents acting to change the social structure of Caribbean life. Lovelace and Anthony point us toward a richer theory. Both the Dragonmaker and Ghidaree 'encounter the world with their consciousness already given form, but not entirely determined, by the pervasive structuring properties of everyday practice'.[31] In other words, the imagination of both writer and character is determined not by social structure alone, but also by cultural practice, by what Pierre Bourdieu has called 'habitus'. Habitus, or Bourdieu's theory of practice, has recently been applied fruitfully to the debate on ethnicity by G. Carter Bentley in an attempt to resolve the kind of contradictions Lovelace and Anthony throw up. Bentley claims that 'the theory of practice provides a means of explaining the conjunction of affect and instrumentality in the phenomenon of ethnicity.'[32] He quotes Bourdieu, who has not himself applied his theory specifically to ethnicity or nationalism, who writes that 'the habitus is the product of inculcation and appropriation necessary in order for those products of collective history, the objective structures (for example, language, economy, and so on) to succeed in reproducing themselves.'[33] Bentley suggests that shared habitus is realized in 'the same rhythm of life'; and he notes that Bourdieu 'leans heavily on descriptions of the rhythms of dance, ritual, and calendrical succession'.[34] Although Bentley does not make the connection, Bourdieu's use of the body as a storehouse of cultural practice is echoed in Paul Connerton's work and in Daniel Miller's essay on carnival dancing in Trinidad: both see the body's daily practice as the source of cultural patterns and persistence.[35] Bourdieu's words recall the rhythms of Ghidaree in his forest garden, or the Dragonmaker as he sews together his yearly costume. What Lovelace and Anthony appear to be sensing is what some linguists have referred to as a deep structure. The same theory of a deep structure is applied by Bourdieu to practices of everyday life, and by Bentley, through Bourdieu, to ethnicity.

This deep structure or habitus means that Lovelace and Anthony do not have to enter the debate over primordial versus instrumentalist conceptions of national and ethnic identity. If ethnicity or nation is simply the product of living in a place, thinking in a place, with the other people of that place, then the struggle becomes not whether or not there is a perfectly imagined nation or ethnic group, but rather how the individual can liberate himself or herself from the destructive and constraining parts of habitus. This liberation is what the Dragonmaker begins to feel, and what Shellie feels just before the Hindu wedding ceremony, and what Pariag and his wife feel finally. Ethnicity and nationhood, like Jameson's national allegory, are the history carried in the body and the consciousness of these characters, but they are not bound by that practice or that ideology. Bentley and Bourdieu have been attacked for not using enough history, enough social fact, in their theories of identity and daily behaviour. Kevin Yelvington, using Caribbean examples, has argued that ethnicity must be seen as a social identity originally constructed with the help of the ethnic other.[36] But the clear lesson of Lovelace and Anthony is that the Trinidadian must struggle internally with his practices, as well as externally with his fellow nationals, to arrive at a liberated imagination and a liberated nation. The Dragonmaker must break his daily practice to break his habitus, and move beyond the question of how to talk to Pariag, the other, to how to talk to oneself, made the other by habitus. Not to make that break from the habitus that reproduces the metadiscourse on race has serious implications for citizens and writers in Trinidad, and also for gender relations, as the next chapter will attempt to underscore. Both Lovelace, seeking a new relationship between citizen and nation, and Anthony, insisting that a new relationship is already in the making, understand those implications; and, as they displace the official discourse on nationalism with their personal acts of imagination, they also take the nation a step further toward breaking debilitating forms of its habitus and imagining a new nation-space.

Notes

1. Fredric Jameson 'Third World Literature in the Era of Multinational Capitalism', *Social Text*, vol. 15, no. 1, 1986, pp. 65–88. See also the response by Aijaz Ahmad in *Social Text*, vol. 15, no. 2, pp. 3–25, and Jameson again in ibid.

2. Kenneth Ramchand, *The West Indian Novel and Its Background*, London: Faber, 1970.

3. Benedict Anderson, *Imagined Communities: Reflections on the Origins and Spread of Nationalism*, London: Verso, 1983, p. 12.

4. Anthony D. Smith, 'The Myth of the Modern Nation and the Myths of Nations', *Ethnic and Racial Studies*, vol. 11, no. 1, 1988, p. 19.

5. William O. Douglass, 'A Critique of Recent Trends in the Analysis of Ethnonationalism', *Ethnic and Racial Studies*, vol. 11, no. 2, 1988, p. 204.

6. Reinhard Sanders, ed., *Kas-Kas*, Austin: University of Texas, 1972, p. 21.

7. C.L.R. James, *The Artist in the Caribbean*, Mona, Jamaica: Open Lecture Series, University of the West Indies, 1965, p. 8.

8. Victor Questal, 'Views of Earl Lovelace' (interview), *Caribbean Contact*, vol. 5, no. 3, pp. 15–16.

9. Malcolm Cross, 'Colonialism and Ethnicity: A Theory and Comparative Case Study', *Ethnic and Racial Studies*, vol. 1, no. 1, 1978.

10. David Horowitz, *Ethnic Groups in Conflict*, Berkeley: University of California Press, 1985, p. 315.

11. Colin Clarke, 'Society and Electoral Politics in Trinidad and Tobago' in C. Clarke, ed., *Society and Politics in the Caribbean*, London: Macmillan, 1991, p. 71.

12. Selwyn Ryan, *Race and Nationalism in Trinidad and Tobago*, Toronto: University of Toronto Press, 1972, p. 320.

13. John La Guerre, ed., *Calcutta to Caroni: The East Indians of Trinidad*, Trinidad and New York: Longman Caribbean, 1974, p. 106.

14. A full discussion of gender and the metadiscourse on race can be found in Chapter 2, and is elaborated in Steve Harney, 'Men Go Have Respect For All O' We: Valerie Belgrave and the Invention of Trinidad' *World Literature Written in English*, vol. 30, no. 2, 1990, pp. 110–19.

15. References are to Michael Anthony, *Green Days by the River*, London: Heinemann, 1973; and Earl Lovelace, *The Dragon Can't Dance*, London: Longman, 1979.

16. Ian Munro and Reinhard Sander, 'The Return of a West Indian Writer' (interview with Michael Anthony), *Bim*, vol. 14, no. 56, p. 217.

17. John Mendes, *Cote Ci Cote La: A Dictionary of Trinidadian English*, Port of Spain, Trinidad: College Books, 1986.

18. Alistair Niven noted the critical reaction in 'My Sympathies Enlarged' *Commonwealth*, no. 2, 1976, pp. 45–62.

19. Richard Smyer, 'Enchantment and Violence in the Fiction of Michael Anthony', *World Literature Written in English*, vol. 21, no. 1, p. 148.

20. Alternatively, non-Caribbean critics on Caribbean literature, in recent 'post-colonial literary theory' (discussed in Chapter 6), force Anthony's works into post-colonial struggles between 'centre and periphery' in which his easy style is said to 'abrogate the authenticity' of the empire. See Gareth Griffiths and Helen Tiffin, eds., *The Empire Writes Back: Theory and Practice in Post-Colonial Literature*, London: Routledge, 1989, pp. 91–7.

21. 'The Homesickness of Michael Anthony' (interview), *The Literary Half-Yearly*, vol. 16, no. 1, 1975, pp. 95–124.

22. Rhoda Reddock, 'Women and Slavery in the Caribbean: A Feminist Perspective' *Latin American Perspectives*, vol. 44, no. 12, 1985, p. 78.

23. Anson Gonzalez, *Trinidad and Tobago Literature On Air*, Port of Spain, Trinidad: National Cultural Council, 1973, p. 89.

24. Gilles Deleuze and Felix Guattari, 'Kafka: Toward a Minor Literature', *New Literary History*, vol. 16, no. 3, 1985, pp. 591–608.

25. Michael Kaufman, *Jamaica Under Manley: Dilemmas of Socialism and Democracy*, London: Zed Books, 1985. Kaufman notes that the continuing political violence during elections in the Manley years suggested both internal and external instigation.

26. Robert Hamner, 'The Measure of the Yard Novel: From Mendes to Lovelace', *Commonwealth*, vol. 9, no. 1, p. 101.

27. Anthony Giddens, *A Contemporary Critique of Historical Materialism*, Berkeley: University of California, 1981, p. 90.

28. *Trinidad Guardian*, Port of Spain, Trinidad, 23 March 1990, p. 14.

29. Kenneth Ramchand, 'An Approach to Earl Lovelace's Novel through An Examination of Indian–African Relations in *The Dragon Can't Dance*', *Wasafiri*, vol. 1, no. 2.

30. V.S. Naipaul, *The Middle Passage*, New York: Macmillan, 1963.

31. G. Carter Bentley, 'A Reply to Yelvington', *Comparative Studies in Society and History*, vol. 33, no. 1, January 1991, p. 174.

32. G. Carter Bentley, 'Ethnicity and Practice', *Comparative Studies in Society and History*, vol. 29, no. 1, 1987, p. 28.

33. Pierre Bourdieu, *Outline of a Theory of Practice*, Cambridge: Cambridge University Press, 1977, p. 72, quoted in Bentley 'Ethnicity and Practice'.

34. Bentley, 'Ethnicity and Practice,' p.33.

35. See Paul Connerton, *How Societies Remember*, Cambridge: Cambridge University Press, 1989; and Daniel Miller, 'Absolute Freedom in Trinidad', *Man*, vol. 26, no. 2, 1991, pp. 323–41.

36. Kevin Yelvington, 'A Comment on Bentley', *Comparative Studies in Society and History*, vol. 33, no. 1, 1991, pp. 158–68.

CHAPTER 2

Men Go Have Respect For All O' We:
Valerie Belgrave's Invention of Trinidad

This chapter takes its title from the chorus of a song by the Calypso Queen of Trinidad and Tobago for 1990, Eastlynn Orr. Her calypso exhorted women to respect themselves in order to win the respect of Trinidadian men. She herself earned the respect of a notoriously tough audience in San Fernando, in the south of Trinidad. Only twenty-four, she had a quite beautiful dark-skinned, slightly gap-toothed African look. It was not the kind of look that appears often in BWIA flight magazines or on Carib beer posters. Trinidad, not unlike Brazil, imagines itself – indeed markets itself – as a nation of mixed heritage. The relation of this national rhetoric to its people is an odd and deceitful one. And to understand both a Carib beer poster and the enthusiastic response Eastlynn Orr received at her Skinner Park performance, I think it is necessary to recall again the metadiscourse on race that runs through the modern nation-state of Trinidad. As already discussed in Chapter 1, this metadiscourse is a privileged text in Trinidadian culture and politics, and is often held as a transcendent tool for understanding that culture. But to investigate the metadiscourse itself is to come face to face with its hegemonic power. The meta-narrative of race in Trinidad finds full expression in a recent novel by Valerie Belgrave called *Ti Marie*.[1] A look at her novel as a text within the metatext of race in this Caribbean nation can help uncover both the beauty of Eastlynn Orr and the perverse power of a discourse over the imagination of that nation. Lovelace and Anthony moved confidently beyond the metadiscourse by denying its hegemony. Belgrave demonstrates the danger of not recognizing the existent national community, and thus not addressing its real needs. Indeed, she falls into the trap of pursuing a peoplehood built on racial commonality and respect, rather than revealing a nation in need of new projects for understanding class and gender.

Inventing the Mixed Nation

There are few women with Eastlynn Orr's look in what the author describes on the opening page as an attempt 'to promote a positive image of West Indian culture through the popular medium of the historical romance'. There are even fewer examples in the novel of men respecting all women. The novel is an unabashed and wholehearted attempt to reimagine Trinidad at the turn of the eighteenth century. And it is a project with obvious cultural ambition, including a foreword that describes the geography of Trinidad, a note on language, and a chart of further historical events. The acknowledgements thank the eminent historian of Trinidad Dr Bridget Brereton, and Trinidad's foremost literary critic, Professor Kenneth Ramchand. The book is published in the Heinemann Caribbean Writers Series and already appears on a course book-list at the University of the West Indies, St Augustine. In her foreword, the author informs the reader that the people of Trinidad 'are drawn from many races, and indeed today the twin-island republic of Trinidad and Tobago prides itself on being an exceptionally cosmopolitan and racially harmonious nation'. (The term 'harmonious' will be an important one in both Belgrave's work and in the many texts of modern Trinidad that make up the metatext on race in the nation.) Belgrave continues, telling the reader that the 'early history of Trinidad has contributed greatly to its cosmopolitanism and also to its rich outpourings of art, for even in the dawn of its modern-day period [the late eighteenth century], it was a haven of liberalism and racial and cultural tolerance' (p. vii). Thus the scene of writing is set for the metanarrative of the difficult birth of racial harmony in Trinidad. The author has been forthright about her purposes, but she begins writing her narrative of race already in the grip of a metanarrative that will force itself on her story, making her both conspirator and victim in the hegemony of the metadiscourse. And what ensures the dominance of the metadiscourse, both in Belgrave and in the public discourse of the nation, is the invented and real harmony of races in Trinidad, a harmony that for this multiracial nation, unlike other multiracial nations like the United States or Guyana, is a source of communal pride. But the relative degree of socio-cultural peace masks deep economic and political stratification and limits all discourse to the boosterism of racial harmony. This is the regime of truth, as Foucault would say, a regime patrolled by the metadiscourse on race. Valerie Belgrave's novel is written under this regime, and indeed, perhaps unwittingly, written for this regime, because the power of the metadiscourse lies in the apparent goodwill and optimism of its speakers – the faith that holds that, if racial harmony prevails, the nation's people will be free and equal is a difficult sentiment to attack, even if that sentiment masks an attempted negation of political and economic fact.

Ti Marie is, first, what Eric Hobsbawm has called a constructed tradition. Valerie Belgrave has set out to invent the cosmopolitan roots of Trinidad today, and to lend both literary and historical legitimacy to the dominant discourse of racial harmony in this post-colonial West Indian nation. 'Modern nations and all their impedimenta generally claim to be opposite of novel, namely rooted in remotest antiquity, and the opposite of constructed, namely human communities so "natural" as to require no definition other than self-assertion', writes Hobsbawm.[2] But this novel is not, as will be seen, an invented tradition in control of its own ideology. Rather, like much of the journalism and scholarship in Trinidad, the invention comes to dominate its master, and the metadiscourse of race creates a monstrous distortion.

A sketch of the novel's plot would not, at first, reveal anything but the most uplifting tale of the triumph of tolerance and enlightenment over the forces of oppression, just as a reading of the historical events detailed would only permit the conclusion that Trinidad's history is pregnant with hopeful omens of racial harmony. The story is set on an estate north of Port of Spain, just after the French Revolution. The estate is owned by a Spaniard, Don Diego de Las Flores. He lives with his son and daughter, and is attended by a half-Amerindian, half-African, who saved his daughter at birth and who is said to possess healing powers. She has twin daughters, Carmen and Elena (ti Marie); the first almost white, the second described as 'mulatta'. Unknown to them, their father is a French republican who works as a tutor on the estate. Two young British aristocrats find their way, reluctantly, to the island just before the British capture it. One of them, Barry, son of Lord Vantage, falls in love with Elena, and she with him, but he wavers because of his love for his grandmother, who, despite being an outspoken liberal, might not accept a mulatto as his wife. Several other love stories surround this central one, following the laws of the genre. The dilemma of Barry and Elena is sharpened by the rising racial intolerance and civil strife that takes place following the British takeover of the island. The characters converse on the Haitian revolution, Wilberforce and the abolitionists, Napoleon, and Lord Nelson. In the end, Barry marries Elena and takes her back with him to inherit his estate, having gained his grandmother's consent. One of the last historical events, one based on fact, has the British Governor signing a torture order for Louisa Calderon, a slave woman whose death would result in his trial and conviction for torture. But the fight to end racial bigotry is constructed in a traitorous discourse.

The Metadiscourse of Race

To unmask the hegemonic metadiscourse in this seemingly innocent romance, it might be useful before proceeding with a textual analysis to remind ourselves of the history of the modern nation-state for which Belgrave is inventing this tradition. Or, to phrase it differently, it might be helpful to search out other texts in the metatext of race in Trinidad, texts of the modern Trinidad that Belgrave invented. Such a search will indicate the pervasive influence of the metadiscourse, and its destructive tendencies, both in Belgrave's narrative and in the nation. Such a search does not have to reach far beyond the Sunday newspapers. In one short editorial section of the *Trinidad Express* of 11 March 1990, there are three columns on race and racism, all referring to previous columns or editorials on the subject, and there are two long letters to the editor on the subject, also in response to previous instances of discourse on race.[3] A column by a European Trinidadian on the subject of a bill to introduce mandatory national service criticizes Hindu leaders for whipping up fears of miscegenation brought on by Hindu–African contact in a national service corps. Set off in bold print in his column is the question: 'What is so significant about the fact that it is a society of diverse races that merits constant repetition from public platforms' (p. 2). An African Trinidadian columnist, Geoffrey Frankson, distinguishes two types of Indo-Trinidadian intellectual: those who rightly call for more understanding of Indian culture among non-Indians, and those who, 'like any petty politician of any race', are simply seeking votes along racial lines (p. 5). Finally, the most thoughtful column comes from Kevin Baldeosingh, who asserts that being East Indian and Trinidadian makes him more Trinidadian. He ends his column hoping that, 'as long as East Indian food is so popular, prejudice fights a losing battle' (p. 20). Like Belgrave's novel, the sentiments in these columns might seem admirable for a nation struggling to achieve a sense of itself as a single, modern nation-state, united in its imagined community. Belgrave's novel concerns itself with racial harmony between Africans and Europeans, but sets itself up as a precursor of harmony between the two dominant groups in modern Trinidad, the Indians and Africans, who represent roughly equal segments of the population today. But Belgrave's novel inhabits an invented tradition, having been written after the rise of Indians and Africans to social and political dominance – not at all a natural and antiquated precondition for that rise, but rather a prisoner to the metadiscourse of that rise and its subsequent infection of the national discourse. In order to understand the crucial importance of denying the ahistoricity of Belgrave's book and the invented traditions that form the journalist's imagining of Trinidad today, a quick return to the birth of metadiscourse at the birth of the independent nation (and not at the turn of the eighteenth century) will be helpful.

The Counter-discourse of Class

In *Black Intellectuals and the Dilemmas of Race and Class in Trinidad*,[4] Ivar Oxaal traces the rise of nationalism in Trinidad. His excellent study recalls the working-class movements of the 1930s in Trinidad, and particularly their interracial nature. At the time of the labour strikes known as the Butler Riots in Trinidad in 1937, the dominant discourse in Trinidad was clearly one of class struggle. Mainly Afro-Trinidadian, and often Grenadian oilfield workers, joined with predominantly Indo-Trinidadian farm labourers to call for better conditions and home rule. But following the Second World War, with the dissolution of the British Empire, the discourse became a less class-based independence movement. At the same time, Oxaal notes, the emergent Afro-Trinidadian middle class, closely connected by education, culture, urban environment and workplace to the British colonial government, began to assert itself, under Dr Eric Williams, as the natural successor class to the departing British colonial administrative class. Thus the rhetoric of nationalism became tied both to a discourse of anti-colonialism (Williams's famous 'Massa day done' phrase) and to a subterranean one of African succession. The Indo-Trinidadian population, in the 1950s still largely rural and locked out of the colonial education system and bureaucracy, saw little advantage in independence and indeed feared the unchecked power of an Afro-Trinidadian administration. Nonetheless, using the rhetoric of race and nationalism, Williams and his urban Afro-Trinidadians seized the young nation. But Williams, never the Marxist of his scholarship, had no intention of expelling either Creole or foreign massas. The British colonial clerk class was replaced by an Afro-Trinidadian one, and Williams's stratified nationalism led to a rhetorical vacuum that was filled by the pernicious discourse on race, now twisted from African versus European to African versus Indian. This metadiscourse on race thrived on the discourse of nationalism, which insisted that unless a Trinidadian was in favour of the nationalist movement he was not truly Trinidadian. The lines of racial politics were drawn, and the wicked marriage of nationalism and race was celebrated. What was lost, as John La Guerre has pointed out, was the possibility of class politics, and the opportunity for a political discourse on equality of workers and individuals, rather than hierarchical ethnic groups.[5]

The better and brighter day that labour leader Uriah Butler had envisioned in Trinidad was sacrificed to a hollow nationalism exhorting racial unity against the massa, while practising the massa's colonial politics of division and stratification. In fact, the career of 'the Chief Servant' to the people, as Tubal Uriah Butler was known, is a career illustrative of the national tensions of race and class, from his role in the First World War, all the way to independence and beyond to the Black Power movement of the late 1960s and early 1970s. It was Butler, Black and radical, who was continually singled out by colonial authorities, as Richard Jacobs notes in his fascinating study of the Colonial Office records in *Butler Versus the King*. There were attempts after the riots of 1937 to split Butler and his Indian partners, particularly Adrian Cola Rienzi, by both local elites and the Home Office, and later, by a treacherous 'coloured' middle class that feared his populist socialism. All these agents saw early the benefits to racial politics; and they saw, with the coming of independence, a chance to hook that politics to the politics of anti-colonialism and nationalism. But, more than anything else, Butler stood against the multi-class politics of Cipriani, Albert Gomes, Williams, and eventually Rienzi himself, despite in fact winning the pre-independence elections in 1950. As Jacobs notes, Butler's 'colour and his class origins betrayed his true sentiments and the professionals in his 1946 and 1950 campaigns could now be seen to have used the Butler bandwagon to achieve their narrow goals.'[6] Butler's political history points to another aspect of race-based politics in Trinidad: the irony of a truly multiracial elite, like the one that used Butler in 1946 and 1950, sitting atop a racial politics partly of their making. Interestingly, it took until the 1970s and the threat of a new class-based coalition and a politics of race that had turned on its creators and begun to distinguish between Blacks and 'coloured' elites, for the Trinidadian government, in panic, to recognize this true founder of independence.

Against this history of the metadiscourse, the quality of the journalism of contemporary Trinidad is sadly telling. To hope that a common love for Indian food, the exposure of petty ethnic politicians, the erasure of race as a social category, can make Trinidad a more prosperous and just nation is to write within the meta-discourse of race. The economic and political consequences of such an issue as national service are subsumed in the rhetoric of national culture and harmony between races. The noble aims of these journalists and academics make the hidden ideology of their criticism all the more insidious. A letter to the editor of the *Sunday Trinidad Express* on 11 March 1990, defending West Indian cricket captain Viv Richards for describing his team as 'of African descent', criticized instead Indo-Trinidadian leaders for chastising him, noting that the Indians boasted of dominating recent island scholarship competitions without being accused of racism (p. 22). Such a letter represents not the giddy rhetoric of a carnival nation of all peoples, but the darker side of race as a dominant discourse. While intellectuals like Dr Selwyn Ryan of the Institute of Social and Economic Research seek to address the cultural gap that leads to such accusations, publishing polls that are really ethnic mobility studies,[7] virtually no one escapes the metadiscourse on race long enough to ask about the class of those receiving island scholarship, or the reason for their very limited number. Still fewer escape the metadiscourse to ask why the West Indian cricket captain has had to retreat to the issue of race to praise the West Indian team, or, finally, whether an end to such comments can ever be expected without new attention being given to economic justice and access to power. The fate of Trinidadian women is tied to that giving of new attention to justice and power, and not to the harmony of the races. The metadiscourse of race reproduces its own hierarchy: the very discussion of race in Trinidad falls into the trap Williams unwittingly set, and the economic stratification and power structures under the metadiscourse sabotage any chance of equality, regardless of the sincerity of the speaker. Nationalism becomes a project of cooking the big pilau, not examining who cooks, who eats, and who does neither. Perhaps it should be noted, however, in defence of these journalists, that the roots of the metadiscourse on race reach deep into the history not only of Trinidad but of Trinidadian journalism. Bridget Brereton, in her classic study of race relations in Trinidad in the nineteenth century, noted that

> whenever questions of colour and race were discussed in the press, correspondents and editors divided into two camps. There were those who argued that it was important to bring into the open the existence of race feeling and discrimination, in order to destroy it; they were nearly always coloured or black ... and there were those, often but not exclusively white, who argued that to discuss race questions was to fan the fires of ill-feeling and that the best policy was simply to ignore them.[8]

What is interesting is that neither Brereton nor the journalists connect race to class in this discourse, although elsewhere Brereton

is quite explicit about the interdependence of the two in the socio-
economic hierarchy in colonial Trinidad. Contemporary journalists inherently operate the same boundaries in their conversations
on racial equality. One can highlight the subject for nationalist
purposes, or downplay it for the same purpose. But one cannot tie
progress on racial equality too closely to progress on economic
equality.

History against Itself

To test the thesis that the nationalist quest for racial equality in
Trinidad is inscribed with the malevolent hierarchy of the metadiscourse on race, with its destructive consequences for women,
let us return to Belgrave's novel to see if her novel privileges race
over class, and whether that privileging distorts the possibility of
racial equality. Her novel covers roughly the same historical period
as the classic book and play by another Trinidadian, *The Black
Jacobins* by C.L.R. James.[9] In Valerie Belgrave's novel the
plantation system in Trinidad is never called into question, and
indeed Barry, the abolitionist hero of the novel, talks of creating
a colony where 'free labour is encouraged' to come to work on
the estates (p. 114). Such an attempt to attract free labour to the
plantations did, of course, occur after emancipation, resulting in
what Hugh Tinker has called a 'new system of slavery', and bring-
ing East Indians, Chinese and Portuguese to Trinidad. By contrast, in C.L.R. James's play about the same period in Haiti, one
of Toussaint's generals demands: 'Break up those accursed big
plantations. As long as they remain, freedom is a mockery. Distribute the lands carefully among the best cultivators in the
country. Let everybody see there is a new regime.'[10] But in *Ti
Marie* it is the old regime that is benign and threatened. The
kindly patriarch of the novel, Don Diego, tells his young son near
the beginning of the novel that,

> Trinidad is a refuge for anybody on the run. Slaves or no, they live just
> like us anyway. None of us have anything. How many of us are here?
> A handful of whites? And so many of us already intermarried with
> Africans and Indians. My son, in a companionship of misery, there's
> little room for discrimination. (p. 4)

Don Diego's particular misery is that he needs 'strong black slaves to work the cocoa' (p. 3).

Nor is the Spaniard Don Diego alone in his view of Trinidad as a hapless and innocent place. Much of the novel focuses on the erosion of the rights of coloured plantation owners, mixed French and Spanish creoles who throw social balls at which they allow the slaves the day off to celebrate as well. None of this island portrait is given an ironic tone by Belgrave. In fact, she invests an emotional attachment in this ethno-specific class and invites the reader to do the same with many heart-wrenching moments. Her mulatto heroine sees to the needs of the slaves every Saturday and is viewed as especially sensitive and kind by her coloured friends. In short, the novel takes as its subject the imperilment of a land-owning coloured class, which is trying to forge an allegiance with a landowning white class, but subject to the rigid racial rule of the British. The only two African slave characters are the overly loyal personal slaves of the heroine and hero, both of whom were bought by their unlikely masters to save their lives and then to give them their freedom. It is perhaps in this action – the buying and freeing of Tessa and Fist – that the class dimensions of the novel, and of the invented tradition, take on their most obvious appearance. In stark opposition to the slave uprising of Saint Domingue, it is the white abolitionists and the enlightened mixed class that agitate and effect change in the novel. (Anachronistic memories of Cipriani and Williams are hard to avoid – though at least the European Trinidadian labour leader Cipriani had some understanding of class struggle.) The loyalty of Tessa and Fist, therefore, comes to represent their debt to their struggling masters, a coloured woman tutored by a French republican émigré, and a young British noble aligned to Wilberforce. It is only too easy to recall here the theory of Orlando Patterson in *Slavery and Social Death*. Patterson develops what he considers a worldwide theory of slavery that includes manumission in its structure. Though the theory appears to have little application to *The Black Jacobins*, it fits *Ti Marie* all too well. Patterson asserts that

> the master gives the slave physical life either directly (if he was the original enslaver) or indirectly (if he purchased or inherited him), in return for which the slave is under obligation to reciprocate with total

obedience and service.... With manumission the master makes another
gift to the slave, this time the gift of social life, which is ideologically
interpreted as a repayment for faithful service.[11]

Caught in the dialectic of slavery, the relationship between Barry
and Fist or that between Elena and Tessa never transcends the
gift of social life. The metadiscourse on race inscribes a paternal-
istic and inhuman order in the harmony between master and freed
slave. The novel includes an episode where Fist puts his drunken
master to bed before curling up on the rug below him, and one
where Tessa gives herself to Fist on their first encounter alone, in
marked contrast to the lengthy courtship of Elena and Barry. In
the metadiscourse of race, Barry and Fist swim and ride together,
and discuss abolition, but the distance of class remains. Fist has
moved from slavery to the working class; and, while Elena might
be destined for an English country estate, Fist must ask upon his
arrival in England, 'So much o' misery in England and you does
worry so 'bout black man?' Barry replies that slaves 'are in a state
of physical bondage, and that does put them in a worse position'
(p. 218). Reinhard Sander notes that C.L.R. James would hardly
be content with such an answer, would hardly be part of the
metadiscourse on legal and cultural racial harmony. He suggests
that James saw no freedom for the Haitian people in the final
results of their revolution; he saw only that 'white masters were
exchanged for black ones; slavery, though abolished in name,
persisted.'[12]

Nationalism without Equality

There is no talk in Belgrave's novel, even from the idealistic French
tutor or the now persecuted coloureds, of the need for people to
have their own land, or the need for all to participate in their
government. The book invents a Trinidad for the Afro-Trinidadian
nationalists born of the independence period, a Trinidad in which
the call for cultural wholeness and harmony prevents the national
discourse from returning to issues of class and empowerment.
C.L.R. James has described this middle class and its tenacious
insistence on a hierarchical discourse: 'They are horrified at being
considered a part of that huge black mass and they are excluded

from being part of those who really master the economic and political life of the country.'[13] It is useful here to recall Anthony Smith's distinction between 'aristocratic lateral and the demotic vertical types' of premodern ethnic communities upon which Smith believes nations are both primordially founded and imaginatively constructed.[14] Smith's attempted resolution of that primordial/instrumentalist debate is an interesting one. But, for our present purposes, what is most jarring in light of Belgrave's effort is his distinction between lateral and vertical premodern ethnies. The irony of Belgrave's work, controlled as it is by the metadiscourse on race, is that it focuses on a lateral aristocratic antecedent to the present Trinidadian nation, attempting to locate national traits in the liberalism of the elite minority. Alternatively, as a nationalist intellectual interested in constructing a tradition of tolerance and multiracial harmony, Belgrave could have used what Smith termed 'ethnic historicism' as an 'educator-intellectual' using 'communal culture' to reconstruct and reconstitute Trinidad 'through a national and civic appropriation of ethnic history, which will mobilize members on the basis of a rediscovered identity.'[15] Belgrave might have chosen early forms of carnival or the labour movement to represent that communal culture. Instead, she chose to concentrate on the lateral aristocrats of the plantocracy because the metadiscourse on race emptied her task of class and demotic cultural forms.

If this metadiscourse causes Belgrave to choose the lateral aristocrats, just as it subverts the honest attempts to prevent racial strife by journalist and academics alike, its effects on the politics of gender are no less devastating. Here the metadiscourse orders not only men and women, but women and women. The dominant discourse of racial harmony and cultural blending, their national pilau, writes a history of gender full of hierarchy and ignorant of class prejudice. This is nowhere more apparent than in Belgrave's constructed romance.

> We too – all we feminist critics – may desperately wish to find an adequate past, a family romance sufficient to our longing, and we too may fear the inadequacies of the past which we now unequivocally possess. Is it possible that we have rewritten and reappraised history in order to give the positive inflections we desire and require?[16]

These are the doubts of the prominent literary critics, Sandra M. Gilbert and Susan Gubar. It is worth comparing their thoughtful criticism of the feminist project with Valerie Belgrave's own construction of the past. Intoxicated with the discourse of many races happily playing an elite form of mas together, has Belgrave rewritten the past, doing more damage than good to her slave character, Tessa? How does the metadiscourse on race enslave Tessa, as surely as it enslaved Luisa Calderon?

Inventing the Rules of Class

In Belgrave's historical romance there are many minor love stories swirling around the difficult love of Barry and Elena. One would have thought that one of these would cross class boundaries, if not for the politics of race, then at least for the politics of good fiction – a love between slave and noblewoman would have offered intense drama and suspense. But no cross-class love can be found in any of the relationships except, significantly, in the one that produced Elena. The young French republican tutor reveals that he is the father of the twins with their half-African, half-Amerindian slave mother, whom he describes as 'young, beautiful, and easy to be with. She once took pity on a broken-hearted man' (p. 69). The relationship is said by the author to have meant nothing to either of them – and is the only relationship in the novel about which such a thing is said. The republican goes on to find his true love, an Irish absentee landowner, and the slave mother continues to live as a slave and bring up her daughters in the house of her master, Don Diego. Her daughter Carmen, educated and refined by life as a surrogate daughter of Don Diego, attends balls held by estate owners and marries the Spanish son of Don Diego – she has little class distance to cross. Because there is no inter-class love, we can never know the significance of her lighter colour – only those of lighter colour have escaped to the owning class, and Belgrave cannot achieve a more thorough harmony without breaking the laws of class, the inscribed laws of the hegemonic discourse.

As a result of Belgrave's inability to encounter class struggle in her invention of racial struggle, Carmen and her mother are sepa-rated not only into different classes but into different classes of women. The daughter requires courtship and marriage, the mother is a temporary concubine. No amount of mystification about the mother's healing powers or strong silent Amerindian blood can obscure her status as slave to man and estate owner alike. But *Ti Marie* contains an even more central hegemonic gender relation, born of racial rhetoric and class silence. Early in the novel, the carnival celebrations brought by the new French white and coloured slave-owning immigrants are described. One such coloured elite 'in his generosity had granted his slaves the permission to celebrate by performing that morning' (p. 20). This narratorial comment opens a discussion on the carnival celebration among the characters in which one French coloured wonders about 'the white man's notorious penchant for coloured mistresses' (p. 21). Later in the novel, Barry reasons that 'every white man here had a black woman or mulatto mistress hidden away somewhere', and he concludes that he 'just happened to find a black woman who could fulfil more than bedroom needs' (p. 173). The hero's idea that these other women are fulfilling only in the bedroom denies their humanity in a particular classist manner. First, it assumes that the bourgeois education that Elena has received makes her more than a sexual object, more than these other women. Second, it assumes that the system of mistresses is the result only of racial prejudice, and thus that the mistresses must be hidden. The hero's comments deny the class (and gender) relationship between master and mistress – if the master's servants were Irish, or even Cockney, he would still undoubtedly have forced one into such a semi-secret position. No doubt being a Black mistress made the power more complete. But Belgrave's particular obsession with the origins of race-mixing in Trinidad denies the class order of that mixing, leaving those without bourgeois education fulfilling only bedroom needs.

Mistresses to the National Body

These are not the only references to mistresses, and indeed the motif of this historical romance is the mixing, within unstated class boundaries, of races in love or in sex – the constructed tradition of the face on the Carib poster. From Dr Selwyn Ryan to former prime minister A.N.R. Robinson, to the national anthem in which 'every creed and race has an equal place', the Trinidad rainbow is praised as a model of societal harmony in the making; and Belgrave's class-bound construction of voluntary and coerced race-mixing invents a tradition for this rainbow. But what of the land below the sky, and the women who hold up half that sky? Belgrave's discourse sweeps up the Trinidadian woman and offers her to the cause of racial harmony. The metadiscourse on race forces Belgrave into a reification of woman as cultural exchange. Mistresses and mulatresses become evidence of tolerance or intolerance, whether slept with, married or raped. Their bodies become the scene of writing, and on them is inscribed not only the discourse of racial harmony but also the class nature of that attempted harmony. Their essential significance as characters is to be taken by an abolitionist man or a slave-owning man, a freed slave or a coloured land-owner, to prove the existence of racial harmony, or, conversely, racial hypocrisy. In short, they become commodities in the narrative exchange of race, sent where and when they are needed, to stand for aspects of the struggle between the pro-slavery and anti-slavery bourgeoisie. In this system the value of an African slave, whose class will not enable her to accompany an aristocrat to England, is less than a mulatress who can prove the nobility of her race, and the nobility of the rainbow discourse, by speaking Latin with her French tutor. The metadiscourse of race in Trinidad invents a tradition that makes the preference for a light-skinned mulatress on a Carib poster seem natural. The metadiscourse also renders any attempt to address that colour preference useless without a concrete historical analysis of the class prejudices that incorporated colour prejudice in Trinidad. Instead of exposing class rigidity in a plantation society, *Ti Marie* celebrates an alleged race mobility, and one of the casualties of this invented tradition is gender relations. Hazel Carby, an American Black female literary critic, has addressed precisely this use of mixed women to signify race relations. In a perceptive essay challenging the construction of the Black female literary tradition in the United States, she notes that one school of American Black women writers has tended to inscribe the mixed Black woman with all the current debates on race relations, and that tendency has often been joined by a tendency to idealize 'rural folk' and ignore the Black urban working class. But she notes that there is an alternative tradition of such writers as Nella Larsen, Ann Petry and Toni Morrison, who do represent both race and class in the city, 'through a prism of black female sexuality'. Carby accuses the ascendant tradition of engaging in a discourse of race, without attention to class, and of fearing Black female sexuality for its own sake, focusing 'on defending their morality or on displacing sexuality onto another terrain'.[17] It is a charge that must also be levelled at Belgrave. Her Black female women have no sexuality but that of the racially and nationally symbolic (perhaps her men do not either.) And the use of the mulatto trope, without some concomitant attention to the pernicious relationship in Caribbean history between colour and class, constructs a tradition for the official nationalism in Trinidad and Tobago that does such a disservice to Eastlynn Orr and her fans.

But Valerie Belgrave is not alone in her official nationalism. Much of the sociological work on Trinidad, such as the classic studies by Lloyd Brathwaite and M.G. Smith, though containing class considerations, became so enmeshed in the complexities of race and skin colour that their work became susceptible to the metadiscourse.[18] Today, the works of both are immersed in nationalist debates that concern themselves not with the problems of social stratification or plural societies, the subject of their studies, but with how to distribute races, and thus racial harmony up and down the stratified society or inside the ruling class in a plural society.[19] A few, like Stuart Hall, have tried to extend the class analysis. Hall developed a 'complexity–unity' model that would concentrate on Althusserian 'structures of domination' in Caribbean societies. But his analysis led him to conclude that, 'if there are no predictable class solidarities [in sophisticated Marxist analysis], then there are certainly no ethnic or cultural solidarities either.'[20] Hall perhaps breaks the stranglehold of the metadiscourse on race by insisting on a general rule of unpredicatability. But his voice is an unusual one.

Far more usual is the front page of the Trinidad Guardian on 19 March 1990, in which Basdeo Panday, the Hindu leader of the opposition party, United National Congress, was quoted as saying, 'there can be no economic progress in Trinidad and Tobago unless and until we first resolve our socio-political problem.' This ultimatum is sad testimony to the continuing dominance of the metadiscourse on race. It is a discourse that takes as its national project a constructed community not of men and women working together for economic and political empowerment, but of groups seeking to share racial representation in the hegemony of the current political society. In his classic play about the Haitian Revolution, one of C.L.R. James's Haitian generals defines his revolution thus: 'Liberty, slavery abolished; Equality, no dukes ... no counts, no marquises, no princes, no lords, everybody equal. And Fraternity, everybody gets together and be friends, nobody takes advantage of anybody, everybody helping everybody else.'[21] Valerie Belgrave's *Ti Marie* invents a tradition of liberty in Trinidad. But the metadiscourse that surrounds liberty, whether voiced by Dr Eric Williams or Basdeo Panday, makes the writing of equality difficult, and the regime of fraternity only a dream in Trinidad.

Despite the political mood of the intelligentsia and the constructed traditions that strengthen it, the applause showered on Eastlynn Orr, against the wisdom of the metadiscourse, gives hope, hinting that the people of Trinidad may be imagining a community of their own. Valerie Belgrave fell into a trap in her novel; but can the writer in Trinidad imagine ethnicity, race and peoplehood without falling into this trap? Perhaps the fault lies more in the political intention of the writer than in the execution of the act. It might be worth recalling Frantz Fanon's words at the end of his agonizing study *Black Skin, White Masks*. 'The discovery of the existence of a Negro civilization in the fifteenth century', wrote Fanon, 'confers no patent of humanity on me. Like it or not, the past can in no way guide me in the present moment.'[22] Belgrave's effort to construct such a past may, in the end, be of little help to the people of Trinidad and Tobago, no matter what its deficiencies. In the next chapter I will try to show that Willi Chen has beaten back the metadiscourse on race while talking repeatedly about race and culture, precisely because he has not taken it as his task to uncover a great civilization. He does, in fact, reject the imperative of racial harmony and of a singular national identity, not, like Lovelace, out of personal creative vision, and not, like Anthony, out of hope for local communities. But he avoids

Belgrave's regime of racial harmony by celebrating the communal and individual resistance to any harmony – political, racial or sexual.

Notes

1. Valerie Belgrave, *Ti Marie*, Oxford: Heinemann, 1988.

2. Eric Hobsbawm and Terence Ranger, eds., *The Invention of Tradition*, Cambridge: Cambridge University Press, 1986, p. 14.

3. *Sunday Trinidad Express*, 11 March 1990, Section Two, pp. 1–24.

4. Ivar Oxaal, *Black Intellectuals and the Dilemmas of Race and Class in Trinidad*, Cambridge, Mass.: Schenkman, 1982.

5. John La Guerre, *The Politics of Communalism*, Port of Spain, Trinidad: Pan Caribbean Publications, 1982.

6. W. Richard Jacobs, ed., *Butler Versus the King: Riots and Sedition in 1937*, Port of Spain, Trinidad: Key Caribbean, 1976, p. 26.

7. *Sunday Trinidad Express*, 5 November 1989, Port of Spain, Trinidad, pp. 27–8.

8. Bridget Brereton, *Race Relations in Colonial Trinidad, 1870–1900*, Cambridge: Cambridge University Press, 1979, p. 199.

9. C.L.R. James, *The Black Jacobins*, New York: Vantage Books, 1963. References to the play are from *A Time... And A Season: 8 Caribbean Plays*, edited by Errol John, St Augustine, Trinidad: University of the West Indies, 1976.

10. C.L.R. James, *The Black Jacobins*, p. 339.

11. Orlando Patterson, *Slavery and Social Death*, Cambridge, Mass.: Harvard University Press, 1982.

12. Reinhard Sander, 'C.L.R. James and the Haitian Revolution', *World Literature Written in English*, vol. 26, no. 2, 1986, pp. 277–90.

13. C.L.R. James, *At The Rendez-Vous of Victory*, London: Allison & Busby, 1984, p. 154.

14. Anthony D. Smith, 'The Origins of Nations', *Racial and Ethnic Studies*, vol. 12, no. 3, 1989, p. 361.

15. Ibid., p. 362.

16. Sandra M. Gilbert and Susan Gubar, 'Forward Into the Past: The Complex Female Affiliation Complex', in Jerome McGann, ed., *Historical Studies and Literary Criticism*, Madison: University of Wisconsin Press, 1985, p. 244.

17. Hazel V. Carby, 'The Quicksands of Representation', in Henry Louis Gates, ed., *Reading Black, Reading Feminist: A Critical Anthology*, New York: Meridian, 1990, p. 87.

18. Lloyd Brathwaite, *Social Stratification in Trinidad: A Preliminary Analysis*,

Kingston, Jamaica: University of the West Indies Press, 1975; and M.G. Smith, *Stratification in Grenada*, Berkeley: University of California Press, 1965. Smith and Brathwaite disagree about the degree of cultural and social interaction and stability in the Caribbean states, with Brathwaite seeing creolization as an effective cultural unifier, and Smith viewing elite coercion as the unifying element of these states. However, the class analysis in both works is overwhelmed by the discourse of race, peoplehood and nationalism.

    19. A conference held by the University of the West Indies, St Augustine, to honour and reconsider Brathwaite's work, entitled 'Under the Rainbow', on 4–6 December 1989, took as its mandate the problems of race in Trinidad in 1989, as the conference title would indicate, largely ignoring the Marxist inspiration and class relations of much of Brathwaite's work.

    20. Stuart Hall, 'Pluralism, Race, and Class in Caribbean Society', in John Rex, ed., *Race and Class in Post-Colonial Society*, Paris: UNESCO, 1975, p. 179.

    21. James, *The Black Jacobins*, p. 367.

    22. Frantz Fanon, *Black Skin, White Masks*, London: Pluto Press, 1986, p. 225.

CHAPTER 3

Willi Chen and Carnival Nationalism in Trinidad

In a lecture at the Collège de France in 1970, Michel Foucault argued that the Greek sophists practised 'a discourse which in prophesying the future not only announced what was going to happen but helped to make it happen, carrying men's minds along with it and thus weaving itself into the fabric of destiny'. But by the time of Plato, 'truth no longer resided in what discourse was or did, but in what it said: a day came when truth was displaced from the ritualized, efficacious and just act of enunciation, towards the utterance itself, its meaning, its form, its object, its relation to its reference.'[1] Perhaps contemporary writers, writers from developing countries, do want a discourse that weaves itself into the fabric of a nation's destiny. But writers, and politicians, too often find themselves imprisoned in the second discourse, or what Foucault calls the will to truth. Trinidad's writers have not escaped this will to national truth, although in its pursuit they have often subverted it. The novel has been a dominant art form in post-independence Trinidad and literature has reflected the efforts of a nation to distinguish itself, to use its culture to prove its existence. Sometimes, culture not employed to prove existence is accused of proving oblivion. Thus the will to nationalism can threaten literature. And literature, as Benedict Anderson writes, is a difficult place from which to root out this will to nationalism.

> What the eye is to the lover – that particular, ordinary eye he or she is born with – language – whatever language history has made his or her mother-tongue – is to the patriot. Through that language,

encountered at mother's knee and parted with only at the grave, pasts are restored, fellowships are imagined, and futures dreamed.[2]

It is in the language of the novel that Trinidad has been imagined; but it is in the negotiation of identity in language that it has resisted imagination, and withstood the threat of a will to nationalism. The writer considered in this chapter uses the resistance of identity to disarm the will to nationalism. And, in the process, he defeats the metadiscourse of race embedded in that will.

Trinidad, of course, is not unique among new nations in its search for national identity, but its abundance of writers, and what Stuart Hall has called its 'overdetermined' social structure, make it a heavily imagined, and imaged, community. And it can be reiterated that it is a country where the writers have taken up the call to nationhood, and where those who have not have often been vilified. Earl Lovelace has not been alone in saying that he 'would want to feel that the writer is the most important citizen in the state'.[3] And the works of many other Trinidadian novelists share this commitment to reading community, even when, like Lovelace they eventually question that community. Some of Michael Anthony's novels are designed almost as regional portraits, and his series of popular histories confirm his confidence in a common national discourse. Anthony, like the best of the creative artists in the Caribbean, has bent the will to nationalism to his own – expressing his faith in the historical commonality of people. Samuel Selvon's *Moses Trilogy*, discussed in the next chapter, is perhaps the most self-conscious and writerly examination of the writer and community in Trinidad, and certainly the funniest – but again he uses the will to nationalism to emplot his own history of that nationalism. Going back further in the literary history of the island, the Beacon Group of the 1930s, led by C.L.R. James and Alfred Mendes, sought specifically – as Mendes has maintained in recent interviews – to ground their literary discourse in indigenous language and culture, taking on an overt nationalist project. Even V.S. Naipaul's work can be seen as a directed antinationalist discourse. Novels like *Guerillas* and *In a Free State* are attacks on the representation of nationhood, the citizen as national referent; but does that mean they escape the discourse?[4]

Naipaul's recently conferred knighthood passed through the Trinidadian press like a minor obituary, so tied in the mind is nationalism and righteousness, nationalism and care for fellow men (although the event was perhaps more significant than the press at first admitted, as I will discuss in Chapter 6). But, despite the cultivation of nationalism, and the many costumes made to fit it or make it look ridiculous, critics and writers alike still face a nation whose citizens by and large do not imagine themselves chiefly as members of a modern nation-state; perhaps fewer still imagine the same nation-state. Again the recent World Cup football qualifying match against the United States illustrates too well the fragile state of national commonality, and the breathless efforts of the intelligentsia to find that commonality. The press and the advertising industry successfully whipped up excitement to the point of a hysterical public discourse of sure victory, and columnists and university lecturers misidentified the frenzy as the birth of a nation, celebrating the common cultural value of football and fete (kaiso soccer) among the diverse 'ethclass' groups. But, as one dissenting journalist noted the day after the heartbreaking defeat, when striker Russell Latapy left the field, all the same old divisions among Trinidadians were still there.[5] 'In the inevitable integration into a national community, one of the most urgent needs, sport, particularly cricket, has played and will play a great role', wrote James.[6] But if kaiso soccer will not fulfil the urgent needs today that C.L.R. James sensed for cricket in the Black–Coloured–Creole (and emergent Indian) dynamic of the 1950s, where will nationalists find a habitable text for the island? In 1988, Willi Chen published a collection of short stories called *King of the Carnival*.[7] The stories read the many texts of Trinidad as a way to write that text. They enunciate what they see. They start to re-ritualize the discourse of the Trinidadian text by freeing identity from prescriptive nationalism. And they subvert the will to nationalism and its privileging insistence on racial harmony by suggesting that the habitable text for the Trinidadian nation may be multiple, far more diverse than race, and far more secure than nation.

Chinese Text of Identity

Kenneth Ramchand points out in his spare and informative introduction to the collection that 'Willi Chen's parents, John Chen (1906–79) and Iris Chen, came to Trinidad from the village of

Tien Tien in the Guandang Province of China.' The Chinese presence in Trinidad is a result of what Hugh Tinker has called the 'new system of slavery', in which the British moved to import labour from other colonies and dependent territories to replace freed slaves who refused to stay on the land. Some two and a half thousand Chinese, a thousand Portuguese, a thousand Syrians and Lebanese, and 144,000 East Indians made the journey to Trinidad in the post-emancipation era.[8] Inserted into the colonial Creole world of Trinidad, the smaller groups like the Chinese, after brief and unhappy turns on the land, became shopkeepers and business-men. They, like the Syrians and the Portuguese, have been termed 'middle minorities' because of their intermediary status both socially and economically, though these two are not always in step.[9] Their presence, together with the East Indian community, which now equals slightly more than half of the population, makes talk of Black and White and comparison with other West Indian societies, except Guyana and Surinam, misleading. This diversity is similarly manifested in the religions of the nation, where pastoral letters on matters of politics and culture are often signed jointly by Anglican, Catholic, Hindu, Muslim, and (Shango) Baptist clerics. This multicultural, multiracial population also means that searches for national identity that do not take this diversity into account, such as Negritude, fail utterly. But perhaps most im-portantly, their presence and the presence of those who came after them transformed Trinidad a from British plantation society to an immigrant society, as similar to Brazil and Canada as to Grenada and Jamaica. Of the Caribbean islands, Trinidad alone is a nation of immigrants; and, however coercive the immigration, images of the receiving country, and its opportunities, played some role in the decision to become a new member of that nation, even temporarily. Such nations are subject to many imaginations – immigrant countries are read differently by different groups, and the country's past often does not receive a privileged reading by its new citizens. For instance, contrary to the anger of African Trinidadians (and the disappointment of some nationalist cheer-leaders), when Indian Trinidadians cheer for the Indian cricket team against the West Indies, they may not be expressing treasonous allegiances so much as giving different readings of what Trinidad is or should be. It is against competing readings, rather than competing writings, of the will to culture, that Willi Chen's stories should be seen. His stories do not deny the history of slavery and disenfranchisement that Trinidad shares with the rest of the Caribbean, but they do affirm options of identity not available to Caribbean people in more homogeneous states.

The appearance of these stories in 1988 must also be addressed before we can see them as the readings they are. Major West Indian literary critics like Kenneth Ramchand and Gordon Rohlehr, if they agree on little else, seem to agree that the golden period of West Indian fiction was the 1960s. In the early 1970s, most of the major novelists were still active and present in the nation's consciousness. By the late 1970s and through the 1980s, these novelists were producing fewer novels and drawing less attention, inside Trinidad or in the metropoles. To some extent poetry has replaced fiction in the West Indies. Few young novelists have arrived to replace those of the golden age, but some poets have. A Bakhtinian argument about the different political meanings of form could be made, particularly in light of some of the disappointments in the Caribbean of the 1980s. But since West Indian poetry tends to stick close to narrative form, and not much of the attention has been given to Trinidadian poets, it is difficult to see poetry as alternative writing, or reading, in Trinidad.

One significant exception to this trend was Earl Lovelace's *The Dragon Can't Dance*.[10] This novel is significant not only because of its intertextuality with Chen's collection of stories, but also because Lovelace took direct aim at the possibility of the cohesive Trinidadian text, using carnival both as a people's incessant text and as a national writer's elusive text. Because the novel came out in 1979 when few other novels of Trinidad did, and because the novel was clearly, on the surface, an epic attempt at capturing a nation's text, the book drew much critical attention, some of it both perceptive and vaguely wistful.[11] For what Lovelace's novel cannot give is a reading of a new synthetic nation. The inability of the Afro-Trinidadian Dragonmaker and the Indian shopkeeper to communicate suggests for Lovelace the failure of all citizens to inhabit a common national text. Lovelace writes about the role of a writer in stitching together a national costume, a costume that is habitable for all citizens, poor and rich, male and female, African and Indian. As suggested in Chapter 1, when the Dragon turns his back on his costume and on what he perceives is the uninhabitable text of being that is carnival, the author is partly recording his reading of the historical emasculation of carnival and its cooptation by business and the middle class.[12] But the Dragonmaker's abandonment of carnival is also Lovelace's abandonment of the shifting – and, for him, debilitating – identities of carnival as a basis for national imagination. At the end of the novel, with the Indo-Trinidadian Pariag's speech to his wife about his failure to let the African Trinidadians see him as he really was, and with the Dragon's redemptive search for the young girl from the Laventille yard, Lovelace calls for a new discourse. Lovelace's call is for a new inclusive imagination of Trinidad that will allow for shared texts of identity, that will allow the Dragon to speak to the shop-keeper, and allow the young girl from Laventille to imagine a better life, a better Trinidad. In short, as I concluded in Chapter 1, Lovelace ends up insisting on a nation where individual creativity can flourish independent of a will to national culture, and that this very independence will remake the nation. But such a discourse, like Lovelace's novel, despite its strengths, is still burdened with the will to truth. It still insists on the need for an imagined community, still maintains that the texts of Trinidad are unintelligible, that the Dragon and Pariag have yet to find a nation and a true self with which to read that nation.

At bottom, Lovelace's vivid prose is still trapped in the act of writing national culture, still viewing the present nation as less than whole, still looking for the day when African and Indian texts read each other, and all citizens read a new Trinidad. Willi Chen's writing stands against this writing and against the will to national culture. Chen, like Lovelace, has heard Pariag cry that he must be seen as he really is; but for Chen that reading of identity is not for the purpose of realizing a national culture or sharing a common text, nor can it be. Chen's stories reveal the error of the will to nationalism, the impossibility of its task. The texts of identity in Trinidad pass by the writer's eye like a carnival; and like a carnival costume each text can be read differently, discarded, or picked up by another; and a nation will appear from this uncertainty, but it will be a nation of competitive imagination where only a discourse that celebrates the multiple rituals of identity in Trinidad will weave itself into the costumes of men's destiny. Only a discourse that does not try to complete men's imaginations, or restrict texts to agreement and consistency, can glimpse the nation of Trinidad. For Chen, that young girl from the Laventille yard is already reading a text of Trinidad, but the good news is that tomorrow she may inhabit another.

Nation of Imagi-nations

Octavio Paz has said that each man has many imaginations. Willi Chen confirms this in these stories, as his discourse confirms the right of citizens to have many imaginations, and the possibility of a nation with many imaginations. Chen picks up and puts down many Trinidads in his collection, all complete but all solitary readings in a field of identities. His title story, which appears last in the book, is a direct rereading of Lovelace's Dragonmaker, and the character with the costume is even named Santo Lovelace. But the story in itself is representative of the collection precisely because it is not representative of the cohesive whole; nor is this merely a consequence of the short story form. This last story, 'King of the Carnival', tells the tale of a Carnival King who works obsessively on a traditional costume of a dragon. Like the character in Lovelace's novel, he is identified and praised by his community because of the costume, and he comes to identify himself with the character of that dragon. When the contest arrives, the Dragon is upstaged by 'the white man' whose costume 'came on the stage, part man, part robot, its coordinating movements mechanized, the eyes sparked, it spoke, it buzzed, sang, emitting clouds of tinted smoke, a perfumed spray.'[13] The story then ends with the disillusioned Dragon standing in the wings, haunted by the vision of the white-faced judges, and listening to the mechanical noise of the rival's costume. In isolation this story is little more than a text of post-colonial disenchantment with the colour and style of power in the Caribbean. But such a will to truth does not hold in Chen's work. Other readings in other stories will not permit an interpretation of the text of carnival as a ritual of resistance or a scene of social conflict. Or, rather, if they permit this text to stand for Trinidad, other readings refuse to privilege the Dragonmaker's Trinidad.

Before the reader comes to the last story of the Dragon, he or she will have read a very different text of Trinidadian identity in a story called 'Caesar'. Caesar is the pet mynah bird of Margot, a woman who marries a white pilot and who eventually, despite their happiness and wealthy lifestyle, has an affair with a Portuguese Trinidadian in the neighbourhood, loses her husband, and commits suicide. The story is told in the first person, by a narrator named Mr Chen. There is an intimacy to the voice of the story which betrays an emotional attachment in the narrator's (or author's) telling. Although, as readers, we do not know the precise ethnicity of Margot, we can guess by the fact of her walking a small dog in the Port of Spain botanical gardens, and her ease in the exclusive hillside neighbourhood, that she is upper class, presumably French Creole or light-skinned African. I stress a reading of ethnicity here precisely because the voice in this highly sympathetic story is as familiar, comfortable and concerned, as it is bitter, alienated, but still attached, in the Dragon story. Moreover, the details of daily life in this story are as precise and separate as the details in the Dragon story or the several stories of farming and working-class Indians in central Trinidad.

'There was that thick brown rug he had brought from Mexico, all aflame in red and orange rays of sunset over a head motif which was the central theme of the decor.'[14] Descriptions like the one above of Mark and Margot's class culture, here concerned with house motifs, are delivered without judgement or malice, without writing the text of Trinidad as a nation with a dominating elite, in marked contrast to the Dragon story. Conflicting Trinidads are read without conflict. Chen's readings of Trinidad do not denature any other readings of Trinidad. There is little room here for M.G. Smith and his pluralist models of society.[15] Sally Falk Moore has recently raised questions about Smith's models. She uses the work of both Smith and Barth to question Ernest Gellner's contention that modern nationalism will end genuine pluralism, through industrialization and the standardization of education. She notes that diversity and repluralization are in evidence everywhere, not only in the Third World case studies of Smith, but also in the new multiracial Europe of Gellner's imagination. But she also notes that for Smith, 'the organization of the state is the beginning point.'[16] Informal cultures, resistance cultures, residual cultures, or Chen's multiple identities play no central role in this kind of pluralism. Whether or not Trinidad is a nation of different cultures

held together only by the coercive force of a minority is un-
important to Chen; what is more, Smith's will to truth would be
a restriction on Chen's freedom to find the texts of Trinidad. For
Chen, Smith's pluralism and all sociological texts are only more
readings of Trinidad. This is because, crucially, it is Chen's
readings, and the readings of other citizens, that hold Trinidad
together. A privileged text of coercive minorities, or benevolent
investors, dismantles the rights of other texts, other Trinidads.
Chen's stories set in the predominantly Indian town of Bustahall
reinforce the discourse of competitive readings.

An Indian Text of Identity

In the politics and social life of Trinidad, as John La Guerre has
documented, the Indian community, never completely imagined
as a whole, shows instances of integration and instances of
segregation.[17] This erratic reading of nationalism in the Indian
community has preoccupied those writers and thinkers trying – to
use Yeats's double meaning – to forge a nation. Writers have either,
like the early Naipaul, or Sam Selvon, tried to make Indo-
Trinidadian culture more available to other Trinidadians and
outsiders, or, like Lovelace and Anthony (in *Green Days by the River*),
they have tried to understand how the culture will meet the
creolizing African culture around it. But in both cases, Indo-
Trinidadian culture is viewed structurally, defined against (segregation) or with (integration) the other imagined community in
Trinidad, the creolized African text. The circumscribed world of
Mr Biswas is an example of the first – the creolized African text
is the dark territory beyond his tight world; Shellie's reluctant
acceptance of the doogla girl and rejection of a perceived African
creole trait of pre-marital irresponsibility in Michael Anthony's
novel is an example of the second. It is not the brevity of Chen's
pieces that eliminates this narrative; rather, it is the decentring of
any dominant text of Trinidad, the free play of readings, the open
competition for the imagining of Trinidad. For Chen, communities
do not come together or move apart; they do not encounter each
other or ignore each other for any predestined project of nationhood, for any attempt at the unification of the imagination, or

under any dominant text of potential identity. History has not privileged any texts in an immigrant society; nor has the legal state mandated its own imagination. For Chen it is not an overstatement to say that even carnival itself cannot be a reliable referent for identity. The growth of festivals such as the Muslim-derived celebration Hosay have taken on their own level of national theatre, and jostle carnival as alternative acts of public and personal identity for Trinidadians.[18]

The village of Bustahall is also read without any will to truth. The village of Bustahall is not a sociological problem, a discourse to be understood. Willi Chen invokes the violent husband Lalloo, or the taciturn shopkeeper Wong, for the terror or the comedy of the reading. This is not to say that the writer is without politics, of course, but to insist that his is a politics freed from the will to truth, the need to define the text of Trinidad as either fully imagined or barely imagined. Chen has many imaginings, many Trinidads; and even many Trinidads is not for Chen the necessary reading of the nation. The story 'Lalloo's Wrath' may be seen and read against stories of carnival or of 'Chinee' shopkeepers, or it may not be. Different texts do not dominate each other or rely on each other for meaning. 'Yesterday, Lalloo had struck her trembling cheeks, drawing blood, over an argument about food. Cold food she had served him, sitting cross-legged in the crocus bag hammock. His eyes blinked steadily from his bouts of rum drinking at Allong's shop, high up in the village.'[19] So Chen writes, with tense economy, of the violent husband whose wife Dulcie has left him after the most recent drunken beating. When Lalloo goes to his mother-in-law's house to plead for his wife to return, she refuses. ' "Ah not coming! Everytime is the same ting and you goh beat me again." '[20] At this Lalloo begins chopping down the stilt house of his mother-in-law with an axe.

> He was attacking the last stilt with the same savage fury of the madman, the crumbling, decaying boards collapsing in a heap over him, the dust rising in clouds. She rushed out of the yard at top speed, this time down the road which she had come the night before. She did not look back.[21]

Chen achieves a clever confusion in Dulcie's flight. On the one hand, the phrase, 'she did not look back' suggests her permanent flight from Lalloo. But the direction, 'down the road which she had come the night before', raises the possibility that her frightened flight is to Lalloo's house. Her liberty or entrapment remains to the end uncertain. The story is impressive for its brevity and the clarity of the text. But that clarity does not suppose a definition of rural Indo-Trinidadian life. Like the text of the dragon and the text of the parrot, Lalloo's text imagines its own nation; and, like Italo Calvino's invisible cities, one text may live atop another unaware of the other's nation, living in it one moment, and out of its imagination the next.

The several appearances of Chinese Trinidadian shopkeepers in the stories lead the reader, and the critic, to think of Chen's background, one of his lived texts in Trinidad. The fact that 'the Chinee' appear as quiet observers, or spectators to the action, brings to mind the writer's own position as an observer and teller, as the maker of a discourse. Does the writer's own text of identity, the identity of a Chinese Trinidadian, a middle minority, help him to make a discourse that can avoid the will to truth and make equal readings of the nation's text? In an article entitled, 'To Be Or Not To Be Chinese', Thomas Shaw writes that Chinese settling in Jamaica chose to emphasize their identity and remain ethnically solidified. By contrast, those in Trinidad chose quick acculturation into creolized life, retaining some cultural traits but committing themselves to Trinidadian culture.[22] But as Chen's story 'No Pork, Cheese' nicely recalls, this acculturation faced two questions. What should the Chinese keep, and to what were they acculturating? Of course, the processes of migration, adjustment and acculturation are never so rationally negotiated, except sometimes by ethnic group leaders. Even so, the question of to what were they acculturating remains a thrilling one, and one, I believe, that explains some of Chen's openness and his rejection of a will to truth.

In the story 'No Pork, Cheese', three Indians come into the rum shop and grocery of a Chinese named Wong. Two of the Indians are Hindus; the third, Ahamad, is a Muslim. From 10.30 in the morning they begin drinking cheap rum, spilling some, shouting for more, disrupting Wong's business. Codes of ethnicity, readings of identity in Trinidad, fly fast as another reading of the national text takes place in Wong's rum shop. "'He is Muslim, Wong. You know what dat mean?" Balraj said. "Salt Kine good meat, Amat", Wong smiled. "Dat good for creoni", Ahamad grumbled.'[23] Ahamad's repulsion at the salt kine and his relegation of it to the status of African Creole food amuses both his Hindu companions and Wong. But, unlike the two drunk Hindus, Wong sells to everyone, stepping in and out of different discourses and different texts. There is no sense given in the story that Wong has any particular reading of community. The reader never knows Wong's imagined nation. But as bartender, and as owner of the shop, he facilitates the action and is the filter through which action must move. In the end, he mistakenly feeds all three pork and cheese sandwiches on hops bread. Ahamad realises too late that he has eaten pork in his severely drunken state. He lurches to the door vomiting violently while his friends laugh and Wong stands behind the counter baffled. More than his Chinese-inflected English or his economic niche in the petty bourgeoisie, the violence of Ahamad's retching and the laughter of his companions set Wong apart. He stands behind the counter in a sudden separateness, watching the adamancy and extremity of different identities writing and rewriting the nation. From behind the counter he reads these writings. He can inhabit all the texts, but finds none fully habitable. Chen, like Wong, sees too many texts to privilege one. For Chen, the imagined community goes the way of the characters coming together to drink or going apart to close up shop, reading the nation every day again, inhabiting changing texts of identity. Ahamad might, on another day, listen to calypso and praise the taste of the Trinidad mango. On another day, Wong might attend a People's National Movement meeting, or marry an African Trinidadian. Or Ahamad might curse Eric Williams, and Wong marry an immigrant from Hong Kong. Chen understands the number of national costumes available to every Trinidadian.

Nation as Street Theatre

Willi Chen's experience as a playwright helps to explain his willingness to see the costume changes in Trinidadians; whereas Lovelace, though also interested in multiple readings of Trinidad, forces his characters to search for a true self. Chen is comfortable with the fickle nature of the Trinidadian text. His readings of identity are always subject to revision, and his stories reveal that no fewer options for identity would be tolerated by Trinidadians. The story 'Trotters' proves a good example of the fluid nature of identity in Trinidad. Chen tells the story of an old Muslim Indian woman whose son has recently married a girl named Zobida, whom the old woman and the son suspect is part African. One night Zobida serves them soup with pork trotters, in an incident that at first recalls Wong's feeding of pork to Ahamad. But Chen plays here with the multiple texts of Trinidad, and in this story the son concludes:

> he loved Zobida and that was that. After all, she was his wife and if she wanted to eat pig foot at times, why not? That was her own business. And who cared whether she was Dougla, part Creoni or even full bloodied Creole. Azard probed into the murky depths of his bowl.[24]

And in the end, the old woman asks her daughter-in-law for more 'chotters', enjoying the creoni food, still unaware of the blasphemy. Here is a single instance of cultural melding, of identities and imaginations spreading beyond the familiar into the murky depths of new texts. But Chen guards against any interpretation of this reading as emblematic of a future nation. It is not necessary for the writer to see this exploration as cultural atrophy or creolization. The creolized African world is not the only referent for this story; it is only one possible text in the identity of these characters, only one imagined text among many in a nation of immigrants. Chen's country need not move in any direction to complete itself – it is complete in its competitive imaginings.

There is a another type of story in Chen's collection, and this other type is full of a discourse beyond prescriptive nationalism. These are texts in which the multiple readings of Trinidad are no longer the topic but are now the fabric of other readings. They represent a triumph over the will to nationalism. They recommend to other writers the project of recovering a discourse that does not rely on the will to truth or burden itself with the alchemy of nationhood. These stories are 'Death at Coramandel' and 'The Killing of Sanchez'. Chen also wrote and directed a play in Trinidad called *Tainted Blood* that should be mentioned alongside these two stories. The play told the story of drugs and corruption in the Trinidad police force and was a chilling success in a country just coming to grips not only with its drug problem but also with corruption and the immunity of the powerful to common justice.[25] Like the play, these two stories are readings of the cloaked and vicious world of drug-runners along the mangrove swamps of Trinidad. Their world has its tradition, its past texts of contraband kings like Mumtaz, 'that ferocious dougla with the longest dread', who brought from Venezuela 'Carupano whisky, fat morocoys, bags of tobacco, spiky iguanas with their hind claws pinned into flesh behind their own tails, kegs of honey'.[26] But the profession had grown much more deadly and profitable with the smuggling of drugs.

In these stories of cut-throat smugglers, the identity of the characters takes on the quality of theatrical costuming, of carnival texts. Chen plays with various readings of Trinidad and the characters do battle like 'ole time' carnival characters. Chen even presents his characters as characters, listing them, and next to their names, their costume. There is 'haughty Lopez' with his 'shock of red beard dangling like his scrotum past his knees', and 'Manickchand and Jojo, robed in dashiki'. Chen continues: 'there was Ganga with four hundred pounds of ganja', and 'Marquez slouched; he was of Spanish extract – deadly with his knife.'[27] There are texts of identity here, hinted at by the red beard or the dashikis, or stated in the playfulness of the Indian Ganga and his ganja and the stereotype of the knife-wielding Spaniard. But their identity is part of a parade of texts, now clashing, now reading each other, now changing in full or part. 'Death at Coramandel' ends as the police find the body of a drug lord one evening when the 'chulas had long begun to blaze under tawas sizzling with hot oil and garlic, at Coramandel'.[28] The Indian cooking is only a buried text of identity in this story. In both stories, Chen reads many identities and watches many texts. Each drug smuggler is both an imagining of Trinidad and an imaginer. The flux of texts and the competition of identity produce the discourse of a carnival nation, in which images of the nation are tried on and discarded, worn together and separately, and where the carnival, far from being a detrimental symbol of confused identity or what The Mighty Sparrow called a Creole celebration, as it is in Lovelace's work, becomes the process of identity itself, becomes the scene of jostling texts and concurrent imaginings of Trinidad.[29]

Stories of drug smuggling may seem an odd place to locate this carnival of texts. But even in their perverse way, by tossing texts of identity into the anarchy of criminal life, they displace constructive texts of nationalism and they summarize Chen's commitment to open readings. Ironically enough, these stories are best explained by V.S. Naipaul, who quotes the Spanish writer Ortega:

> People don't live together just like that. That kind of cohesion exists only within a family. The groups who make up a state live together for a purpose. They are a community of projects, desires, big undertakings. They don't come together simply to be together, but in order to do something tomorrow.[30]

Willi Chen has come to understand that the will to nationalism cannot capture the free play of identities in the carnival text of Trinidad. Trinidadians may come together to smuggle drugs, to make money, to build a school, or fête in the streets, but they will not be read in a discourse of nationalism where identities and imaginations must be agreed upon and their carnival costumes marketed. Willi Chen, at least, is willing to let the unruly texts of identity rule in Trinidad.

Even Benedict Anderson's elegant theory of the power of language in the national imagination cannot contain the sliding scale of choices of identity and ethnic boundaries. Chen's nation-language disturbs any attempt to agree on a national imagination. But Chen's Trinidad does not necessarily remain still for theorists of ethnic relations in the state – theorists who would substitute models of comparative ethnic relations for models of nationalism in multi-ethnic states. Such models might at first seem to fit with Chen's reading of Trinidad because they do not require the common imagination of nationalist thought. Indeed Trinidad has often been the subject of comparative ethnic relations, often together with Guyana, most famously in the work of Donald Horowitz.[31] Recent theory on comparative ethnic relations in multi-ethnic states has since cautioned against a comparative structural analysis that overlooks the specificity of meaning in the socio-historical context of each society in the search for a master narrative of ethnic relations in the modern world. Fardon's article 'African Ethnogenesis' questions all projects of comparative ethnic relations on the basis of this faulty symmetry, and, by implication, the project of creating a transcendent theory of ethnic relations.[32] And as I have tried to show, comparing Willi Chen's Trinidad to multi-ethnic Tanzania or Jamaica would be of little use without a thorough examination of Trinidad's unique history and cultural legacy. It would appear that any theory of ethnic relations in Trinidad would have to rise from Trinidad's soil, observing everything from carnival to Trinidadian plantation culture. How else to contain Chen's criminals?

Theories on Containing Chen

But such a model of ethnic relations, built within a specific historical context but capable of wide comparative application, has been attempted by Thomas Hyland Eriksen in a recent article. Can his model of a multi-ethnic society contain Chen's imagined Trinidad? Eriksen calls his proposition a 'multi-dimensional model of ethnicity' and he draws on both Anthony Giddens's theory of structuration and on Ludwig Wittgenstein's language-games to fashion his flexibility. Eriksen identifies the central reification in past theories of ethnic relations and suggests that theories have concentrated on formalist theories of social process in which ethnicity is communicated to those inside and outside the group and the object of study becomes the structure of group and communication, not the content of that group's properties or ethnic signs. Eriksen maintains that, 'if there are contextual imperatives for the production of ethnic signs – and it would be foolish to suggest otherwise, then the contexts in question must be understood along with the acts of inter-ethnic communications.'[33] Eriksen writes that 'a concept of culture which fully acknowledges the contextual character of shared meaning in any society must be dual: culture is continuously created and re-created through intentional agency, but it is simultaneously a necessary condition for all agency to be meaningful.'[34]

The influence of Giddens's theory of structuration is obvious here, and Eriksen further refines his model by suggesting that people of East Indian and African descent in Trinidad, and comparatively in Mauritius, play a Wittengensteinian language-game when talking about each other that can only be understood if the concrete historical relationship between the groups is understood as well. Eriksen's theory, though among the most elegant, would appear to help us more with a reading of Earl Lovelace's Trinidad than with Willi Chen's. In Lovelace's novel the Indo-Trinidadian character Pariag misunderstands the ethnic language-game when he buys a bicycle. The bicycle is an affront to the Afro-Trinidadian people of the Hill, who reject the concept of owning valuable durable goods. They smash the bicycle and with it Pariag's desperate attempt to make cross-cultural contact. In Eriksen's paradigm, there is a historically specific tradition of mistrust of property among one ethnic group (and one class within that group) in Trinidad. In fact Pariag, trying only to give off ethnic signs friendly to the Afro-Trinidadian majority of his adopted neighbourhood, fails to understand this historically specific tradition, illustrating Eriksen's insistence on reading inter-ethnic communication in the context of previously produced ethnic signs. One could argue that Lovelace underscores this vision of ethnic relations in his imagined Trinidad. However, the end of the novel, rejecting radically historical context and calling for a post-millennium search for the true self in all his characters, contradicts if not the reality of Eriksen's conceptual framework in Trinidad, then at least the desirability of it as a way of thinking.

Chen's Carnival

The case for Chen's Trinidad may be even harder to make. The contextual history of ethnic exchange and identity in Chen's Trinidad mutates at a pace Eriksen expects of inter-ethnic communication itself. Rather than employing concrete historical analysis to understand the context of ethnic semiotic exchange (or language-game exchange), the reader of this imagined Trinidad is left hanging on to the semiotic exchange while the historical context changes like scenery from the back window of a car speeding from Pitch Lake to the Northern Range. Chen's characters resist a sturdy historical context as scene of the inter-ethnic signification. Competitive and contradictory contextual readings of shared meaning suggest not that we should retreat to the ahistorical models of formalists like Karl Barth, but that Chen's reading of Trinidad insists that multiple contexts must be equally subject to acts of inter-ethnic communication just as surely as the reverse – Eriksen's model of understanding ethnic semiotic exchange by noting specific historical context. There are too many histories in Trinidad for Chen to privilege that of one individual, class, or ethnic group for more than a single reading. And, by implication, there are too many kinds of ethnic relations for any Trinidadian to confirm or predict the next relation. The theoretical model closest to Chen's decentred Trinidad might be found in a recent article by Arjun Appadurai. Unfortunately, the model is only outlined in the article, based on a forthcoming book. Appadurai appeals (at this stage only in what are called 'macrometaphors') for set theory, fractals, polyethetic classifications, and chaos theory to revamp social theory sufficiently for the purpose of coping with what he calls the disjunctures of the 'ethnoscapes, finanscapes, technoscapes, mediascapes, and ideoscapes' that stream and flow as cultural material across ethnic and national boundaries.[35] Appadurai expresses admiration and wistfulness only about scientific theories of chaos and set theory in this article; but the impulse to free oneself from even the most flexible model of agency versus context must be one that Chen and his Trinidadian citizens would recognize as carnival freedom. The sparse elegance with which Willi Chen creates his theory of national chaos in Trinidad stands, however, in contrast to the convolutions of theorists like Appadurai, and reinforces the value of the creative artist in the Third World as a social observer and thinker on nationalism.

Chen's rejection of the will to nationalism, of the metadiscourse on race, and of a simple binary view of Trinidad, and also of knowable metahistory of the nation's ethnic relations, is, for me, a high point of freedom and responsibility for the writer in the nation. Chen democratizes the discourse on nationalism by insisting that it is made and remade daily by each identity. His stories echo the nationalist project of C.L.R. James, who also seeks definitions and initiatives in the daily life of the people. And they guard both against the intrusion of outside models of ethnic interaction and against the dominance of a literate and official nationalism, no matter what its metadiscourse. If the nation requires every citizen to define him- and herself, it is helpless without them. Samuel Selvon celebrates some of this same popular creativity. As the calypsonian David Rudder sang: 'the people are always ahead of their leaders/ that's why the people will always survive.' Selvon, like Chen, has great faith in the people, and no fear of their carnival of identity.

Notes

1. Michel Foucault, 'The Order of Discourse', in Robert Young, ed., *Untying the Text*, Boston and London: Routledge & Kegan Paul, 1981, p. 55.

2. Benedict Anderson, *Imagined Communities*, London: Verso, 1983, p. 140.

3. Victor Questal, 'Views of Earl Lovelace' (interview), *Caribbean Contact*, vol. 5, no. 3, 1977, pp. 85–7.

4. For an analysis of how Naipaul's creativity undoes his attempt to escape national identity, see Mark McWatt, 'The Two Faces of El Dorado: Contrasting Attitudes towards History and Identity in West Indian Literature'; in M. McWatt, ed., *West Indian Literature in its Social Context: Proceedings of the Fourth Annual Conference on West Indian Literature*, Mona, Jamaica: University of the West Indies, 1985, pp. 33–47.

5. See *Trinidad Guardian* and *Trinidad Express*, 8–18 November 1989; and Lennox Grant, 'A Nation Seduced into Believing Own Rhetoric', *Guardian*, 23 November 1989.

6. C.L.R. James, *Beyond A Boundary*, New York: Pantheon, 1983, p. 243.

7. Willi Chen, *King of the Carnival*, London: Hansib Publishing, 1988.

8. Malcolm Cross, *Urbanization and Urban Growth in the Caribbean*, Cambridge: Cambridge University Press, 1979, p. 106.

9. Ivar Oxaal, *Black Intellectuals and The Dilemma of Race and Class in Trinidad*, Cambridge, Mass.: Schenkman, 1982, pp. 83–4.

10. Earl Lovelace, *The Dragon Can't Dance*, London: Andre Deutsch, 1979.

11. See, for instance, articles by Marjorie Thorpe in Erika Smilovitz and Roberta Knowles, eds., *Critical Issues in West Indian Literature*, Parkersburg, Iowa: Caribbean Books, 1984; or Maureen Warner-Lewis, *The Journal of West Indian Literature*, December 1987.

12. See Errol Hill, *Trinidad Carnival: Mandate for a National Theatre*, Austin: University of Texas, 1972.

13. Chen, *King of the Carnival*, p. 153.

14. Ibid., p. 125.

15. M.G. Smith, *Plural Society in the British West Indies*, Berkeley: University of California, 1965.

16. Sally Falk Moore, 'The Production of Cultural Pluralism', *Public Culture*, vol. 1, no. 2, 1989, p. 43.

17. John La Guerre, paper given at the Institute of Social and Economic Research conference 'Under the Rainbow: Social Stratification in Trinidad', 4–6 December 1989, Port of Spain, Trinidad.

18. See Noor K. Mahabir and Ashram Mahraj, 'Hosay as Theatre', *The Toronto South Asian Review*, vol. 5, no. 1, 1986, pp. 118–21, for a historical and processual interpretation of the festival in the diaspora.

19. Chen, *King of the Carnival*, p. 37.

20. Ibid., p. 41.

21. Ibid., p. 43.

22. Thomas A. Shaw, 'To Be or Not To Be Chinese', *Ethnic Groups*, vol. 6, no. 2, 1985, pp. 155–85.

23. Chen, *King of the Carnival*, p. 52.

24. Ibid., p. 122.

25. Kevin Yelvington, "Vote Dem Out', *Caribbean Review*, vol. 15, no. 4, 1987.

26. Chen, *King of the Carnival*, p. 143.

27. Ibid., p. 144.

28. Ibid., p. 97.

29. Circumstantial observation will reveal that carnival now crosses almost all ethclass lines, as the growth of Indian soca music also indicates. But common participation does not mean common readings, only common participation in the act of reading; hence my use of the term 'carnival nationalism'.

30. Quoted in 'British Policy Toward a Separate Indian Identity in the Caribbean, 1920–1950', in Hugh Tinker, ed., *East Indians in the Caribbean*, Millwood, New York: Kraus, 1982, pp. 33–48.

31. Donald Horowitz, *Ethnic Groups in Conflict*, Berkeley: University of California Press, 1985.

32. R. Fardon, 'African Ethnogenesis: Limits to the Comparability of Ethnic Phenomena', in L. Holy, ed., *Comparative Anthropology*, Oxford: Blackwell, 1987.

33. Thomas Hyland Eriksen, 'The Cultural Contexts of Ethnic Differences', *Man*, vol. 26, no. 2, 1991, p. 129.

34. Ibid., p. 125.

35. Arjun Appadurai, 'Disjuncture and Difference in the Global Cultural Economy', *Public Culture*, vol. 2, no. 2, 1990, p. 19.

CHAPTER 4

Samuel Selvon and the Chronopolitics of a Diasporic Nationalism

The novels of Samuel Selvon present a number of new questions about the nature and development of nationalism, peoplehood and race in Trinidad and Tobago. If the dominant discourse of nationalism in this post-colonial Caribbean state can be said to privilege the search for racial harmony over the search for economic justice (thereby decentring ethnic and creative individualism), what does one make of an East Indian Trinidadian with a Scottish grandfather who writes a masterly satirical trilogy set in London and Trinidad which features an Afro-Trinidadian protagonist and a scathing narrative style that mocks Trinidadian, African, East Indian and English culture alike? Samuel Selvon creates the same havoc with political theory as he does with the lives of the poor characters in his satirical narratives. He adds the confusions of the diaspora, the mother country, and greater West Indian brotherhood to the questions of national culture and Trinidadian identity. His *Moses Trilogy* forces many new issues onto the negotiating table. Why is West Indian unity only achieved in the immigrant ambience of Shepherd's Bush? What is an East Indian Caribbean immigrant in Britain? What role did immigration play in the decolonization of country and mind? What role does the migrant writer play in the formation of national identity back home? And finally, and most importantly for Selvon, what is this Caribbean culture upon which this new nation is to be built? His three Moses novels address all these questions, and, I believe, begin to outline a coherent faith in Caribbean culture that flourishes in the anarchy and satire of

Selvon's story. It is a faith not unlike that of C.L.R. James or
Michael Anthony or Willi Chen – it fights nationalism with nationalism, rejecting the official nation and the official narrative of nation.

Keith Warner in his study of the Trinidad calypso wonders how
The Mighty Sparrow could have written his immensely popular
calypso 'Model Nation' to celebrate the nation's independence,
featuring the lines, 'still no major indifference/ Of race, colour,
religion or finance', so soon after the racially split election of 1961.[1]
Leaving aside the conundrum of 'indifference', Warner is right to
question the programmatic nationalism of some calypsonians (although Francisco Slinger, The Mighty Sparrow – considered by
C.L.R. James to be the Caribbean's greatest social scientist – wrote
his share of pessimistic assessments). The nation that was born
during Samuel Selvon's absence in England was not in the least
harmonious. But, as the work of Selvon reminds us only too well,
political disharmony does not always mean cultural weakness.
Selvon, like the thousands of Trinidadians who danced to
Sparrow's 'Model Nation' and whose children continue to dance
to calypsos celebrating Trinidad, felt the power, and the power of
resistance, in the popular culture of the island. The calypso's true
assertion is not of racial harmony (or 'indifference of finance') but
of itself, as a form of demotically practised political comment.
Selvon's early short story 'Calypso in London' indicates some of
the power of West Indian culture to assert itself even in London,
where Mango dreams of his new calypso about Abdul Nasser
blasting from every English radio.[2] What runs throughout Selvon's
work, like a calypso on every radio, is the unruly strength of identity that does exist for West Indians in London and Trinidad, an
identity that defies the boundaries of harmonic nationalism and
the heritage of ethnic enclaves. It is the source of Selvon's strength,
the key to his conception of national culture and the West Indian
diaspora. It is also at the heart of his uncertain position in the
West Indian literary canon, and his uncertain position in both the
East Indian community, the Trinidadian nation, and the West
Indian diaspora. He presents a challenge to West Indian intellectuals and to others studying Caribbean societies. His novels
suggest that the weakness of the Caribbean nation-states does not
lie with the culture of their population, but with the invented
traditions of their political literati.

Selvon Rediscovered Discovering Trinidad

Samuel Selvon was asked to give an opening address at a conference on 'East Indians in the Caribbean' at the University of the West Indies at St Augustine, Trinidad in 1979.[3] Selvon's first novel, *A Brighter Sun*, is often considered the first novel of the West Indian literary renaissance.[4] George Lamming, the prominent Barbadian novelist, who coincidentally left on the same boat for England as Selvon, also points out that, unlike most of the great West Indian novels to follow, *A Brighter Sun* was published while Selvon was still living in Trinidad. But, despite his early success, Selvon has been among the most wayward of all West Indian writers, fiercely tied to the island in his novels, but, except for a period in the 1970s, never ending his self-imposed exile. His satirical style and his unfashionably long absences have sat uneasily with critics and nationalists who would use him. Indeed, despite his dedication to Trinidad as subject matter, and his position as a founding father of modern West Indian literature, he is conspicuously absent from some studies of Caribbean literature, such as O.R. Dathorne's *Dark Ancestors* and Selwyn Cudjoe's *Resistance and Caribbean Literature*.[5] He received far less critical attention than many of his contemporaries through the 1960s and 1970s, despite a steady output of novels. Jean-Paul Durix, editor of the journal *Commonwealth*, recently made just this point. 'It was surprising', he said, 'that Samuel Selvon, one of the founding fathers of Caribbean literature in the 1950s had not been the object of any full-length critical survey ... his present stature in the literary canon does not correspond to what he has achieved in terms of innovation and artistic sophistication.' With his usual perceptiveness, Durix adds that 'perhaps when the most sterile aspects of the debate concerning "national language" or the "folk tradition", with their limiting nationalistic overtones, have disappeared, readers will discover that Sam Selvon is simply one of the best contemporary novelists in the English language.'[6] Durix is here reviewing a new collection of essays on Selvon, and he does not have the space to explore the limits of the nationalistic overtones. But I will try to make that exploration here, and show that Selvon displaces the emplotment of the Caribbean nation on both sides of the Atlantic.

The reasons for Selvon's unclear position in the Caribbean literary canon, and for the relative lack of critical attention paid to his work, are closely connected to the vision of the island he carries with him in his travels from Trinidad to England, and now to Canada. For Selvon, Trinidad and the Caribbean are fabulously rich with native, if not nationalist, folkways and culture. Lamming calls him the Caribbean's greatest folk poet. And it is true that Selvon asserts a Caribbean man bursting, though sometimes in confusion, from the husk of the old colonial islands, and from the Old World memories that shackle him. His characters struggle with past identities, but they also dance in the inevitable new identities of a multicultural colony becoming a multicultural nation. But it is here, in Selvon's folkloric energy and his populist national- ism, that he presents problems for the nationalist discourse and difficulty for critics committed to more solemn and pessimistic assessments of the region, bound up with economic and cultural dependency theories and their counter-theories of resistance and de-linkage. A good example of this kind of nationalist thinking on cultural underdevelopment can be found in the work of Paget Henry, who co-edited one of the prominent academic anthologies of the Caribbean in the 1980s, *The Newer Caribbean*. In an essay in that volume he insists that 'the Indian heritage shows all the marks of cultural colonization: hybridization, dialectization, and under- development. As a result, the Indian in the Caribbean has experi- enced a marked degree of creolization, and it is the above processes of cultural colonization that have been largely responsible for this process of creolization.' Selvon would not necessarily disagree that East Indians in Trinidad had become creolized. But I will argue that he would not use creolization in such a disparaging way, and that, in fact, he sees it as something significantly more than decay and colonization. Paget goes on to conclude that 'hence, the extent to which the society successfully decolonizes itself must become the broader framework for evaluating the strides made in the direction of a national culture.'[7] But for Samuel Selvon, creolization, however imperfect, however unevenly mixed and credited at any given moment in the country's political discourse, is national culture, is the hope of strong populist culture capable of leading a people to higher development and happiness. His work offers a challenge to dependency nationalists like Paget

Henry. (This challenge has also been taken up by Cuban scholars, making a strength of the borrowing and remaking of other cultures and the destabilization of inherited cultures.[8]) Sam Selvon's Caribbean man insists not on the rejection of European values or the recovery of Indian culture, but on a toe-to-toe stick fight with all cultural influence, and the cooptation and transformation of every influence into something creolized, something impure, something Trinidadian. 'As a child I grew up completely creolized,' he confirms in an interview published in 1979, 'which is a term we use in Trinidad, meaning you live among the people, whatever races they are, and you are a real born Trinidadian, you can't get away from it.'[9] This challenge of an abiding creolization as the very seed of national culture has often led to the misreading or neglect of Selvon by all those who demanded that a discreet cultural past be recovered or invented.

However, in the late 1970s and the 1980s, Selvon enjoyed a kind of personal renaissance. A series of important younger critics picked up on his work and offered reassessments of his contribution and his vision. Frank Birbalsingh in Toronto, Victor Ramraj in Calgary, and Susheila Nasta in Britain all wrote intelligent new appraisals on Selvon in the principal international journals of what is now called 'World Literature'. (I will turn to those articles in more detail later.) Their attention proved to be more than justified by Selvon's talk at the 1979 conference on East Indians, and in subsequent interviews with the author. His talk at the conference offered the kind of complex and subtle insights that help make the case for the Caribbean novelist as supreme social observer in his society. But those insights also sharpen his conception of a creolized national culture in Trinidad and remind the audience why Selvon's work seemed to lie dormant for much of the 1960s and 1970s. And it is clear from his talk that it was more than his humour and his absence that caused the neglect. Rather, it was the challenge he presented to critics and political essayists – a challenge not unlike that of C.L.R. James, a challenge to all those who would claim that colonialism had produced only a plural society, in M.G. Smith's sense of the term, of disparate groups held together by coercion and geographical limits. Sam Selvon grew up in something more than that, something more than a culturally dependent, manufactured society, something that had risen above obscene oppression long before (as Naipaul would say) cultural nationalists recognized that oppression and politicians sought to exploit it as an excuse for their own mimicry.

Selvon entitled his talk 'Three Into One Can't Go: East Indian, Trinidadian, West Indian'. His style was humorous and anecdotal. He jokes that,

> we find Columbus had a brother who was a tally clerk counting the first East Indians who ever came to Trinidad as they land off the ship. He can't understand them when they talk, so he spelling and writing down the names what he think he hear, and allocating groups to the sugar cane plantations regardless of skill or craft, caste or religion.[10]

His humour hides the deadly accuracy of colonial cold indifference to skills and cultures of non-Europeans. He admits the confusion of Trinidad today, and that 'under the surface of affluence there is resentment, bitterness, tension and dissatisfaction between the Blacks and the East Indians, and all the old handicaps standing in the way of a peaceful settlement.'[11] Selvon speaks of a Trinidad here much like the one that Lovelace's characters, Dragon and Pariag, inhabit. But he also speaks of his own upbringing in the 1940s. His easy and unconscious creolization and how he lived 'among the people', as he often repeats in interviews, is his definition of being a Creole, of being a Trinidadian.

> It is important to point out that all the races in Trinidad were involved in this processing and coming under the influence of western culture, and there were as many Blacks ignorant or indifferent to the Shango cult, to stick for example, as there were Indians to their own ritual.[12]

Selvon, in his sly fashion, is beginning to stake out the kind of cultural and national dialectic he demonstrates in his fiction. He has little doubt, despite racial tension and group politics, that there is such a thing as a Trinidadian – he himself is one. He sees the renewed East Indian consciousness of the 1980s (which helped refocus attention on him), not as a rejuvenation of a minority culture or a militant nationalism, but of a group of people struggling to gain full credit for their contribution to Caribbean life, to feed Trinidadian culture and work for West Indian unity. He concludes that this struggle to contribute and have those contributions respected 'will be an inspiration to the new generation, and supply the impetus we sorely need in these times to put our house in order and work together for the benefit of the people of the Caribbean'.[13] Sam Selvon is bound to the people of the Caribbean.

The Challenge of Trinidadian Identity

The challenge of Selvon, found most stridently in his *Moses Trilogy*,[14] is crystallized in his address. Selvon believes in East Indian identity as a contribution to Caribbean identity, as he believes in African, European and Chinese identity as influences in Caribbean life. His cultural politics stem from his own upbringing among the people – an upbringing he admits was full of colonial misconceptions and prejudices, but an upbringing that held the sweet surprise of friendships in the face of the confusion of cultural amalgamations. 'I was one of the boys, doing my jump-up at Carnival time, giving and taking picong, liming for a freeness, drinking coconut water around the Savannah or eating late-night roti down St. James', writes Selvon.[15] Gordon Rohlehr, in one of the best essays in *The Newer Caribbean*, confirms that Selvon grew up on the multicultural streets of Port of Spain in the 1940s, when steelbands would feature a Chinese iron man and young African Trinidadians could play the tassa drum, and all of them went together to see John Wayne movies. Selvon's faith that there was, and is, a 'there there' in the Caribbean is a kind of optimistic nationalism based on his experiences as a youth, and reconfirmed by his bonding experiences with other West Indians in the cold hostels of London in the 1950s. This assertion of nascent identity is not the same as West Indian federal unity or racial harmony, or even national pride; it is, rather, the assertion that in cultural politics the Caribbean man could hold his own, and had produced a popular culture that withstood colonial pretension, and ethnic roots-searching, and even nationalist invention. Selvon himself often laments the limits of this popular culture; but in an age of mass culture, mass migration, and mass production it is precisely that popular culture and its language that are strong enough to do battle with Hollywood movies and the Oxford Dictionary. Ulf Hannerz's work on the 'global ecumene', the continued popular

cultural difference in the face of totalizing conceptions of centre
and periphery, echoes Selvon's faith in popular creolizing agents of
cultural difference.[16] As John Figueroa insists at the end of his
refreshing article on 'The Relevance of West Indian Literature',

> one of the ways in which Caribbean literature is relevant to Caribbean
> heritage people in Britain is in underlining the varieties of cultural
> heritage that have made the Caribbean something new – not some-
> thing perfect or necessarily something very pleasant; but something
> new. Worthy of study and contemplation in and through its literature.[17]

And this newness is precisely Selvon's point of departure. Critics
and nationalists of all kinds either misunderstand or ignore Selvon
from this point of departure onward. His *Moses Trilogy* is an assertion
of the power of a new popular culture, from its first coming to
consciousness in *The Lonely Londoners* to its growing confidence in
Moses Ascending, to its maturity in *Moses Migrating*. The trilogy covers
three decades in the history of independent Trinidad and colonized Britain. It covers three decades of nationalist thought, cultural
theory and race relations. The trilogy is a document of these times
– a tool for understanding these times – but it is also a challenge
to them, and to the hegemony of the written word in the history
of Caribbean culture. Selvon will challenge the notion that the
nation begins with its writing. He will also challenge the notion of
immature and mature national cultures, the evolutionist notion of
the childlike development of culture in the periphery versus the
immutable cultures of the centre. In short, Selvon subverts the
chronopolitics of anthropology and race relations in Britain.

In his book *Time and the Other*, anthropologist Johannes Fabian
writes that 'geopolitics has its ideological foundations in chronopolitics.'[18] Fabian believes that anthropologists have forced non-
Western cultures back into history, back into time, even when those
cultures, like the West Indian culture of the 1950s in London, is
contemporary with modern European culture. The purpose of
this chronopolitics is to increase the anthropologist's objectivity
and authority. But the effect is to represent European culture as
more mature, further evolved. Non-Western cultures then take on
an artificial history of development, a development beginning with
their encounter with the more mature European culture. Selvon's
challenge to this chronopolitics is evident throughout the trilogy

– his West Indian culture will not be forced out of the present. It is developed, is contemporary, is coeval.

Selvon has already hinted at the Trinidad that he left behind – a pre-independence Trinidad in which the ideologies of race and nationalism had not yet been fully articulated by independence politicians, intellectuals and journalists, but also one with a vibrant street and rural culture. It was a Trinidad that could not support much artistic or intellectual life – a lack of resources such as printing presses, enlightened patrons or governments, and restricted higher education prevented much more than the energetic but limited efforts of men like James and Mendes in the 1930s. Although Selvon had managed to find a publisher for his novel, he knew he would have to migrate, like so many others in the postwar period, to pursue his way of life. But his migration, like that of thousands of others who went to work for British Rail or the Post Office if they were lucky, for light manufacturing if they were unlucky, was part of a long tradition of migration, for both intellectual and working-class labour.

Elizabeth M. Thomas-Hope reminds us that migration had been a way of economic life for the Commonwealth Caribbean for a century before the mass migrations to England, and then to Canada and the USA in the 1950s and 1960s. At least 14,000 Barbadians had migrated to neighbouring Trinidad by 1891, and 24,000 Jamaicans migrated to Panama to work on the railroads in just the one year of 1883. Barbadians and Jamaicans also came in great numbers through Ellis Island during the great migrations to the USA at the turn of the century. The relative prominence of West Indian doctors, lawyers and intellectuals in the Harlem renaissance testifies to the migration of skilled labour as well. Even England bears evidence of a prehistory of migration, followed by a migration.[19] C.L.R. James left Trinidad at the invitation of Trinidadian cricketer Learie Constantine – one of a number of West Indian cricketers to play in the English county leagues, with varying success, but in Constantine's case, with legendary effect. By the time that intellectuals like Selvon, and workers – like the hundreds who landed in 1948 on the famous *Windrush* steamer – arrived in Liverpool, Bristol and London, they found small communities of ex-seamen, boxers, vagabond intellectuals and entertainers already living in small 'coloured quarters'.

Nonetheless, the shock and dislocation of coming face to face with the myth, ideology and reality of the mother country (and paradoxically with Caribbean culture in a new light) pervades the first instalment of Selvon's trilogy *The Lonely Londoners*.[20] This first book has received renewed evaluation and praise twenty and thirty years after its publication. Critics seized on Selvon's search for community and West Indian identity. The pioneering literary critic Kenneth Ramchand strikes a common tone, saying that,

> for Selvon ... it is only through the development of consciousness that the group, tribe, clan, community or whatever can preserve its essential qualities while living as twentieth-century people ... the birth of consciousness is the beginning of our participation in the perennial effort to sing simultaneously our songs of innocence and experience.[21]

Frank Birbalsingh adds that 'it is easy to see why Selvon and Lamming, who had emigrated to London together, were such good friends: they are both inspired by a similar compassion for the cultural rootlessness and political despair faced by West Indian people.'[22] Victor L. Chang also notes that Selvon 'is creating his tradition and its heroes'.[23] While it is certainly true that *The Lonely Londoners* explores identity, community and roots, I wish to argue also that, contrary to pessimistic, or dependent nationalistic, accounts of this search, Selvon, from very early on in this novel, and with increasing confidence in the subsequent novels, has already found those roots and asserted their strength. In fact, his novels are aggressive acts of creolization and heralding of West Indian identity. That is not to say that this identity is unproblematic – Selvon, in fact, often dwells on its imperfection – but rather that, as John Figueroa understands, West Indian, and in sharpest form in this study Trinidadian, culture is something new, something formidable.

Challenging the Sociology of Race Relations in Britain

The new Caribbean culture about which Selvon writes encounters a new cultural influence in Britain. What effect on Selvon's conception of West Indian identity and nationhood did this movement and collision of peoples have? Clearly, despite the prehistory of migration to England and the history of migration to other parts of the Caribbean and Latin America, the move to England, co-inciding with independence movements and a rise in political consciousness throughout the Third World, produced opportunity and desire for cultural activity and West Indian exploration of a new level. What is interesting and bold about Selvon's work is that his novels show the encounter to be a cultural triumph for the West Indians – not an economic or political one, but a triumph of Caribbean identity, a proof of its abiding existence. In this encounter, Selvon offers an alternative not only to West Indian nationalists who doubt the power and authenticity of popular Caribbean culture, but also to the British academics and politi-cians who observed this encounter. Race relations in Britain has never been a calm arena. It is a difficult task to give a brief history of the field in Britain, although it clearly rose with the growth of immigration and settlement, clearly was and is dominated by Caribbean immigrants and their children as subject or object matter, and clearly continues to produce a massive amount of literature. But the clarity ends there. In fact, central to the problem is the debate about whether there is or should be a field, or even a bookstore section, called Race Relations. But it is worth pointing to a couple of major works that stake out territory in the discourse, if only to indicate the havoc Selvon's work visits on all of them. Selvon's robust Caribbean characters appear to 'heckle', to use a favoured Trinidadian term, those students of race relations and their paradigms, in much the same way as they throw Caribbean literary critics into confusion. But these same Caribbean characters nonetheless do much to explain the encounter with the mother country.

To begin with, I will avoid being drawn into a discussion of racial theory, though many who write on race relations have also written race theory and tried to make that theory useful to race relations, among them, John Rex, Michael Banton, Robert Miles and Pierre van der Berghe. Instead I will stick to what some have called, deridingly, the Sociology of Race Relations – keeping in mind the genuine value of some of this work to migrants and host society alike. Within this field there are at least four kinds of writing. A pragmatic approach to studying the racial encounter can be found in a book like *Colonial Immigrants in a British City* by

John Rex and Sally Tomlinson.[24] Rex and Tomlinson believe in
the value of studying the encounter and its aftermaths in order to
understand prejudice, its cultural and economic basis, and to help
overcome these rooted problems. By contrast, Chris Mullard's *Race,
Power and Resistance* rejects any study of race relations as a reification of an artificial category. He argues that race is socially
constructed and should thus be treated, in a Marxist manner, as
just another social relation.[25] Finally a third book, *Multi-Racist
Britain*, edited by Philip Cohen and Harwant S. Bains and published in 1988, presents two more approaches – a progressive anti-
racism that both studies the encounter and prescribes programmes
for its eradication in British institutions like schools and social
services, and a Black nationalist approach, typified in articles like
that by Paul Gilroy, championing a resilient resistance culture in
the Caribbean ethnie.[26] These publications only represent prominent tendencies, but evidence needed of the splits in the field
could certainly be found in the most famous incident in its short
institutional history, that in the Institute for Race Relations in
1972. In that year, a radical Sri Lankan librarian, A. Sivanandan,
led a 'palace coup' in Britain's leading institution of its kind, forcing
out pragmatic academics and radicalizing the purpose and nature
of the Institute. The split also led to the publication of two new
journals: *Race and Class*, edited by Sivanandan, and *New Community*,
edited by pragmatic rivals. That Sivinandan was able to defeat
prominent academics in this coup can be seen now as partly due
to the luck of the times, and partly to the tenacity and intelligence
of the coup leader. Selvon's *Moses Ascending* will provide a good
way into this particular reversal of fortune in 1970s Britain. Jenny
Bourne and A. Sivanandan produced their own history of these
times, and of 'the dangerous sociology of race relations', in a 1980
article in *Race and Class*.[27] All of these arguments among intellectuals and academics occurred against the backdrop of a changing
Britain, and followed on the heels of cultural and popular stirrings
like the Caribbean Artists Movement, the battle against neo-Nazi
skinheads, and the growth of Notting Hill Carnival.[28]

The reason for recalling this troubled history is that Selvon,
tellingly, throws up opposition to all these writers. In an analysis
of *The Lonely Londoners*, and subsequently of the other volumes in
the trilogy, I will try to show that his challenge is not just to

Caribbean dependent nationalists like Paget Henry, but also to British conceptions of race, colonialism and nationhood. His novels are as subversive to A. Sivanandan's project as they are to John Rex's work; as difficult for Paul Gilroy's resistance culture as they are for traditional Marxist analysts. And all the time they challenge Caribbean intellectuals to take stock of the new culture, to beware, as Trinidad's new great calypsonian David Rudder warns, that 'the people are always ahead of their leaders/that's why the people will always survive.'[29]

The Lonely Londoners tells the story of a group of young, working-class West Indian males in London in the 1950s. The protagonist is a Trinidadian named Moses Aleotta, who by the time of the telling has already been in London ten years. The novel weaves a number of retold incidents around the initiation by Moses of a new migrant, nicknamed Galahad for his bravado on arrival. The concerns and difficulties of adjusting to life in London, finding housing, jobs and social comfort in a hostile city, are mixed with humorous but ultimately sad anecdotes of the collection of characters,

> coming together for oldtalk, to find out the latest gen, what happening, when is the next fete, Bart asking if anybody see his girl anywhere, Cap recounting a episode he had with a woman by the tube station the night before, Big City want to know why the arse he can't win a pool, Galahad recounting a clash with the colour problem in a restaurant in Piccadilly...[30]

Kenneth Ramchand has written a detailed introduction to the Longman Caribbean Writers Series. He cautions in it that 'to praise a novel for its fidelity to social or historical facts is to praise it, as some critics do, for being secondary.' Ramchand continues: 'its relevance to the social world from which it draws its material is enhanced by our first responding to it as fiction, something that has been made up, in this case, out of fairly recognisable material.'[31] But despite Ramchand's warning, his essay, like the rival essay by Gordon Rohlehr that he criticizes, tends to rely on the dominant concepts of West Indian migration to Britain, and of the sociology of race relations. Ramchand claims that the skilful use in *The Lonely Londoners* of a narrator who gradually takes on the identical perspective of the main character, Moses, is an example of 'individuation', and that the 'birth of consciousness is the beginning' of the preservation of the essential qualities of the group. By contrast, Ramchand notes that Rohlehr thinks of Moses as a kind of high priest of his group. The critics' differences, as with many other issues between them in West Indian literature and culture, centre on conflicts over the responsibility and liberty of the individual in communal culture. But what both critiques have in common is an assumption that the book tells the story of a displaced group of colonial working men, searching for conscious-ness – either group, or group mediated by individual. They both lean on the paradigm of migration, settlement and acculturation in which nascent West Indian group culture is pushed and pulled into a Black British minority culture. The critiques imply that an ill-suited colonial mentality and unformed national identity are hardened and defined by the encounter with the mother country. The obvious implication – in the sociology of race relations, and unfortunately in both the classic criticism of Rohlehr and Ramchand and the newer wave criticism of Ramraj, Birbalsingh and others – is that an entertaining but hopelessly underdeveloped Caribbean culture is only brought to consciousness and maturity in collision with the steel of British national culture. Moses then becomes either the father of resistance culture, or of mobility studies, or of anti-racist education. But this line of criticism, es-pecially for Caribbean critics, assumes the dominance of British culture in the clash, and denies the lonely immigrants the diasporic imagination of West Indian culture that holds the British encounter as only a small incident in an evolving sense of nationalism and peoplehood that centres, as it should, on the home islands. In short, it assumes that the beginning of the written history of Caribbean culture in the 1950s, by great novelists and dedicated British social scientists, is the beginning of a progressive history of Caribbean culture.

The Chronopolitics of Creolization

The idea is of a robust Caribbean man encountering and challenging the British way of life directly, not by adapting and evolving a Caribbean consciousness but by dealing with British

culture as an equal or even lesser force. And it is here that the
challenge to the chronopolitics of British academic thinking on
the subject is joined to the challenge of Caribbean nationalist
thought on the subject of national consciousness. Jagdish Gundara
puts it well when he says that 'it is insufficient simply to chronicle
the enormity of the injustices perpetrated. Colonialism needs to
be explained in economic and political terms and colonial history
recorded from the perspective of the oppressed. Resistance to
colonial domination and control occurred virtually everywhere...'[32] It is, consequently, presumptuous to view national or
group consciousness as beginning with the British encounter, or
to assign too much significance to that encounter in considering
the growth of Caribbean culture and resistance. For Selvon it is
important to see the wider West Indian unity, but not necessarily
for inventing West Indian culture. That invention, as C.L.R. James
constantly reminds us, was begun centuries ago by the people of
the Caribbean. Seen from this angle, Selvon's *The Lonely Londoners*
is an even contest between two dynamic cultures, and each story
of one of the boys is, rather than a fable for a disabled colonial
consciousness coming to realize oppression, a confident satire of
what is to Selvon a dour and emasculated host culture coming
face to face with the weight of centuries of Caribbean popular
culture.

There are three levels upon which Selvon builds his challenge
to the traditional paradigm of the encounter. First, the stories
themselves call into question the value and validity of British culture,
while at the same time highlighting the value and resilience of
West Indian culture. The most obvious examples of this kind of
challenge are the many stories of the boys encountering and
pursuing British women, and forming relationships with them.
Commonly, as with Frank Birbalsingh, these stories are viewed as
bitter-sweet tales of loneliness and Black colonial obsession with
white women, and partly they are just that. Less commonly, these
stories, such as Bart being thrown out of his girlfriend's house by
her father, or Moses being offered £3 to accompany a British
couple home, are viewed as the self-assured sexual culture of the
Caribbean and the malleability of British sexual practices under
the influence of the Caribbean tradition. (Strong or weak,
Caribbean national culture is not all good, and whatever reading

is finally privileged, the objectification of women remains perniciously inscribed in these texts.)

Similarly, the disillusionment and weary manner of Moses is often put down to his famous vision of

> the black faces bobbing up and down in the millions of white, strained faces, everybody hustling along the Strand, the spades jostling in the crowd, bewildered, hopeless. As if, on the surface, things don't look so bad, but when you go down a little, you bounce up a kind of misery and pathos and a frightening – what?[33]

The easy interpretation of this passage is of a minority floating aimlessly and desperately in a sea of the majority. But this interpretation would not take into account the principal source of that despair, which is not blackness or minority status as such, but the existence of that river of millions of 'white, strained faces'. The source of misery and fear is this white flow, and it is for this flow that Moses can find no meaning. The black faces in this flow only react in the correct manner to the meaninglessness of the condition. Moses is weary of London, not the black experience in London, and he recognizes the superior status that his humanized Caribbean culture gives him to look out upon this flow and write about it.

In fact, the assumption implicit in Selvon's comic portrayals of all the hardships and prejudices encountered, and the Anglophilic behaviour of characters like Galahad, is not only that these hardships are the mark of a dehumanized European society but also that they are felt most severely by those who have the most humanity to lose, those black faces in the crowd. Selvon's much quoted passage of Galahad confronting the colour of his skin as a culprit cannot simply be interpreted as a schizophrenic reaction to racism. Galahad watches his hands, and begins 'talking to the colour Black', saying

> You know is you that cause a lot of misery in the world. Is not me, you know, is you! I ain't do anything to infuriate the people and them, is you! Look at you, you so black and innocent, and this time so you causing misery over the world![34]

Here both Selvon and his character Galahad let on that they are aware of the innocence of those black hands. It is impossible for

Selvon to have made this joke without already having made his choice about a guilty and an innocent culture. It is equally impossible for critics or social theorists to couch interpretations of Selvon's work, or the sociological phenomenon from which it is drawn, as a progressive history of cultural discovery and decolonization of the mind. It is clear that from the outset of this novel Selvon has already placed full faith in Caribbean culture and in what Ramchand rightly calls its songs of innocence and experience – from long before those first trains pulled into Paddington Station, Selvon is confident of Caribbean innocence, itself a kind of superiority.

A better strategy for historians of the field of race relations might be an examination of the neglected cultural chauvinism and influence of Caribbean immigrants – that is, an examination of the clash of stubborn equals. The boys boast about seeing Marble Arch and meeting a woman at Charing Cross or Trafalgar Square, but when asked to choose between their own popular culture, their own social style, and that of the British, they choose their own. Caribbean culture shows a muscle no organized political nationalism could ignore. At a fête in St Pancras Hall in London sponsored by one of the Anglophilic characters, Harris, the others refuse to behave 'like proper gentlemen' just because 'there are a lot of proper English people here tonight'. One of the characters, Five Past Twelve (because he is five minutes blacker than midnight), reminds Harris who he is:

> You remember them lime we used to coast by Gilda Club in Charlotte Street in Port of Spain? You remember the night when Mavis make you buy ten rum for she, and then she went behind the rum shop and tell you to come?[35]

Pretty soon, the West Indian social style, the Caribbean popular culture of fêteing comes to dominate the night, just as the music and style of their offspring dominates the dance-club nightlife in the 1980s and 1990s. It seems difficult to make the case for nascent group identity or besieged and unformed cultural behaviour in this context. Samuel Selvon recognized that economic and political subjugation cannot necessarily be linked to cultural colonization, and consequently economic and political struggle cannot assume that culture starts from the same disadvantage, though it may well be interpreted that way by both group nationalists and host social scientists imposing the sociological condition on cultural interpretation and emplotting the written narrative of nation.

Perhaps sensing that the progressive view of communal and cultural becoming is disrupted even more decisively in Selvon's subsequent novels of London, Ramchand dismisses them by saying that, 'while the latter books are amusing, they suggest a disengagement by the author from his protagonist which at times, especially at the climax of *Moses Migrating*, feels like cynicism or evasion.'[36] By contrast, Michel Fabre writes that,

> whereas reviewers tend to consider *Moses Ascending* as a mere sequel to *The Lonely Londoners*, it represents a unique attempt, along the lines of post-modern fiction, to unite the iconoclastic techniques of the West and the iconoclastic techniques of the calypso in order to liberate Trinidadian fiction by negating the monopoly of the 'great tradition'.[37]

In his introduction to the Heinemann edition of *Moses Ascending*, the Jamaican critic and poet Mervyn Morris concludes that in this book Moses has developed into 'a set of attitudes affording Selvon some well taken opportunities for literary burlesque, for provoking laughter against snobbery, racism, deceit; against English assumptions of superiority; against people – often Caribbean people – who would prescribe how writers should work.'[38] It could be that what Ramchand is reacting to, and what Fabre and Morris are sensing, is a kind of good-natured Caribbean triumphalism that laces these subsequent novels. In spite of documented socio-economic hardship in Britain in the 1970s, and the regression of early Thatcherism, Black Britain exerts tremendous cultural force in these novels, dominating the life of the city in Selvon's account. Fabre and Morris point out the literary technique of this domination. But both nationalist literary critics and those in British race relations might well be disturbed by Selvon's observations regarding Caribbean cultural hegemony: that a colonized culture does not impede economic progress and civil rights, and that it does not follow that a strong Caribbean culture can defeat racism. Caribbean cultural hegemony exists side by side with oppression in these two novels, suggesting that culture is not a sufficient or controllable weapon in the struggle for the nationalist goals of economic well-being and political respect.

For instance, A. Sivanandan, a radical critic of the race-relations industry, might still be uneasy with the bawdy confidence of Selvon's West Indian language. Rather than representing cultural triumph, for Sivanandan, Caribbean culture appears to be only an inconvenience. 'The black man must go back and rediscover himself – in Africa and Asia – not in a frenetic search for lost roots, but in an attempt to discover living traditions and values.' Sivanandan adds: 'some of that past he still carries with him, no matter that it has been mislaid in the Caribbean for over four centuries.' No wonder Sivanandan sees the culture in which Black people in Britain find themselves as only a 'culture of competition, individualism, and elitism'.[39] Selvon turns his Moses into a laughable and somewhat ignorant character in the second two novels, but he does so in the confidence of an abiding Caribbean culture whose reality might unnerve Sivanandan.

Nor would these novels serve the purposes of more mainstream anti-racist analysts like Ernest Cashmore and Barry Troyna. Selvon has said that he created the Moses character, and modified him subsequently, because he 'wanted to have a voice belonging to the old generation, the first immigrants who came to this country'.[40] But that voice, in *The Lonely Londoners* and in the buffoonery of the next books, is not a voice from the prehistory of West Indian consciousness, and this fact tends to undermine the thinking of scholars like Cashmore and Troyna. The degree of cultural completeness, of national consciousness, and of cultural chauvinism and resistance, is remarkably high both in the mellow first book and even more so in the riotous second book. In an essay entitled 'Growing Up In Babylon', Cashmore and Troyna tell us that the history of Rastafarianism in Britain is 'a revealing glimpse at the contrasting orientations of first- and second-generation West Indians' and that the movement towards the open defiance and rejection of society suggests massive changes in consciousness'.[41] But what is merely apparent in the first novel becomes obvious in the second: the first generation of Caribbean migrants both defied and rejected British culture, keeping or reinventing their own dress, food, music, social behaviour, world-view, language and sexual relationships. Sivanandan might not find that retention desirable, and Cashmore and Troyna might not find it political enough, but Selvon's books argue that it survived and flourished nonetheless.

Predatory Creolization

Moses Ascending picks up the life of Moses Aloetta twenty years
later. At the beginning of the novel, now written in a bold and
often blundering first person, Moses buys a house, deciding that
it is time to be a landlord living upstairs, after being a tenant
living downstairs for so many years. He also decides that he will
write his memoirs – though this hardly seems to be the book he
is dreaming about at the end of the first novel. In fact, his character
has undergone tremendous change, from a wise, world-weary and
introspective leader to a marginal buffoon. The change has transformed him from a sympathetic character to a pathetic one, but
Selvon's reasons for this change might well be his confidence that
various forms of Caribbean culture have won out in London, as
the novel shows, and so he as an author feels less political responsibility to the group. Whatever his reason for abandoning the
redeeming side of Moses' character, he has a great deal of fun
with him. He plays off colonial archetypes and myths, using
Prospero and Caliban, Robinson Crusoe, the Crusades, and British
imperial history. Moses' house becomes a hilarious symbol of the
multicultural ferment of London in the 1970s. His basement
becomes the headquarters of the local Black Panther Party. Two
Pakistanis run an illegal immigration ring from his first floor. And
he takes in a working-class handyman from 'the black country' of
the Midlands to whom he resolves to teach the Bible when he has
time. Needless to say, most of this activity quickly spins out of
control.

Critics are right to focus on the language of this extraordinary
novel. The first novel possessed a beautifully elegiac feel, born of
the elongation of standard English with long strings of dialect
woven into the narrative. This novel loses some of that beauty, but
surely makes up for it in Rabelaisian excess. Maureen Warner-
Lewis calls it 'Samuel Selvon's Linguistic Extravaganza' and writes
of the narration and the would-be memoirs, that 'the socio-
historical tensions underlying Moses' aspirations are reflected in
the incongruity of his language codes, in the concomitant severity
of his register shifts, in inconsistent grammatical forms, and in
extravagant metaphoric comparisons.'[42] But the clash in language
between Caribbean dialect and rarefied forms of the Queen's

English is a good place to reconfirm Selvon's belief in the power and creativity of creolization, and his belief in a national Caribbean culture.

Most commonly, as in the introduction by Morris, *Moses Ascending* is interpreted as an attack on pretentious, Anglophilic colonized minds, like that of Moses, aping British ideologies of peoplehood and language. Morris asserts that 'the whole of the novel is largely a response to the assumption that the culture of Europeans is superior to the culture of others, whether Africans, Asians, or Caribbean people.'[43] Morris is not wrong, but his emphasis suggests a struggle to respond that is largely absent from Selvon. There is a triumphant quality to Selvon's effort to 'confute and redirect' stereotypes. I would argue that this is born of a confidence in the ability of Caribbean culture to meet domestic British culture, as it has met many cultures before it, and leave its obvious mark in the process of creolization, a process that for Selvon is the essence of Caribbean being. Morris is right to say that Selvon lampoons Black nationalism in his book with the shady character of a corrupt American Panther leader who absconds with the funds. But behind this lampooning is a heady confidence in its effects, in the inevitable mark it will make on domestic British culture. Moses comments, in typical fashion, that

> some white men are taking the initiative and snatching up black things before the black man has a chance. Whereas it used to be the top of the social ladder to be seen escorting a white piece in the Dilly or the circus, brothers are scorning that sort of thing nowadays, and as these black beauties grace the scene, it is to be noted that they are fecundated soon enough.[44]

Moses usually misunderstands the political point, as in his comment in the same passage: 'Blessed be the coming of this new generation of Black Britons, and blessed be I that I still alive and well to witness their coming of age from piccaninny to black beauty.' But Moses is witness to the creolization of urban British culture, not merely an illicit miscegenation but a wholesale cultural marriage. Behind Moses' paean, 'Like you see an ordinary girl tits jump up and down if she is running, thus a black backside merely pedestrianizing', is Selvon's paean to the strength of Caribbean culture and its reincarnation in Black Power. And despite Moses' sexist ignorance, Selvon gives us a Black woman who runs the Panther office in the house in Shepherd's Bush – and Selvon has her outwit Moses routinely.

Selvon's style in *Moses Ascending* is to have Moses half-understand the impact of Caribbean culture on urban British life (symbolic perhaps of the grasp of some British academics on the subject) but observe fully the ever-present creolization of life in London. Marches, demonstrations and movements dominate the news headlines; his white Man Friday becomes a Panther; the only contemporary authors mentioned by Moses are Caribbean or Black American writers like Lamming, Salkey and James Baldwin; and Moses himself begins taking on aspects of Muslim culture from his tenants, repeating after a number of conversations that there is no God but Allah. Selvon's novel is concerned with more than prejudice. It is a delighted record of the creolization of London: the making Black of white British, and the making white of Caribbean peoples. For Selvon, it is a process that indicates the strength and durability of Caribbean culture. He has witnessed the effect of his generation of Caribbean men on British society and on the next generation of Black British. The staunch Caribbean preferences of *The Lonely Londoners* described how, rather than losing Caribbean identity or finding it in reaction to loss, the early cultural nationalism of the first generation of people of Caribbean descent forced British urban culture into a process of creolization that they can be proud to have instigated. *Moses Ascending* tells not just the story of Black Britain, but the story of Blackened Britain. Critics have underestimated the nationalism of this book. Coming to England in 1952, Selvon saw just how culturally closed much of London was, and his pride in the role Caribbean peoples played in transforming that parochialism into a cosmopolitan creolism is obvious in this novel and the next. It becomes clear that Selvon cannot limit himself to recording the ethnicization of the Caribbean migrant, but must address the creolization of the Caribbean migrant's surroundings – what used to be called, quaintly, 'the host society'. In this sense, Selvon subverts the term 'creolization' as Nancy Foner tries to use it, to speak of an ethnogenesis among West Indians in Britain. Foner speaks only of British culture transforming West Indian ethnic identity. Selvon knows that creolization affects everything it touches; and consequently he concentrates on mutual transformations – not the break-up of Britain, but its reinvention.[45]

Critics considered *Moses Ascending* a response to Black nationalism and the orthodoxy imposed on the writer by Black militancy. But in fact the novel is a response to an earlier and deeper Caribbean nationalism and its success in the creolization of urban culture. Such a response refuses to see nationalism as a product of British attention to the subject of race relations, decolonization and independence. Black nationalism is only the expression of a rise in consciousness among Caribbean people if centuries of popular resistance in culture, politics and war come to nothing. Selvon, like C.L.R. James, will not deny this history in order that nationalism might begin with the migration to Britain and the attention of the British. In Trinidad, the trade-union movements of the 1930s, and the carnivals of the same time indicate the level of cultural nationalism already rampant in Trinidad before the migration. The West Indians who came to Britain were not lost colonial souls, but Jamaicans, Trinidadians, Grenadians – perhaps not politically, but culturally. Selvon's work confirms this nationalism and its protection mechanism, creolization. But it is not only white British academics who have misread this development. Several Black British analysts also fall into the trap of believing resistance and nationalism to be new phenomena, born in the migratory experience.

Ron Ramdin's weighty and admirable work, *The Making of the Black Working Class in Britain*, passes over an essentially radical point. He notes that in the 1960s and 1970s, 'the West Indian teenager was "very West Indian". The working-class Jamaican, for example, was drawn closely to Jamaican heritage, preferring to speak patois and listen to bluebeat music, and think of himself as Jamaican.'[46] But what progress in nationalism is that – to think and act Jamaican? It is Selvon's first generation that thought and acted Jamaican, Trinidadian, and so on. If Ramdin is right that such behaviour among youth is a sign of rebellion and worker alienation, then surely the efforts of the characters in Selvon's first work to keep their cultural style, their music, food, dance and social behaviour, was also rebellion, refusal to assimilate, protest at inferior human relationships found in the host country – in short, a cultural radicalism to match that of today's youth. Selvon understood that there could be nothing more radical than being Jamaican in Britain, nothing more radical than preferring not to be British. Similarly, Ken Pryce's good anthropological study of Black Bristol is marred by a false timeline of Black nationalism. He identifies, in 1970s Bristol, two kinds of Black British youth: workers and hustlers. He also places his hopes in 'disruptive-articulates' who refuse to join the system, but who express that refusal with cultural preferences for West Indian lifestyle and philosophy. But Selvon could surely tell him that such hustlers, particularly articulate ones, have a long tradition both in Britain and in the West Indies. As the leader of the *Race Today* collective, Darcus Howe, often notes in speeches and conversation, the conditions Black people found in Britain were not that different from the ones they found in colonial regimes. It is not surprising, then, that nationalist resistance should predate its supposed rise in West Indian literature or Black nationalism in Britain. It certainly does so in Selvon's fiction.

The third novel of the trilogy, *Moses Migrating*, is worthy of attention for these same reasons. This novel features the return of Moses to Trinidad; but Trinidad, ever creolizing and developing, has passed him by – he is now a creolized Englishman. The novel demonstrates the transforming power of creolization, its dynamic, rather than progressive, energy. Selvon takes a sly poke at the reification of migrant community culture – the holding on to old country ways after the old country has long abandoned those ways. Much work has been done on the cultural effect of returnees on the old country: some of it emphasizing them as change agents, other studies emphasizing the cultural fossilization of their ways. A body of literature on *ritornati* in Italy is perhaps the most sophisticated and developed. But Constance Sutton has done some of the same work in the Caribbean context.[47] *Moses Migrating* would be a good text for examination in this context. But that is another study.

Taken together, the novels indicate that Selvon's base in the street culture of Port of Spain gave him the insight to reject the chronopolitics of British race relations, and to see the history of a diasporic nationalism in the Caribbean as a new phenomenon powered by the inevitable creolization of Trinidad, and one which suggested that the Trinidadian nation, and the Caribbean nation, would continue to devour and transform cultures local and alien.

This idea of a predatory creolization as national culture is Sam Selvon's contribution to the national community of Trinidad.

Notes

1. Keith Warner, *The Trinidad Calypso*, London: Heinemann, 1982, pp. 74–5.

2. Samuel Selvon, 'Calypso in London', in *Ways of Sunlight*, London: Longman, 1987, pp. 113–19.

3. Samuel Selvon, 'Three Into One Can't Go', in David Dabydeen and Brinsley Samaroo, eds., *India in the Caribbean*, London: Hansib Publishing, 1987.

4. Samuel Selvon, *A Brighter Sun*, London: Longman Caribbean, 1979.

5. O.R. Dathorne, *Dark Ancestors*, Baton Rouge: Louisiana State University, 1981; Selwyn Cudjoe, *Resistance and Caribbean Literature*, Athens, Ohio: University of Ohio Press, 1980.

6. Jean-Paul Durix, reviewing Susheila Nasta, ed., *Critical Perspectives on Sam Selvon* (Washington, DC: Three Continents Press, 1988), in *Commonwealth*, vol. 13, no. 2, pp. 125–6.

7. Paget Henry, 'Decolonization and Cultural Underdevelopment in the Commonwealth Caribbean', in Paget Henry and Carl Stone, eds., *The Newer Caribbean: Decolonization, Democracy, and Development*, Philadelphia: ISHI, 1983, pp. 105 and 119.

8. The novels of Alejo Carpentier have most often been studied as part of a Latin American tradition, but his active creolizing fits easily with Gustavo Perez Firmat's *The Cuban Condition*, New York: Cambridge University Press, 1989.

9. Peter Nazareth, 'Interview with Samuel Selvon', *World Literature Written in English*, vol. 18, no. 2, 1979, pp. 420–36.

10. Samuel Selvon 'Three Into One Can't Go', p. 21.

11. Ibid., p. 23.

12. Ibid., p. 16.

13. Ibid., p. 24.

14. References are to *The Lonely Londoners*, Harlow: Longman Caribbean, 1985; *Moses Ascending*, London: Heinemann Caribbean, 1984; and *Moses Migrating*, Harlow: Longman Caribbean, 1983.

15. Ibid., p. 15.

16. Ulf Hannerz, *Cultural Complexity: Studies in the Social Organization of Meaning*, New York: Columbia University Press, 1992.

17. John Figueroa 'The Relevance of West Indian Literature', in Colin Brock, ed., *The Caribbean in Europe*, London: Frank Cass, 1986, p. 222.

18. Johannes Fabian, *Time and the Other: How Anthropology Makes its Object*, New York: Columbia University Press, 1983, p. 144.

19. Elizabeth M. Thomas-Hope, 'Caribbean Diaspora, The Inheritance of Slavery: Migration from the Commonwealth Caribbean', in Brock, ed., *The Caribbean in Europe*, pp. 15–35.

20. *The Lonely Londoners* was originally published in 1956.

21. Kenneth Ramchand, 'Song of Innocence, Song of Experience: Samuel Selvon's *Lonely Londoners* as a Literary Work', *World Literature Written in English*, vol. 21, no. 3, 1982, p. 654.

22. Frank Birbalsingh, 'Samuel Selvon and the West Indian Literary Renaissance', *Ariel*, vol. 8, no. 3, 1977, p. 14.

23. Victor L. Chang, 'Elements of the Mock Heroic in West Indian Fiction: A Look at *The Dragon Can't Dance* and *Moses Ascending*', in Erika Smilovitz and Roberta Knowles, eds., *Critical Issues in West Indian Literature*, Parkersburg, Iowa: Caribbean Books, 1984.

24. John Rex and Sally Tomlinson, *Colonial Immigrants in a British City*, London: Routledge & Kegan Paul, 1979.

25. Chris Mullard, *Race, Power and Resistance*, London: Routledge & Kegan Paul, 1985.

26. Philip Cohen and Harwant S. Bains, eds., *Multi-Racist Britain*, London: Macmillan, 1988.

27. Jenny Bourne, 'Cheerleaders and Ombudsmen: The Sociology of Race Relations in Britain', *Race & Class*, vol. 21, no. 4, 1980, pp. 331–52.

28. A view of the cultural struggle for pluralism and against racism in Britain, including inside British institutions, as opposed to purely sociological or political accounts of the struggle, can be found in Kwesi Owusu, *The Struggle for Black Arts in Britain: What Can We Consider Better than Freedom*, London: Comedia, 1986.

29. David Rudder, 'Trinidad Boys', 1989.

30. Selvon, *The Lonely Londoners*, p. 122.

31. Kenneth Ramchand in his introduction to *The Lonely Londoners*, p. 7.

32. Jagdish Gundara, Lessons from History for Black Resistance in Britain', in John Tierney, ed., *Race, Migration, and Schooling*, London: Holt, 1982, p. 44.

33. Selvon, *The Lonely Londoners*, pp. 124–5.

34. Ibid., p. 72.

35. Ibid., pp. 96–7.

36. Ramchand, introduction to *The Lonely Londoners*, p. 21.

37. Michel Fabre, 'Samuel Selvon', in Bruce King, ed., *West Indian Literature*, London: Macmillan, 1979, pp. 123–4.

38. Mervyn Morris, in his introduction to *Moses Ascending*, London: Heinemann Caribbean Writers Series, 1984, p. 16.

39. A. Sivanandan, 'The Liberation of the Black Intellectual', *A Different Hunger*, London: Pluto, 1982, p. 89.

40. Susheila Nasta, 'Sam Selvon Interviewed', *Wasafiri*, vol. 1, no. 2, 1985, p. 5.

41. Ernest Cashmore and Barry Troyna, 'Growing Up in Babylon', in E. Cashmore and B. Troyna, eds., *Black Youth in Crisis*, London: Allen & Unwin, 1982.

42. Maureen Warner-Lewis, 'Samuel Selvon's Linguistic Extravaganza: *Moses Ascending*', in Erika Smilowitz and Roberta Knowles, eds., *Critical Issues in West Indian Literature*, Parkenburg, Iowa: Caribbean Books, 1984.

43. Morris, introduction to *Moses Ascending*, p. 10.

44. Selvon, *Moses Ascending*, p. 15.

45. Nancy Foner, 'The Jamaicans: Cultural and Social Change among Migrants in Britain', in J. Watson, *Between Two Cultures: Migrants and Minorities in Britain*, Oxford: Basil Blackwell, p. 121.

46. Ron Ramdin, *The Making of the Black Working Class in Britain*, Aldershot: Gower, 1987.

47. Constance Sutton and Susan Makiesky, 'Migration and West Indian Ethnic and Racial Consciousness', in H. Safa and B. DuToit, eds., *Migration and Development*, The Hague: Mouton Publishers, 1976.

CHAPTER 5

Neil Bissoondath and
Migrant Liberation from the Nation

Benedict Anderson writes that, 'in an age when it is so common for progressive, cosmopolitan intellectuals [particularly in Europe?] to insist on the near-pathological character of nationalism, its roots in fear and hatred of the Other, and its affinities with racism, it is useful to remind ourselves that nations inspire love, and often profoundly self-sacrificing love.'[1] The case of young Trinidadian-Canadian writer Neil Bissoondath provides an interesting test of Anderson's point. There is an attraction to the Caribbean in Bissoondath's work, but no love, and there is much in his artistic philosophy that fears the stigma of Caribbean nationhood, race and origin. His exorcism of Trinidad captures the tension between the desired freedom of a writer, or any citizen, and the pull of imagined nations.

The case of Bissoondath also provides an opportunity to focus on an increasingly vigorous part of the diaspora – Toronto, Canada, a destination of much Trinidadian and Caribbean immigration in the last twenty years and now the cultural scene of what is by one measurement the largest Caribbean festival outside of the Caribbean: Caribana.[2] It might come as a surprise, therefore, to some Canadians that Canada has only recently begun to examine what is hegemonic in its literature. Canadians pride themselves on their official government policies of multiculturalism and bilingualism, and the diversity of the country's demography has become a truism in Canadian politics. And yet, as Robert Lecker points out in a recent issue of *Critical Inquiry*, Canadian literary critics have been hard at work during the last twenty years creating a rigid canon of mimetic texts obsessed with the image of Canada and Canadian values, largely blind to the debates on canonicity raging in the United States and in Europe, and largely ignorant of the growing wealth of literature from migrant populations and Native Canadians.[3]

This instant canon was constructed by self-consciously crusading Anglo-Canadians like Robertson Davies, Northrop Frye and Margaret Atwood, whose resemblance to the privileged, urban Black middle class of Trinidad as a nation-building elite should not go unmentioned, though their sense of injustice and anti-colonialism is far more muted, and their exclusion of other groups more culturally myopic and ignorant, and less a product of ethno-class competitive politics than their Trinidadian counterparts. The chosen literature of this Canadian nation-building *ciudad letrada* could be characterized as full of anti-urban, Anglo-Celtic settler values, wilderness iconography and inward-looking Protestant religiosity. This imagined nation neither acknowledged the historical diversity of the country, nor allowed that diversity to speak for itself.[4] But more recently, with demography in Canadian cities rendering the study and teaching of this Anglo-Canadian literary canon increasingly absurd, new writers have been seized upon in Canada with the same vigour and boosterism that have accompanied new ethnic groups into the proud rhetorical and bureaucratic invented tradition of multiculturalism.[5] Consequently in 1988, when the young Trinidadian migrant to Canada Neil Bissoondath published his first novel, *A Casual Brutality*,[6] he was greeted by a fanfare of nationalist media hype.

The national news magazine called it 'A Novelist's Stunning Debut' and reported in gossip-sheet fashion that he had received a $350,000 advance. The article was part of a larger piece heralding the emergence of Canadian literature onto the international scene.[7] Similar glowing reviews appeared in newspapers and journals across the country, often tying Bissoondath to a growing number of other non-Anglo-Canadian writers.[8] Even more recently, the *Faber Book of Contemporary Caribbean Short Stories* led off its new collection with a short story by Bissoondath, confirming the Canadian critics' contention that he was a young national writer of international stature, the appropriate new face of Canadian

literary achievement, and, at the same time, announcing his initiation into the Caribbean literary diaspora.[9] And Bissoondath is
an obviously talented writer – sometimes stiff, but always in
command of his language. What is odd about the reaction to this
34-year-old Indo-Trinidadian Canadian is that his ideas of community and nation seem antithetical both to a fine Caribbean
critic like Mervyn Morris searching to find Caribbean-ness in each
short story in his collection, and to the new apostles of the multicultural canon in Canadian literature. Neil Bissoondath's words,
both in interviews and in the mouths of his characters, take direct
aim at conceptions of community like the Caribbean diaspora or
the multicultural nation, not to speak of the viability of an
imagined Trinidad-as-nation. In fact, his work is a kind of personal
project of liberation from either migrant communities or home
countries, a liberation that sometimes seems cynical, and that
always, ironically, imagines the nation in order to run from it.
The contradictions of this liberation are manifold if sometimes
subtle, but it is in this search for individual liberation that
Bissoondath's work speaks to political and ethical questions concerning the role of the writer in the community, and presents this
author as a challenge of the writer's responsibility to the places he
writes about and the people he depicts. In this challenge, Bissoondath imagines the nation sometimes as a tattoo or scar; at other
times, in his optimism, as a set of old clothes to be left behind, or
a bad childhood to be overcome.

Neil Bissoondath left Trinidad to attend university in Toronto,
and, unlike the main character of his novel, Raj Ramsingh, he
stayed. In interviews he admits he has never considered going
back, and that he likes Toronto for its openness and its order. But
he is not uncritical of Canada. In fact, he aims a good blow at the
body politic when he says that 'Canadian multiculturalism is ...
aiming at keeping groups separate; it isn't allowing various immigrant groups to get together as simple Canadians, and keeping all
these groups separate makes them easy to manipulate.' And he
openly resents the restrictions of being a migrant from Trinidad,
saying that all multiculturalism does 'is ask you to freeze your
personality, to remain what you once were in order to add to the
colourful multicultural fabric of the country.'[10] Bissoondath has
also appeared on the national television news programme, the

CBC Journal, during the Meech Lake constitutional crisis in Canada, where he voiced similar reservations about multiculturalism, linking it to the failure of the nation to hold itself together.

The Nation Abandoned

But if Bissoondath's words do not serve Canadian multiculturalism, neither do they offer hope to Trinidad. In fact, no writer since his uncle, V.S. Naipaul, has painted a grimmer picture of the nation – in his fiction he calls it a failed attempt at nationhood. 'A lot of former British colonies are worse off since independence but that's not a judgement on independence. You have to look at the lack of political leadership and intellectual direction, at people who have plundered their own country',[11] states Bissoondath in conversation. He goes on to say: 'In Trinidad, you're not just marginal if you're a writer, you're considered crazy. I love Toronto's openness, and its size has given me the anonymity I needed to write.' It is easy to have sympathy for Bissoondath and for his characters, seen by the host country first as ambassadors of a culture and keepers of a nation, before they are viewed as individual imaginations, bearers of a personal history and culture. Fredric Jameson's designation of all Third World writing as national allegory is only the most recent restriction placed on the freedom of Third World and migrant writers to create with the same abandon as First World writers. But, working away from the dominant discourses of the Third World, and indeed under the protection of American exceptionalism, some anthropologists have conceived of a writing inscribed with community identity (ethnicity in this case, rather than nationality) that is nonetheless liberating. In particular, Michael M.J. Fischer in his excellent essay 'Ethnicity and the Postmodern Arts of Memory' makes the point that ethnicity, like peoplehood, is not something passed down, but something discovered and reinvented; and that the 'process of assuming an ethnic identity is an insistence on a pluralistic, multidimensional, or multifaceted concept of self: one can be many different things, and this personal sense can be a crucible for a wider social ethos of pluralism.' This definition of ethnicity, far from being the restriction Bissoondath fears, looks like a pass to personal liberation and individual creativity. That Bissoondath does not see the vehicle of ethnicity or peoplehood as a crucible of pluralism and individual invention in this way speaks to the manner in which he flattens his own ethnicity and peoplehood, and strips the nation of Trinidad of its potential as a crucible of difference.

Other writers from Trinidad, such as Sam Selvon or Ismith Khan, have used the nation 'to activate in the reader a desire for communitas with others, while preserving rather than effacing difference', as Fischer concludes.[12] But, as the rapturous critical response in the Caribbean and Canada suggests, Neil Bissoondath is playing another game, and putting the image of the nation to another use. Unlike Naipaul's famous character Mr Biswas, Bissoondath is willing to burn down his house to escape. He has said that he sees himself as a migrant, not an immigrant, on a journey in which Trinidad and even Toronto are only stops. But in Bissoondath's fiction Trinidad and Toronto are migratory stops of great personal and artistic use (before they are dismissed), and it is here that Bissoondath does join with community, long enough to take what he needs from it. As his main character Raj Ramsingh says, 'self is the prime mover.' Any serious examination of Bissoondath's fiction must make a judgement on its use and abuse of community. It must come to terms with Bissoondath's enigmatic arrival in the critical community, while judging the validity of his rejection of the national project in Trinidad and the Caribbean diaspora in the name of individual liberation.

Arun Mukherjee, in his recent book *Towards an Aesthetic of Opposition,* confessed his doubts about Bissoondath in a volume otherwise dedicated to championing 'South Asian' writers in Canada. Speaking about Bissoondath's collection of short stories, *Digging Up the Mountains,*[13] Mukherjee admitted 'to having experienced a constant sense of unease at the subtle and not so subtle ideological manipulations while reading the stories. It is not so much the violence and corruption that I am disturbed by as by their removal from history and their presentation as the immutable condition of the Caribbeans.'[14] Mukherjee cites a short story in which the narrator encounters an ignorant Marxist student at a university in Montreal. The student wants to return to the Caribbean to start a Marxist revolution, but the writer portrays him as a buffoon, incapable of reading or understanding the books that go flying from his arms in the last scene as he trips and the narrator remarks that 'the future of Trinidad went sprawling to the ground'.[15] Mukherjee suggests that this passage is not only a subtle ideological manipulation, but also the kind of sly manipulation of community and the role of the writer that runs throughout Bissoondath's work and words, even if this episode is farcical and cartoonish. The story mocks those intellectuals who remain committed to some kind of communion with community. Much of Bissoondath's first novel is also devoted to an inscribed manipulation of community, and race, in Trinidad and Toronto, in which the discourses on race, nationhood and multiculturalism mask history, class, and the vitality of difference in Trinidad. An examination of his texts will reveal that Bissoondath's search for liberation from community becomes a negation of history and rejection of social variety in Trinidad, and that this search must fail because the writer cannot find protection outside of a pluralistic national ethos, whether that ethos is part of Canadian multiculturalism or the Trinidadian carnival of identities. But Bissoondath does try precisely to reject these nations through the distortion of their history and the negation of their pluralism.

The first scene in Bissoondath's novel takes the reader to the heart of the matter. Dr Raj Ramsingh is preparing to embark from Piarco airport in Trinidad (though it goes unnamed) significantly with no luggage – his son and Canadian wife having been killed in a confused uprising on the island. As he checks in at the counter for his flight back to Toronto he is disturbed by the surly response of the young African Trinidadian behind the counter. Later, his uncle Grappler explains: 'but don't you see, Raj. He concludes that you can afford to leave with nothing, and then buy everything new.'[16] This opening episode promises to be a investigation into who can leave a community and who cannot. But, unfortunately, far from announcing an inquiry into the privileged position of the writer/intellectual in society, the episode is rejected by Raj and by Bissoondath in the final scene of the book, which picks up sequentially from this first scene. In between, Bissoondath builds his case for Raj rejecting this first episode and choosing to 'go like his forebears, to the future, to the challenge that lies elsewhere of turning nothing into something, far from the casual brutality of collapse, far from the ruins of failure, across thousands of miles of ocean.'[17] Left behind, in what Raj and Bissoondath call a casual brutality, and failed attempt at nationalism, is the young man behind the check-in counter, a young man who could as easily be Indian as African, and who has never been given the economic and educational opportunity of leaving the casual brutality – which has been just as deadly to him as to Raj.

The Caribbean novel has never been without the tension of class difference between writer and subject. In Trinidad, C.L.R James's pioneering novel, *Minty Alley*, featured the middle-class intellectual as voyeur in the unfamiliar world of the poor, working-class yard life. Frederick Ivor Case, in his study of Francophone Caribbean novelists from Guadeloupe and Martinique, makes the necessary point that in looking at any Caribbean text 'the socio-literary analyst has to point out that it is a text in fundamental conflict with its social context' because of the high levels of illiteracy in Caribbean societies, and often because of the use of standardized rather than local speech and writing patterns.[18] With Bissoondath the problem is not the reconciliation of the writer with his less privileged community but the rejection of such a possibility. Bissoondath sees no possibility of forming or saving a community plural and tolerant enough to hold both Raj and the airline clerk. But in his rejection of Trinidad, he indeed burns down the house to leave it, playing loosely with history and fact, and, ultimately, with the life of the resentful clerk. The deconstructive moment in this novel comes outside it, in Bissoondath's decision to call Trinidad by the name Casaquemada, and his claim that Trinidad lies elsewhere. This decision unravels the essential impossibility of the novel and of Bissoondath's quest for liberation from community. It is an attempt to free himself from history and responsibility, but at the same time is purely a reaction to the real history of Trinidad and moves like a shadow of the island itself. As Kenneth Ramchand notes in his review of the novel, 'those who know Trinidad may take a mournful pleasure in recognizing the justice of his observations.'[19] But Ramchand would have done better to represent the simulacra of his observations, because the question of justice, and just representation, is not one Bissoondath is ready to meet head-on.

The Uninhabitable Text of the Nation

'Casaquemada' is Spanish for 'house burn down', and the writer's description of the island is curiously unliberating – except for the name, there is really no attempt to create an imaginary island. In fact, between faithful description of topography and geography and barely masked references to political history in Trinidad, the writer seems to be doing his best to capture Trinidad not reinvent it. The frequent references to Eric Williams, his hearing aid turned off to the sounds of his ministers plundering the oil wealth, are only the most obvious brushes with fact. But if there is an eerie amount of verisimilitude in Casaquemada, there are also some important distortions, made more complex by the attention else-where to historical detail. Or rather, they are less distortions than omissions, omissions that allow Raj Ramsingh to walk away from community and see Casaquemada as a place best burnt down. But he walks away from a society stripped of its polyphony and yet still characterized as emblematic of the Caribbean reality.

The novel presents an island that is racially divided and deeply stratified by class. Raj moves with his Canadian wife through a wealthy Indian subculture on the island, slipping into past worlds – both his university days in Toronto where he met his wife, and his childhood where he was brought up by grandparents who spoke Hindi to each other. His cousin calls the African islanders 'niggers' and lower-caste Indians 'coolies'. But there is a simplification in this imaginary island. Except for the thieves in government – who are black on the outside and green, like US dollars, on the inside, according to one character – the author largely ignores the Trini-dadian fact of wealthy African Trinidadians. And consequently the vaguely homoerotic scenes of Raj as a boy watching a Black youth cut his grass for him become the structural scenario of the island – wealthy Hindu high castes sitting atop lesser Indians and a powder keg of resentful Africans. By emphasizing this link between class and race, and by insisting on a separatist Hindu ethnie as the dominant influence in the lives of these characters, Bissoondath gives Raj ample cause to feel he is not part of the island community – that there is no place for him in a nation where he is neither the right race nor the right class to be loved. When his cousin's 'coolie' leads the revolutionaries to his wife and son, we understand that Raj's removal is one of class as well as race. But both of Raj's reasons to leave, his suspect class and his isolated race, are largely Casaquemada fabrications in the middle of Trinidadian reality. And Bissoondath's map of misreading of Trinidadian society causes him to overlook the heritage of cultural pluralism that he perhaps unwittingly admires in its Canadian form.

In 1988, one of the most popular road march songs of the carnival season was a calypso by Crazy (himself a doogla) called *Nani Wine*, about an Indo-Trinidadian girl and her mother who love to dance, to 'wine down low' during carnival season. Some more traditional Hindu leaders in the community took offence at the song, but for the masses of people who poured into the streets from jouvert morning to the last lap, the song was a tremendous hit. That same year saw Indo-Trinidadian Drupatee's hit calypso, 'Indian Soca', featuring the lines 'rhythm from Africa and India/ blend together is the perfect mixture/ all we doing is adding a little flavour/ then you come up with Indian soca.' And despite Raj's mean-spirited comment that only the tourists dance with every race at carnival, in the real Casaquemada it was evident to any observer that the song marked a further melding and changing of Trinidadian culture and of carnival – still a so-called 'Creole' event, though thousands of Indo-Trinidadians in the streets of San Fernando and Port of Spain were busy changing that Creole event, claiming it.[20] That year featured a new surge in 'soca chutney' – a musical blend of traditional Indian vocals with calypso beat. The first thing that Neil Bissoondath took from Trinidad's history when he renamed it was carnival. And with it, he took not just a nationalist symbol but the right of people to make culture daily and to insist that all culture is man-made and contemporary. But more than that suspension, Bissoondath denied the very sources of diversity that would tolerate individual expressions of identity.

Carnival is Trinidad's central invented tradition. But it is not as tame as the national anthems, flags and rallies of Eric Hobsbawm and Terence Ranger's study *The Invention of Tradition*; for carnival in Trinidad is characterized not by 'formalization and ritualization' alone but also by unpredictability, irreverence, shifts in identity – all qualities dangerous to the official nationalist.[21] Nor could it be said that carnival is the kind of accidental, originally arbitrary act of national life that has been endowed by nationalists with special significance, as Ernest Gellner might argue.[22] In fact, the historical selection of carnival, as well as its continuing character, reflect the unresolved tensions of post-colonial Trinidad and the difference of identity that flourish in the heat of its enactment. As Alvin Magid notes, after World War II,

> Carnival came to symbolize in Trinidad the hope that anti-colonialism would sublimate the passions of communal nationalism, not be engulfed by them. A historic irony marked this development. Where Carnival once underscored the division of colonial Trinidad by class and race, in the era of nationalist struggle and decolonization it symbolized a transcendent nationhood enriched by social pluralism.[23]

But the entire contested terrain of carnival is absent from the lengthy descriptions of life on Bissoondath's island, and from the details of daily life which resemble Trinidad, as Ramchand notes, in so many other respects – from brand of tinned milk to television news. Bissoondath chooses instead to represent an island lacking any appreciable efforts at making daily culture, and he chooses to represent those Indian Trinidadians who reject contact with other Trinidadians. (In fuller dimension, such a portrait would take account of those African Trinidadians who reject Indian Trinidadians, but that would require the support of all the other missing dimensions in this text.)

In fact, what *A Casual Brutality* achieves is the wrenching of culture from history. By removing carnival (not to mention Phagwa) from Trinidad but retaining what Ramchand called the mournful recognition of Trinidad's financial and social ills, Bissoondath cuts the heart out of the nation. He also freezes race and class in precisely the way he does not want to see culture frozen in Canadian multiculturalism. The continuous process of becoming a nation takes place in forums like carnival, in calypso, in chutney, in Hosay. It is in acts of cultural creation like carnival, like literature, like the formation of political parties, that African and Indian Trinidadians, together with Chinese, Syrian, French Creole and mixed peoples, have sought and sometimes found common ground. It is also in these cultural creations that all peoples in Trinidad have imagined Trinidad, have come to belong to the island. And, perhaps most importantly, the sites of these cultural contestations open up the space of individual choice of identity; they are what Fischer has labelled the crucible of demotic pluralism – precisely what Bissoondath claims he needs – openness, anonymity, change. But in *A Casual Brutality* none of these cultural creations have any real presence. It is also worth noting that another potential coalition of experience is denied in Bissoondath's work, an experience that is opposite but complementary to the carnival creations: the common experience of oppression, of enslavement, of continued hardships of poverty, migration, disenfranchisement. As the poetry of David Dabydeen shows us, such commonality does not have to erase difference in Indo-Caribbean and Afro-Caribbean experience, but it can find common, creative ground on which to plan for a common fate. Dabydeen's brittle but full-blooded poem 'The Old Map' is typical of his ability to form coalitions from history. 'Other fragments rot in the sun/ like cane chewed and spit/ from Coolie mouth./ Haiti is a crab with broken claw./ Cuba droops in fear at the foot of America', writes Dabydeen, finding on the same map, perhaps, the hardships of Indian indentured labour, betrayed African Haitian peasants, fearful mixed Cuban workers.[24]

The Politics of Imagined History

In the case of political history, Bissoondath is at his most distressing and least convincing, imagining a nation without political culture in the same way that he read the nation without creative culture. Both in the novel and in interviews he speaks about a lack of 'political leadership and intellectual direction' in the Caribbean. When Raj climbs to the colonial fortifications to contemplate the sadness of the death of his wife and son, he reflects on the Europeans who built the fort, blaming them in no small measure for his fate.

> Those men who had sweated and strained had had other, more valuable lessons to teach, but they had paid only lip-service to their voiced ideals, had offered in the end but the evils of their actions, had propagated but the baser instincts, which took root and flourished so effortlessly in this world they called, with a kind of black humour, new.[25]

This idea of the Europeans planting only their baser instincts in the island – instincts which flourished – underscores the author's universal imperialism. The notion that Trinidad's dominant instincts come from Europe, or that the African and Indian population nurtured base European instincts rather than their own, is a highly paternalist suggestion. But worse, such a notion is also a negation of history, a history in which people were prevented for centuries from pursuing either democracy or economic self-sufficiency. It was not the job of British colonialists, as Bissoondath would have his readers believe, to instruct the colony in democracy and financial management (something they knew little about). It was their job, long before Eric Williams marched in the rain (mocked in this book), to allow the people to practise these arts themselves. Contrary to Bissoondath's assertion about a lack of intellectual direction, it was perhaps the intellectual strength and commitment of men like Eric Williams, Norman Manley and Fidel Castro who salvaged some nationhood from the ruins of Caribbean imperialism.[26] To this list must be added those whose political writings in the postwar period reached far beyond the region, such as Walter Rodney, Frantz Fanon and Aime Cesaire. Postwar Canada – or Britain for that matter – has hardly thrown up greater intellectual leadership than those men represented in their countries, and indeed globally. The Caribbean has thrown up its share of scoundrels in this same period – Vere Byrd, Desmond Hoyte, and Eric Gairey to name a few; but contrary to Bissoondath's reasoning, these leaders neither learned their ways from the baser instincts of Europeans, nor were solely the products of the region's underdevelopment.[27] In Bissoondath's imagination, the Caribbean nation-space is not granted the autonomous agency necessary for a consideration of good and evil.

The novel again plays with fact to Trinidad's detriment in recalling the one real revolt in its post-independence history: the 1970 revolution, or Black Power revolution. (The more recent tragic hostage-taking in July of 1990 reduced itself quickly to a terrorist incident.) In the novel, the event is ripped from its context, emptied of its political meaning. In history, the event was marked by a flurry of intellectual and political writings and teachings, and by a real attempt by middle-class students of both races to enlist the support of poor rural Indians and dispossessed urban Africans (with mixed results). The 1970 revolution was not without its hooliganism or racism (particularly against the Chinese) but it was far from a casual brutality – at least as far away from it as 1968 was in Paris or Chicago. Earl Lovelace, in his novel *The Dragon Can't Dance*, also rewrites the 1970 revolution as farce, but he does so as part of the growth of an artist in Trinidad who ends the novel with a fresh commitment to creating a new culture in the island. The difference is that between a man who makes his life in Trinidad and a man who makes his living from it. And yet Bissoondath is a technically impressive writer and could be forgiven for all of this, for inventing a bleak Caribbean island all his own, if the words of a committed Indo-Trinidadian intellectual did not come back to haunt him – 'those who know Trinidad may take a mournful pleasure in recognizing.'

The liberation of the novelist comes at the expense of all who must recognize their island as it has been denatured and renamed by Bissoondath. The comparison of the author to his character Raj, leaving the country without luggage, is inaccurate: Bissoondath has not, in fact, turned his back on Trinidad for good as Raj resolves to do; rather, the author comes and goes from the country, without luggage, each time antagonizing anew the impoverished airline clerk. The nation for Bissoondath has become not imagination but fantasy, where the logical rules of history and social relations can be broken, and where community has lost meaning but continues to be invoked as a negative referent. The novel takes us on a largely internal voyage through Raj's psychic map of the island, and we are told to dread what he dreads – the violence, the Blacks, his Canadian wife, his dehumanized and violent cousin, and finally the social chaos at the edge of the world. Bissoondath wants to take us to this world, and yet he has denatured it to such an extent that the reader gropes for any human fellow feeling. Bissoondath exhibits an odd possession of the nation he names, a fantastical possession. Mary Campbell, in her book *The Witness and the Other World*, reminds us that 'colonization is in part a linguistic act. At least it is by the linguistic domination of one culture over another that we have tended to define successful political aggression as conquest, colonization, or empire building.' She notes that 'linguistic aggressions' are a central feature of the journals of Columbus, and in fact he 'names everything in sight' and has an 'extraordinary possessiveness displayed in his propensity for naming and his avoidance of native words'. Campbell also notes that Columbus imposed on his 'new heaven and new earth' a 'generic egotism and greed of romance'.[28] There is something of Columbus in Neil Bissoondath's renaming of the nation, and in his greedy use of the nation for romance.

Canada Re-imagined

'In Barbados, I breathe in the smell of the soil, I taste the scandals of the landscape. The mud through which I trample and the sand that pours through my fingers are the roots and ruins I spoke about', writes Barbadian Canadian novelist Austin Clarke. 'It does tend to make my tentative accomplishments in this country empty, and at the same time, over-important and inflated.'[29] Clarke speaks about a lack of what he calls ruins and roots in the immigrants' lives, and how that has left them like Eliot's hollow men, whose voices are reduced to meaningless whispering. In the same collection which Neil Bissoondath leads off with a story called 'Veins Visible', one finds Austin Clarke's 'The Man'.[30] It is important to note that Austin Clarke has recently blasted critical attempts to consider him a spokesman for West Indians in Canada. But the difference in the writers' use of community reveals much about these two migrant intellectuals, something about pluralism and nationalism in the migrant imagination, and something about the nature of multiculturalism in Canada.

In his many short stories and novels, Clarke has dealt extensively with the lack of roots and ruins in the lives of immigrants in Canada, and the consequent damage to the psychological and emotional health of these men and women. In 'The Man' he tells the story of an anonymous man, observed by strangers to be crazy. Clarke describes the man's daily pattern of walking around his neighbourhood within an exact radius of his home, collecting all the newspapers and articles he can stuff into his worn suit, and returning to his furnished room to write letters to the leaders of the world, in the hope of donating his correspondence to the University of Toronto. The man's identity has been stolen by these leaders, and he must write to them to get it back. But this is not

just a postmodern parable. There is tremendous authorial tenderness in the story. Clarke achieves a strange intimacy with the man,
particularly by describing for us the routines of the man's weak-
bladder problem, and his consequent chagrin. In the end, the
man's hotpot burns up his room, probably consuming him. As a
story of a man's faith in the written word gone mad, Clarke's
narrative is first rate and masterly. It is also a tender understanding
of the way personality can be savaged by the immigrant experience. Clarke is more than a West Indian writer in this, as in many
of his stories; this is not because he has burnt down West Indian
identity as unworthy of his imagination, but because he has transcended it, without betraying the roots and ruins so many still rely
on to retain some psychic health. The man's story does not lead
to the conclusion that his roots and ruins are base, but rather that
the roots and ruins of Canadian society have excluded him, left
him a hollow man. Clarke has also called into question the limits
of the open and anonymous nation that Bissoondath praises.

Bissoondath's Raj, for his part, has no sympathy for the hollow
men.

> I had not come to Toronto to find Casaquemada, or to play the role
> of the ethnic, deracinated and costumed, drawing around himself the
> defensive postures of the land left behind. And this display of the rakish,
> this attempt at Third World exoticism, seemed to me a trap, a way of
> sealing the personality, of rendering it harmless to all but the indi-
> vidual. The life implied by Kensington Market gave me nightmares.[31]

And of the Caribbean community in Toronto, Raj says: 'I thought
their behaviour a form of racism, not one that rejected but one
that claimed.... It was the visible minorities who most made me feel
a member of a visible minority, visible minorities who seemed most
to draw the lines of difference.'[32] Neil Bissoondath puts it this way:

> Then you have the professional ethnics who go around screaming for
> this and for that, forgetting that they are in a new country with its own
> historical, political setup. I have a hard time with immigrants and
> immigrant groups who reject learning French for example or reject
> the French fact in Canada.[33]

Bissoondath's rejection of history in Trinidad is complemented by
an appeal to history in Canada. But, as Austin Clarke might be
quick to point out, history in Canada is contested terrain.

Bissoondath seems willing to let Canada dictate the roots and ruins that the immigrant should acknowledge. But despite the hegemonic control of history in Canada, it has become almost impossible to deny that the openness, anonymity and peace which Bissoondath enjoys have been built by immigrants. Moreover, they are as much architects of that openness as they are builders or beneficiaries of it.[34] It comes as no surprise that Canada for its size is now the largest receiver of Third World immigration in the developed world.[35] Canada relies, as it has throughout its history, on immigrant labour not just to expand but to continue to exist. Immigrants are at the heart of its cultural and economic identity. Multiculturalism does not deny that immigration remains the flow of labour to capital, and not the flow of idealists to an idea. But the social agency of multiculturalism has helped Canada to acculturate proportionately massive numbers of what Robin Cohen has called, bitterly, the new helots. Multiculturalism in Canada posits a plurality of origin, of heritage, and of contribution, and if its disadvantage has been the persistence of an Anglo-Canadian central referent, its advantage has been a level of dignity for migrant labour unmatched by any other immigrant nation. Bissoondath and one of his interviewers agree that there are Kensington Markets in North America, but most are accompanied by pathological levels of crime induced by official scorn of immigrant and minority labour in the United States. Bissoondath's rejection of the racism of visible inclusion should not mask the fact that Toronto is perhaps the only residentially integrated multiracial city in North America, and for every professional ethnic there is a child who stayed in school because she received concurrent instruction in English and Bengali, or in English and Greek. (Multiculturalism has not prevented racist police shootings, or racist museum exhibits, but proponents could argue that it has obscured binary tensions like the black-versus-white conflicts in American cities by insisting on difference as a deconstructive social tool. Multiculturalism has not solved the question of whether plurality of origin should lead to plurality of destination either.)

But if multiculturalism has smoothed some of the economic and social shock of immigration by a commitment to recognizing labour resources by recognizing cultural resources, it has not produced the roots and ruins to save Clarke's hollow men, nor those

of Cyril Dabydeen, Pier Giorgio Di Cicco or Dany Laferriere, all
among the most talented migrant voices, all struggling with what
Clarke has called the broken ruins and roots left behind. And in
this sense Bissoondath is right. Multiculturalism is not a blueprint
for one finished nation so much as it is a code for civic and social
behaviour. Taken to its logical conclusion, the policy might indeed
result in a crude Balkanization. But this is where Bissoondath
misunderstands history, as he misunderstood it in Trinidad. It is
not possible to have an immutable condition of casual brutality in
a nation. Nations are always being transformed by their own
people. Similarly in Canada, the people transform the nation
merely by coming to it. There is no constant idea of Canada but
that of the collective and individual image of it in the minds of
the people who have come to it. Ethnic groups are not in another's
country in Canada; they are in their own. Even if they choose to
freeze their culture, which is unlikely in such a cosmopolitan and
economically dynamic urban space, it is theirs to freeze. And yet,
as Clarke shows again and again, it is a daunting task for a community to claim roots and ruins in such a nation, and a saddening
one to leave other broken ruins behind. 'Now I am simply a writer
and if someone knows me he knows I am black. I am not writing
things simply of interest to blacks ... but my point of view can
only be what I am.'[36] There is resignation there, but there is
belligerence too. The belligerence is perhaps inspired by the hope
that the imperfect effort at plural democracy in Canada might
make room for Clarke's hollow men.

But if Neil Bissoondath's critical success has been built so far
on his flying in and out of community with no luggage, there are
some hopeful signs that this technically talented writer may eventually make an uneasy peace with his broken ruins, and begin to
question the ruins he has found in Canada; and perhaps with that
effort will come a new reading of the nation of Trinidad. The
story selected by Mervyn Morris for his anthology, though probably written before the novel, contains the seeds of a new and
more honest vision. Perhaps Morris saw a nascent humanity in
his selection. Bissoondath takes us briefly into an apartment late
at night. A couple receive a call informing them that one of their
friends from home, now also in Canada, has been killed in a
drink-drive car crash. The death comes almost as a relief to the

characters, reduced to poverty after years of success at home. In the brief aftermath of the death, Bissoondath discards what the Indo-British writer Hanif Kureishi objected to in his writing, the 'irritatingly reserved' narration.[37] The reader feels the writer's compassion for the characters; but more than that, the reader feels Bissoondath is really there, with these people. 'All that remained of the world was Jenny's arm, her warmth, her weight pressing against him. And the vein that pulsed in his temple', writes Bissoondath near the end of the story. And he reaches a commonality with his characters, if not a community, when he writes, 'he saw the earth, as from space, streams of people in continuous motion, circling the sphere in search of the next stop which, they always knew, would prove temporary in the end.' The last sentence of the story is, 'he thought: where to next, refugee.' The reader senses Bissoondath seeing something in the faces of other immigrants: not colour, not even roots, but a common past, and a common challenge, and the common predicament of hungry labour. There is little sign yet of recognition of a common predicament in Trinidad; but perhaps, as with Bissoondath's Canadian migrant experience, that recognition will come through imagining choices of ethnicity and identity as part of a plural nation-space. Perhaps Bissoondath recognizes in this story, as Austin Clarke has, that as a writer in community he is different but not separate, and that he has a natural stake in its tolerant and diverse visions.

Notes

1. Benedict Anderson, *Imagined Communities*, London: Verso, 1990, p. 129.

2. Estimates vary because the Canadian census has not distinguished between Blacks and West Indians, nor between West Indian nationalities, but there are perhaps 300,000 people of West Indian descent, the vast majority of these being first and second generation; perhaps a third of these people are from Trinidad – Indian, African and others.

Although the Labour Day Carnival in Brooklyn attracts more people (3 million), partly because it is held in a dense residential neighbourhood, Toronto's Caribana (1.5 million people) now has far more local masmaking – organized carnival bands who prepare elaborate costumes for the parade – and has become increasingly the centre of Trinidadian artistic and cultural activity in North America. See Raymond Breton et al., eds., *Ethnic Identity and Equality*, Toronto: University Press, 1990, for more quantification on Toronto's growing Caribbean population, and comparisons with other ethnic groups.

3. Robert Lecker, 'The Canonization of Canadian Literature: An Inquiry into Value', *Critical Inquiry*, vol. 16, no. 1, 1990.

4. See the introductory conversation between Jurgen Hesse and Ron Hatch in Jurgen Hesse, ed., *Voices of Change: Immigrant Writers Speak Out*, Vancouver: Pulp Press, 1990; and also Linda Hutcheon's introduction to her new volume, Linda Hutcheon and Marion Richmond, eds., *Other Solitudes: Multicultural Fictions*, Toronto: Oxford University Press, 1990. The absence of Canada's aboriginals in the literary canon, together with the cooptation of their voices by Anglo-Canadian writers, is also the subject of fierce public debate, surfacing recently at an international PEN conference in Toronto.

5. Arnold Itwaru's *Invention of Canada: Literary Text and the Immigrant Imaginary*, Toronto: TSAR, 1990, represents the next stage in the battle – other non-Anglo critical voices to match the production of non-Anglo literary texts.

6. Neil Bissoondath, *A Casual Brutality*, Toronto: Macmillan, 1988.

7. Diane D. Turbide, 'A Novelist's Stunning Debut', *Maclean's Magazine*, vol. 101, 3 October 1988, p. 63.

8. See, for instance, Michael Thorpe's sympathetic inclusion of Bissoondath in 'Turned Inside Out: South Asian Writing in Canada', *Ariel*, vol. 22, no. 1, 1985. Thorpe's article also raises the spectre of a South Asian ethnogenesis in Canada in which migrants from Kenya, Trinidad, Sri Lanka and Britain who trace their origins to the Indian subcontinent might create an new ethnie in Canada. For a discussion of ethnicized literature and ethnogenesis, see Steve Harney, 'Ethnos and the Beat Poets', *Journal of American Studies*, vol. 25, no. 3, 1991, pp. 363–80.

9. Mervyn Morris, ed., *Contemporary Caribbean Short Stories*, London: Faber & Faber, 1990.

10. Catherine Bush, 'Immigrant Fictions' (interview with Bissoondath), *What Magazine*, Toronto, December 1988, pp. 17–18.

11. *Maclean's Magazine*, p. 63.

12. Michael M.J. Fischer, 'Ethnicity and the Postmodern Arts of Memory', in J. Clifford and G. Marcus, eds., *Writing Culture: The Poetics and Politics of Ethnography*, Berkeley: University of California Press, 1986, pp. 232–3.

13. Neil Bissoondath, *Digging Up the Mountains*, Toronto: Macmillan, 1985.

14. Arun Mukherjee, *Towards An Aesthetic of Opposition*, Stratford, Ontario: Williams and Wallace, 1988, p. 87.

15. Bissoondath, *Digging Up the Mountains*, p. 29.

16. Bissoondath, *A Casual Brutality*, p. 8.

17. Ibid., p. 378.

18. Frederick Ivor Case, *The Crisis of Identity: Studies in the Guadeloupean and Martiniquan Novel*, Sherbrooke, Quebec: Naaman, 1985, p. 29.

19. Kenneth Ramchand, 'Physician, Heal Thyself', *Third World Quarterly*, vol. 11, no. 2, 1989, p. 176.

20. I have discovered no study of the high representation of Chinese Trinidadians in the arts in Trinidad, particularly in mas-making and the visual arts. Their settlement in the ferment of the lower-middle-class neighbourhoods of Port of Spain, such as St James, is one possible explanation for their high visiblity. It is worth noting as an anthropological point that the high degree of visibility – for a small group – seems to have been transferred to Caribana in Toronto, where, in the 1991 celebration banquet, both the award for best king costume and that for the best individual costume (a more modest but still elaborate piece) went to Chinese Trinidadians. I add to this observation of diversity – a truism for most Trindadians at this point in history – that the reigning queen of calypso for five years now, Denise Plummer, is a French Creole, and that among male calypsonians one readily finds, Africans, Syrians (one of whom calls himself The Mighty Trini), Indians and 'Dooglas'.

21. Eric Hobsbawm and Terence Ranger, eds., *The Invention of Tradition*, Cambridge: Cambridge University Press, 1986, p. 4.

22. Ernest Gellner, *Nations and Nationalism*, Oxford: Basil Blackwell, 1983.

23. Alvin Magid, 'Imperial Adminstration and Urban Nationalism in British Trinidad', *Canadian Review of Studies in Nationalism*, vol. 27, no. 1–2, 1990, p. 99.

24. David Dabydeen, 'The Old Map', in *Coolie Odyssey*, London: Hansib, 1988, p. 14.

25. Bissoondath, *A Casual Brutality*, p. 367.

26. Naturally nation-building boosterism, narrating 'the great men', of the Caribbean, is a discernible strain in its history writing as much as in European and American history. See, for instance, Sir Philip Manderson Sherlock, *West Indian Nations: A New History*, New York: St Martin's Press, 1973; or David Sui-Sang Chin, *The Philosophy of Nation-building*, Port of Spain: Horsham's Printing, 1990.

27. I will consider the abuse of dependency theory in domestic and nationalist contexts in my discussion of V.S. Naipaul in Chapter 6.

28. Mary B. Campbell, *The Witness and the Other World: Exotic European Travel Writing, 400–1600*, Ithaca: Cornell University Press, 1988, pp. 205–9.

29. Austin Clarke, 'A Stranger in a Strange Land', *The Globe and Mail*, Toronto, 15 August 1990, p. 30.

30. Morris, ed., *Contemporary Caribbean Short Stories*, pp. 59–80.

31. Bissoondath, *A Casual Brutality*, p. 221.

32. Ibid., p. 162.

33. Interview in *What Magazine*, p. 17.

34. For a definitive history and analysis of Canada's pluralistic past, see Robert F. Harney, ' "So Great a Heritage as Ours" ', *Daedalus*, vol. 117, no. 4, 1988, pp. 51–97.

35. Alan Simmons, 'New Wave Immigrants', in Shiva Halli et al., eds., *Ethnic Demography*, Ottawa: Carleton University Press, 1990, p. 145.

36. Austin Clarke, quoted in Jeffrey Heath, ed., *Profiles of Canadian Literature No. 4*, Toronto: Dundurn, 1982, p. 100.

37. Hanif Kureishi, 'A Casual Brutality' (book review), *New Statesman & Society*, 16 September 1988, p. 42.

CHAPTER 6

V.S. Naipaul and the Pitfalls of Nationalism

'In the moment of victory,' wrote V.S. Naipaul in *The Mimic Men* in 1967, 'we had wondered why no one had called our bluff. Soon we saw that there was no need, that our power was air.'[1] Who in the Caribbean in the 1990s would not recognize the prophetic truth of these words from two decades earlier. There is a part of Naipaul's pessimism, sometimes repressed, in every Caribbean artist and politician. Nor could this study repress entirely the demons that Naipaul invokes. The work of V.S. Naipaul stands both at the centre and the periphery of this book, as Naipaul himself is always at the centre and the edge of West Indian literature and national consciousness. The further one travels from the Caribbean, the more one hears his name in connection with the place. And so it has been for Naipaul too. He has represented Trinidad and the Caribbean to itself and to the world, in both senses of the word, in deed and in being. No matter that he attempts to distance himself from the 'we' of the narration in novels like *The Mimic Men,* and no matter that there exists frustration or unease on the part of other Caribbean people at the character of that 'we' – neither has escaped the linked destiny. As the Trinidad-based poet and playwright Derek Walcott has said: despite themselves, West Indians claim Naipaul, and Naipaul cannot shake off the West Indies. The history of Naipaul's relationship to Trinidad and the Caribbean, despite the wandering of both his person and his writing, is another narrative of the relationship between literature and nationalism in this Caribbean nation-state. But again, far from Fredric Jameson's national allegory, this narrative has tested the limits, and the growth, of a polyphonic nationalism in Trinidad and Tobago. Trinidadians would not, and probably could not, read Naipaul's later novels, like *Guerillas* (1975) or *In a Free State* (1971), as the allegorical or emplotted history of the region. For, while the early work mixes humour and even hope with disappointment and claustrophobia, by the time of his novel *Guerillas*, Naipaul's work has become too dark to be a fully habitable text of nationalism. His novels continue to be read as national allegories by critics in the developed world,[2] but this is perhaps because these metropolitan critics have the emotional distance and sometimes the cold cynicism to look upon such a sustained negation of a society. In fact, Naipaul's pessimism is so totalizing that any discussion of his situation in the discourse of race and class in Trinidadian nationalism breaks down. His work has to be discussed not as a reading of the nation, but as an attack on the possibility of reading a post-colonial state as a nation at all.[3]

And yet only in 1992 V.S. Naipaul was offered, and graciously accepted, the Trinity Cross from the government of Trinidad and Tobago – its highest honour. There are efforts under way to preserve the Naipaul house upon which he based his most widely praised novel, *A House for Mr Biswas* (1961). In the last few years there has been a movement both in Naipaul's writing and in the writing of some commentators away from a harsh criticism. For instance, the Caribbean linguist, Helen Pyne-Timothy has suggested that Naipaul's subtle use of creole rhythms is in fact a signifier of national commonality, of nation-building.[4]

Dissent in the Nationalist Project

I want to suggest in this chapter that two lessons have been learned by both Naipaul and his critics, and that they are lessons about nationalism. The first lesson is that the provocative nature of Naipaul's vision of the Trinidadian nation, as an archetype of unnatural, European-made, and sometimes ridiculous, post-colonial society, led critics and nationalist intellectuals to inscribe their response with the same kind of rhetorical and ideological excess, and meaninglessness, that has afflicted too many post-colonial governments and regimes throughout the Third World. But the second and more hopeful lesson, characterized by Naipaul's return for the Trinity Cross, is that Trinidadian – and Caribbean – nationalism has reached a level of security and self-assurance that enables the nation to use its harshest critic as France uses Jean Genet, or the USA uses Richard Wright. Whether that national maturity also neutralizes the writer is a matter worth consideration in a larger, comparative study. Eric Hobsbawm's study *Nations and Nationalism* seeks to diminish the importance of nationalism in the global economy and security structure, and suggests that nationalism will linger as sentimentality, or at best one description of identity among many, after it has ceased to become politically useful.[5]

Neither the absorption of the writer through cooptation, nor the absorption of the nation through regional political and economic blocking, can be ruled out in this discussion. But clearly, if Trinidadian nationalism is in decline (and there is no sign of this), it will only be replaced in the immediate future by a Caribbean nationalism already imagined by cultural critics such as Rex Nettleford (though probably not in such an idealized form) competing as a bloc in the international market, and still drawing heavily on culture for its political will. Moreover, the quality of home that might influence the new understanding between Naipaul and Trinidad would only be complicated in a Caribbean definition of home in which his specific East Indian roots in one landscape were dispersed by a more encompassing, and for some ominous, definition of Caribbean peoplehood. But, whatever the future of writer or nation, it is safe to say that Naipaul and Trinidad have conducted a forty-year dialogue on nationalism that has exposed its dangers; and yet ultimately they may have discovered the country's abiding hope. To recall what C.L.R. James said as early as 1960 in a lecture in Trinidad,

> the good life is not to be judged by quantity of goods. What I said at the beginning is the most important: that community between the individual and the state; the sense that he belongs to the state and the state belongs to him.... The citizen's alive when he feels that he himself in his own national community is overcoming difficulties.[6]

Naipaul might have characterized Trinidad as an outpost of empire, abandoned and fragile, but its growing acceptance of him might be a sign that its citizens have started to overcome such difficulties, alive in the security of a national community, and blessed with a polyphonic identity that nonetheless resists whole-sale cultural invasion. Those signs could have been predicted by James, in his lectures on the genius of the Caribbean slave and his place in an international economy, and they could have been foreseen by writers like Michael Anthony and Sam Selvon, who had great faith in the newness and genuineness of Trinidadian culture. Naipaul's difficult relationship with the island should be seen in this perspective. His writing of the nation has, in the end, helped the nation find a habitable text for itself, a text of cultural maturity, confident creolization, and polyglottal national identity; what the Cuban critic Gustavo Perez Firmat has called, in Cuba, critical criollism, or translation style – making everything its own.[7]

It was probably inevitable, given this profound cultural base, that Trinidad and the Caribbean would begin to make their peace with a vitriolic critic like native son Naipaul. But in the process the interference of a more programmatic, political nationalism has brought out some of the same kinds of ideological intolerance that have characterized other new nations struggling to develop habitable texts of existence. The clash between Naipaul and nationalism provides several valuable examples of this kind of nationalist intolerance, and adds another, darker dimension to the discourse on nationalism in Trinidad and in the Caribbean. The best way to detect this dimension is by looking at some of the more prominent critiques of Naipaul's writing; and so this chapter will, in a sense, be more about the dialogues of critics and nation than about writer and nation, with the writer used primarily to interrogate the critics.

Vidia Naipaul left Trinidad in 1950, at the age of 18. He took a degree at Oxford, then stayed on in England, working for the BBC's Caribbean Voices programme from 1954 to 1956. He published three novels depicting life in the East Indian community of Trinidad before publishing *A House for Mr Biswas*, which, as literary critics like to say, secured his fame and reputation. He went back to Trinidad at the request of Dr Eric Williams at the beginning of the 1960s to write a semi-official book on the West Indies.

The result was the notorious travelogue *The Middle Passage* (1962), the first of his many critical accounts of journeys through the Third World (and including the American South, his most recent subject). The book deeply disturbed the nascent Caribbean post-independence nationalist movement, as his subsequent travel books would enrage Muslim Pakistanis, Hindu Indians, Argentinians and Africans, not to mention supporters of Third World causes in the First World. But Naipaul's literary talents also made him immensely popular in the literary circles of the developed world. His novel *The Mimic Men* was the last to meet with positive reaction in the Third World, but subsequent works such as *Guerillas* and *A Bend in the River* (1979) continued to thrill readers and critics in the developed world, and he has now won virtually every major literary prize except the Nobel. This reception, however, has been troublesome for Naipaul. Both in his later fiction and in the travel writing there is great pessimism and impatience with Third World societies, nationalisms and peoples. The unsparing criticism led in turn, from the 1960s onwards, to vitriolic criticism of Naipaul both in the Caribbean and elsewhere in the Third World, as well as from centres of Third World interest and power in the metropoles. English-speaking Caribbean literary critics and cultural nationalists, as we will see, used him to strengthen the case for Caribbean writing, but they used him selectively, concentrating on his early, satirical work, and avoiding the later work so popular among First World critics.

The Janus Face of Nationalism

While First World critics pumped out innocuous introductions to his work, depoliticized or sometimes with a gesture to the ravages of colonialism, leftist and Third World critics hissed their disgust at the betrayal by one of their own.[8] The aggressive criticism of Naipaul is widespread, though probably now slightly on the wane, as if most of the anger has been released. I will concentrate on a few of the more prominent attacks to illustrate the two main dangers of ideological intolerance in critiques, and to suggest that Naipaul, despite his bile, helped dislodge some sinister tendencies among Third World nationalists and some of their metropolitan allies. In his editor's introduction to *Nation and Narration*, Homi Bhabha notes that Tom Nairn, author of a major study of nationalism in Britain, has called the nation 'the modern Janus'. But Bhabha points out that, despite attacks on the totalization of national culture, and the concentration on what Raymond Williams has called 'emergent practices', there is a tendency in heated argument to reduce this Janus-faced nation either to a product of ideological control, or to material conditions. Bhabha suggests instead that we explore 'the Janus-faced ambivalence of language itself in the construction of the Janus-faced discourse on the nation'. Bhabha sees the nation 'as a form of cultural elaboration (in the Gramscian sense) ... as an agency of ambivalent narration that holds culture at its most productive position, as a force for subordination, fracturing, diffusing, reproducing, as much as producing, creating, forcing, guiding.'⁹ I would not want to suggest that Naipaul has ever consciously employed post-structuralist techniques of questioning closure or dwelling in textuality. But Bhabha presents his case for an ambivalent, discursive practice in the nation-space against the rhetorical theories of Third World nationalist utopianism, and against Foucault-derived conspiracies of ideological power. Some of the most insistent critics of Naipaul do, I believe, fall into one or other of these traps. Without wishing to paint Naipaul as a heroic figure, I would like to suggest that his ambivalent, discursive practices of writing in the half-light of the nation-state, as Bhabha would say,¹⁰ dislodge national culture, dislodge Brathwaite's nation-language, from the clutches of an intolerant or static nationalism. Naipaul's texts, and the texts of his critics, present an opportunity to carry this study of the Trinidadian nation into new territory. In at least two important ways, Naipaul's critics unconsciously provide another example of the 'fracturing and diffusing' of nationalism in Trinidad into national culture.

The Politics of Misreading Naipaul

The first dangerous technique that Naipaul's critics have employed, freezing the Janus face of nation, has been the distortion of his views; this has been accompanied by a refusal to recognize his estrangement from the developed world. John Thieme's retrospec-

tive article on Naipaul in *Third World Quarterly* offers a clue not
only to the durability of Naipaul's discursive doubts but also to his
enigmatic politics. 'It is his continuing concern with the consequences of imperialism and its aftermath – particularly the psychological consequences – which makes Naipaul difficult to ignore,
despite his dismissive remarks about the Third World.'[11] Thieme
is right that Naipaul cannot be ignored – there are too few Third
World writers with the attention of the literary centres, and he is
too good to be snubbed entirely by Caribbean critics. And Thieme
also admits a point that Naipaul's detractors rarely remember.
Imperialism and the wicked consequences of colonialism are the
central themes of Naipaul's work. The dismissive comments on
the Third World are made in this context – a Third World dis-
figured by the greed and violence of the colonial powers. His
critics rarely grant him this context. He is a solitary, wandering
figure, not just because of his intolerance toward the Third World,
but also because of his alienation in the First. That is not to say,
as Caribbean critic Gordon Rohlehr has phrased it, that Naipaul
always 'possess[es] the quality of intimacy' that allows him to
understand popular culture and its value to the people of Trinidad; but even when Naipaul is 'superficial' and full of 'sublimated
bitterness', he never fails to indict Britain and the other colonial
powers for the destruction of what he would wish to find – a
cosmopolitan and literate culture.[12] This technique among critics
tends to highlight what Bhabha isolates as the urge to turn nationalism into a solely ideological apparatus, informed by both a
cultural and an economic imperialism, in which local artists and
intellectuals who claim to represent the nation and the people in
fact do the bidding of the power structures.

The second dangerous technique of Naipaul's detractors is the
tendency, when conjuring up the image of post-colonialism and
continued imperial domination, to ignore the complicity of local
business classes, politicians and revolutionaries in the oppression
of ordinary people in post-colonial societies. Official nationalism
or 'the elite culture of nationalism', as opposed to the inevitable
popular nationalism that James identified so often, 'is linked to the
power of writing', as Arcadio Diaz Quinones notes in the context
of the Hispanic Caribbean. Quinones concentrates on the *letrados*
of the twentieth-century colonial period. But the same kind of

ciudad letrada, now backed by a literate middle class, came to view
the post-colonial nation as an imaginary process and construction
under their control.[13] Naipaul has often fallen victim to this nationalism, always proclaimed in the name of a more demotic popular
feeling. This state nationalism is tied in Trinidad and Tobago, as
it is in many other new nations, to the major party of independence; but even after independence the rhetoric of anti-colonialism,
converted to anti-post-colonialism and anti-imperialism, often hides
the complicity of local ruling classes, working in collusion with a
petty bourgeoisie frightened of the masses.[14] Or, just as perniciously,
this nationalist ideology is converted to a revolutionary 'socialist'
one, as in Guyana or Zaire, where the new ruling class is a party
class entirely. Concerning this second group, Manning Marable
cautions intellectuals and politicians in the developed world that
'to falsely encourage such policies because they are clad in a pseudo-
Marxist apologetic only reinforces the general trend towards statist
authoritarianism throughout the entire neocolonial periphery.'[15]
In either case, state nationalism, as opposed to the popular feeling
of belonging to a culture or a landscape, is too often defended at
the price of democracy and freedom of intellectual exchange. And
as Marable notes, 'it is easy to underestimate the factors which
pressure peripheral regimes with anti-capitalist features to suspend
or to eliminate democratic norms.'[16] This sad fact applies to
capitalist governments in the periphery too, as Trinidad's Public
Order Act of 1970 would indicate. This state nationalism is usually
underscored by vague but effective appeals to the special culture
of the land and the people, and to a primordial emotionalism of
place or history.[17] This Third World primordial socialism or its
capitalist equivalent, anti-imperialist nationalism, not only masks
internal hierarchy and difference but – again in Bhabha's logic –
erects a Third World utopian nationalism against which open and
discursive practices of exploring the nation-space operate at their
own peril.

I want to review three prominent critics of V.S. Naipaul's
writing, and suggest that they have taken neither Manning
Marable's nor Homi Bhabha's warnings to heart, notwithstanding
the fact that they may have pointed to some of the fundamental
flaws in official and primordial nationalisms and ideologically rigid
theories of national dependency created in the isolation of the

ciudad letrada or in metropolitan centres – flaws that may fortunately have been overcome, or at least recognized, in Trinidad and Tobago.

These three critics are Chris Searle of the journal *Race and Class*; Selwyn Cudjoe, a well-known critic of Caribbean literature; and Timothy Brennan, whose widely quoted book *Salman Rushdie and the Third World*,[18] presents a general critique of cosmopolitan post-colonial writers. All three, in their zealous efforts to dismiss Naipaul dismissing the Third World, present a distorted nationalist argument that pays too little attention to internal contradictions and conflicts in the very countries they want to defend, and relies on an ideological construct of nation that denies the free play of identity and language in the nation-space, and the historically specific cosmopolitan, critical criollism of the Caribbean region. To these three critics of Naipaul can be added several more exponents of 'post-colonial literary theory', such as Stephen Slemon and W.D. Ashcroft. Post-colonial literary theory, as a kind of anachronistic literary dependency theory, also risks ignoring the internal structures that Naipaul both bemoans and distorts, and certainly falls victim to ahistorical, inflexible systemic thought that denies the shifting and ambivalent margin of the nation-space. In the less credible examples of this post-colonial theory, the nation and the writer are both frozen in primitive Wallersteinian systems theory and exhumed Frankian structuralism. Naipaul's vision of Trinidad challenges this regime of truth too.

Selwyn Cudjoe once explained at an academic conference why he was writing a book on V.S. Naipaul. His reason reveals a good deal about the power of the writer in imagining a community, the importance of the diasporic discourse on the nation, and the continuing power of creation and re-creation from the amorphous boundaries, outposts and metropoles of that nation. Cudjoe, who now teaches in the United States, realized that Naipaul's success in the important sites of the national discourse – North American and European classrooms, publishing firms, and newspapers – guaranteed a certain success and prominence for Naipaul's imagined community (or imagined artifice in his case). Cudjoe had again and again come face to face in the developed world with an imaginary nation of one man's making. Cudjoe, as a dedicated and often orthodox Marxist (despite his Trotskyite claims), believed that such a hegemonic discourse of Caribbean nationalism should be challenged. Naipaul's Trinidad inhabited the imagination of First World intellectuals, and these intellectuals responded accordingly to the Caribbean and its ideas, not to speak of their approach to Caribbean ethnies in the metropoles. In short, Cudjoe perceived Naipaul's prominence as part of a heinous ideological construction of the Caribbean, and he set out to apply a materialist critique which would point out the artifice of Naipaul's vision and replace it with a new imagined Trinidad.

Thus in 1988, Cudjoe published *V.S. Naipaul: A Materialist Reading.*[19] The book is a comprehensive assessment of Naipaul's contribution to both the literature and the nationalist cause of the Caribbean. Cudjoe starts by praising Naipaul's earlier satirical work, set mostly in Trinidad, noting the realistic portrait of ordinary Indian Trinidadians. But Cudjoe begins to level his guns at the point he calls Naipaul's epistemological break. After *The Mimic Men*, Naipaul drifts into nihilism, and, seeking the approval of Europe, sells himself into an imperialist bondage. Cudjoe claims that by the time Naipaul wrote his novel *Guerillas*, he had become 'an apocalyptist of the Third World, and his exegeses were welcomed by the First World'.[20] Cudjoe berates Naipaul throughout the latter half of his book, and he is as relentless in his psychoanalysis of the writer as in his political dissection. In the process, he justly identifies an inability in Naipaul to believe that the colonial subject could become more than a mimic man. It is true, and worth repeating, that Naipaul, unlike Alejo Carpentier of Cuba or Wilson Harris of Guyana, for instance, 'has not been remotely concerned about the developmental possibilities of Third World peoples'.[21] Naipaul's novels and travel writing are characterized by a morbid fascination with post-colonial societies, but never excitement, never thrills. More than the politics of his analysis, it is this lack of excitement about possibility in new cultures and countries – the kind of excitement that still thrills Wilson Harris when he speaks of Guyana, Guatemala or Peru; the kind of sexual and spiritual energy that animates Jorge Amado's sprawling novels of Bahia – that shackles Naipaul's vision. But, rather than stopping there, having identified the limited usefulness of a vision uninterested in the future and afraid of the unknown, Cudjoe, perhaps too indignant to contain himself, ruins most of his best arguments with further distortions of Naipaul's position and further defences of the indefensible in the Third World. In his failure, Cudjoe is guilty of the kind of repressive uses of nationalism and anti-imperialist rhetoric that have plagued Caribbean states, from Eric Gairey's mysticism in Grenada, to Forbes Burnham's state socialism in Guyana, to Eugenia Charles's anti-labour nationalism in Dominica, to the divided souls of the independence movements in Guadeloupe and Puerto Rico. The Janus face is frozen, one side caught in this anti-imperialist rhetoric, the other mired in rigid ideological assessment of Naipaul as imperial stooge.

In discussing Naipaul's quirky history of early Trinidad, *The Loss of El Dorado* (1969), Cudjoe is right to point out that it is absurd, after three hundred pages, for Naipaul to insist that the slave has no story and that consequently he was never real because of this official omission. And Cudjoe is again right to say that Naipaul looked in the wrong places for the real slave. The Trinidadian slave, male and female, has been rendered inarticulate, as Lawrence Levine said of the American slave; but he was quite articulate in his day, and the popular cultures of Trinidad are documents to be studied too (not to speak of acts of resistance, maintenance and assertion among East Indians, Portuguese and Chinese in Trinidad). But, all too typically, Cudjoe then distorts Naipaul's text, equating Naipaul's attitude to the 'Negro underground' in Trinidad with that of the notorious governor Thomas Picton. He implies that Naipaul believed Picton's suppression of this underground was justly done because the undergrounds were fantastic and make-believe. Naipaul does disdain those undergrounds in the book; but he also devotes page after page to the act for which Picton is remembered as one of the most evil men ever to set foot in the Caribbean (no mean competition). The death by torture of Luisa Calderon in fact forms one of the central obsessions of the book. It is described at greater length than the reader can stand, and is returned to again and again. It is dishonest to imply that Naipaul thought such repression was just, simply on the grounds that he is also dismissive of early Negro culture on the island. What is most obvious from the book, but not from Cudjoe's analysis, is that it was precisely such brutality that reduced Negro culture to fantasy in Naipaul's mind. This observation deserves scrutiny – clearly there was much resistance culture in Trinidad that avoided such reduction, and fantasy and reality are not easily separated realms in cultural life, particularly in Trinidad where carnival is contested by ruler and ruled throughout the island's history.[22] But dismissal of the worth of colonial cultural practices in the Caribbean, in light of his contempt for the brutality and, as I noted in my introduction, the intellectual vacuousness of the colonizer, cannot be equated with Naipaul accepting a necessary brutality in colonialism or presuming that 'the colonizer's truth is the universal truth of all societies',[23] as Cudjoe maintains. In fact, Cudjoe's entire reading of *The Loss of El Dorado* constructs a racial schism that is not present in Naipaul's work. Cudjoe repeatedly strives to find Naipaul racist. But Naipaul pronounces European Trinidad a failure, and a copy too. His obsession with European brutality and impotency in the Caribbean is central to his view of those modern nations as cultures brutalized into emptiness. Cudjoe objects to this characterization of an empty culture, and justly, but he denies that Naipaul has also attempted to name the disease of brutality as the cause of that emptiness. The result is an unjust reading of Naipaul. Naipaul imagines Trinidad as a place subjected historically to too much inhumanity to have produced a humane culture. Cudjoe's reading of Naipaul is quick to accuse him of this same inhumanity. But Cudjoe's disservice to Naipaul is a service to us in reading the continuing discourse on the nation of Trinidad. Cudjoe presents a reading that illustrates the unfortunate tendency to develop binary ideological structures, cultural dependency theories in which criticism of the post-colonial state and its nationalist project must mean praise of the centre, and in the process the material base, the people's history that Cudjoe cherishes, becomes brutalized by the selective use of fact.

Reading Internal Oppression

Unfortunately, the distortion of Naipaul's views is not the only means Cudjoe employs. In his attack on Naipaul's reading of African nationalism, he resorts to another pernicious tactic of repressive nationalism – scapegoating. Once again Cudjoe has no difficulty highlighting Naipaul's shortcomings. In *The Mimic Men*,

Naipaul tells the story of an Indo-Caribbean politician who gets caught up in an independence struggle marked by anti-colonial feeling and appeals to racial pride – mostly African with a token gesture of solidarity to the 'coolie' brothers who worked in the cane fields. (Like Eric Williams's People's National Movement in Trinidad, those Indian Trinidadians in the movement of this novel, often Christian or Muslim rather than part of the Hindu majority, were rarely from the class of the 'coolie' cane-cutters.) Things quickly turn sour: the newly energized masses exorcise generations of frustration by scapegoating those Indians, Chinese and Syrians on the island who have risen to become small shopkeepers and merchants. Quickly the main character, Singh, is sent to discuss the nationalization of the sugar plantations to soothe the Indian workers who riot in response to the attacks (and again the class irony of these events is not lost on Naipaul). His plan is laughed at in London. He is humiliated there, and at the same time he is sacrificed by the government back home – rumours spread of him selling out, returning to his bourgeois roots, having love affairs with European Trinidadians, and using nationalization to build a rival Indian power base. He stays in London, exiled to the same weightless, rootless world of his student days in shabby residence hotels. *The Mimic Men* is a prophetic novel. Written in 1966 and 1967, it accused the imperial powers of granting freedom in name only, and it revealed that every nationalist movement could turn to exclusionary definitions under the screws of imperial power or local manipulation. Perhaps the most heartbreaking scene comes ironically and appropriately in Singh's nationalization trip. At the same time that he is being humbled and patronized by the British elite, he is being denounced by the nationalists at home as a traitor. In the 1990s, the power of the IMF or World Bank or Gulf & Western to break apart a national will, on ethnic and class lines, is undisputed. Naipaul saw earlier than many that the power of these nationalist movements was air. But Naipaul never improved upon that prophecy. He has never taken account of other, less political forms of power and resistance; never given credit to what David Lehmann has identified in South America as basismo – grassroots cultural strength. Naipaul recognized long before most in the Caribbean and other parts of the developing world that new nations would not be accepted as equals and could rarely stand on principles of national rights alone. The history of invasion and coercion in the Caribbean should have told most nationalists that story. Cudjoe gives Naipaul credit for these prophecies. But in subsequent novels Naipaul had something quite legitimate to say about the consequences of this neo-colonialism. It is presaged in the discovery of his character Singh in this novel that 'there was no true internal source of power, and that no power was real which did not come from the outside.'[24] There is truth and untruth in this new position, but Cudjoe sees only the untruth, and that leads to readings of Naipaul's African experiences that are plagued by the same kind of scapegoating that befalls Singh.

Naipaul's subsequent novels and travelogues become obsessed with ideas of order, legitimacy, and the power to avoid anarchy. Cudjoe rightly criticizes Naipaul for seeing order in Europe and anarchy almost everywhere else. The order and consent of economically developed democracies is obviously partial and fragile. But rather than making that point at any length, Cudjoe attempts to defend order and power in Africa, against Naipaul's attack. This is an almost impossible task, and one that reveals Cudjoe's weakness – a willingness to scapegoat the developed world for unspeakable crimes committed by forces in the developing world. Ironically, he and Naipaul have already agreed on the malign nature of imperial control. But rather than calling for Naipaul to give this proper weight in his assessment of Africa, he appears to excuse dictators as isolated side effects of that imperial control. The result is not believable. A recent issue of the most prominent left-leaning magazine of French-speaking Africa, *Afrique/Asie*, led with an editorial entitled, 'Ca Bascule'.[25] The editorial spoke of the dangerous 'tottering' of dozens of autocratic regimes in Africa. Pressure from opposition democratic forces to relinquish autocratic party control had been met, almost everywhere, with repression and guns. The lack of democratic rights in Africa only became fully apparent in the call for those rights. Naipaul writes of Zaire in one of his travelogues. He condemns its 'Mobutuism' – the strange combination of African socialism, anti-imperialism and charismatic one-man-rule mysticism. He points also to Uganda, where the persecution of East Indians and Africans alike characterized Amin's murderous rule (and subsequent regimes as well).

Simon Malley, editor and publisher of *Afrique/Asie*,[26] notes that Zaire claims to have fifty-four political parties, and yet is among the least democratic countries on earth.

Selwyn Cudjoe is understandably uneasy with Naipaul's implication that the Zairian people were susceptible to this despotism. Naipaul has never made the same point about German or Italian culture. But Cudjoe also appears quite willing to support the scapegoating techniques of these regimes, and to underestimate or apologize for numerous others. Again, he displays the repressive and dishonest possibilities of a nationalism inscribed with excessive anti-imperial rhetoric and ethnic mysticism. Cudjoe writes that 'the atypical nature of Mobutuism and Aminism cannot be emphasized too strongly.'[27] Such an emphasis might surprise many who languish in jails elsewhere on the continent. Cudjoe quotes Walter Rodney to emphasize the disregard for African history before colonialism, and to suggest that African states should not accept the European models as superior. This line of reasoning is sadly reminiscent of the words of Daniel Arap Moi or Julius Nyerere in defending one-party states and suggesting that Western democracy is not appropriate to Africa and its heritage. Whatever his intention, Cudjoe echoes Mobutu's use of the past to legitimize anti-democratic behaviour. Cudjoe's attack on Naipaul's national readings confirms in the end Naipaul's fears: that a rejection of Europe might also mean a rejection of democratic rights like the freedom to make unfair judgements of a nation's culture. Of course, the rejection of European cultural values does not have to result in either Mobutuism or Aminism, but there is no indication that nationalist critics like Cudjoe are capable of preventing that outcome. The nation of Trinidad is perhaps fortunate to have such a self-hating son – he brings out the worst in others, for all to see.

Bill Warren wrote that 'the fact that the theory of neo-colonialism helped bourgeois nationalism to sweep away many retarding influences impeding the development of capitalism and to forge modern nation-states does not eliminate its crucial weakness.' And he notes that the theory of neo-colonialism has also had 'serious negative political consequences'. In the Third World, 'populist nationalism has been reinforced by the ideological outlook of neo-colonialism, which tends to divert and dampen internal class struggles by orienting discontent towards external alleged enemies.'[28] This diversionary neo-colonialism is employed by Cudjoe in his attacks on Naipaul. Unfortunately, such tactics can also be used by revolutionary nationalists to obscure internal power relationships. Chris Searle's attack on 'Naipaulacity' is an example of such negative political consequences.

Reading Revolutionary Grenada

Chris Searle taught in Grenada in the aftermath of the overthrow of the dictator Eric Gairey by the New Jewel Movement. He joined hundreds of Caribbean and European committed intellectuals and artists, such as George Lamming and Merle Hodge, who came to the new Camelot of Grenada. The Grenada revolution was cause for much hope in the region and beyond, and its acknowledged leader, Maurice Bishop, inspired faith far beyond the Eastern Caribbean. He became a symbol for change from US campuses to the favellas of Brazil. Shortly after the US invasion of Grenada in 1984, V.S. Naipaul was asked by the *Sunday Times Magazine* to go to Grenada and write a report on what he saw.[29] Naipaul's article focused on the language of the revolution, the plethora of slogans and graffiti. It was a natural focus for a writer, and it was to be expected that Naipaul thought that language, as in his book *In a Free State*, had gone out of control, lost its meaning, or had been misapplied in the beginning. It is easy to recognize the familiar pessimism of his views, and particularly the theme of a big revolution on a very small island. It was the kind of Naipaul assessment sure to draw fire. And it did, from Chris Searle.

Searle, like many who took part heart and soul in the experiment of real democracy in Grenada, sounds deeply bitter in the article on Naipaul, and Naipaul bears the brunt of a much larger anger. Perhaps due to anger, Searle neglects the full history of the Grenada experiment, but the result, whatever the motive, is an attack that mocks the tragedy of Grenada and does nothing for its cause. However, his attack on Naipaul does permit a fresh look at the discourse of nationalism in Trinidad, particularly at the borders of national inclusion.

The irony of Chris Searle's article, an irony that would not be lost on Naipaul, is that the author does to Naipaul precisely what Bernard Coard and his faction did to 'Maurice'. Chris Searle concludes his article with the indictment that Naipaul is a 'pawn' of imperial journalism, 'whose only service to his people is to give them a word to describe this new form of cultural imperialism: Naipaulacity.'[30] But Searle would hardly recognize the irony of this accusation because he has neglected to tell the whole story of Grenada; in fact, he has neglected to tell the truth. The interesting part of this dialogue between writer and Caribbean nation, and its mediation by a critic, is that Naipaul offers a strongly pro-Caribbean line in it. Naipaul's claim is that the revolution was imported and made to fit an economy and a culture not prepared for or suited to its foreignness. The argument could have been that of Tapia Party leader Lloyd Best of Trinidad, or of Guyanese economist Clive Thomas of the New World Group on Caribbean plantation economies and the need for special, home-grown models to fit them. Searle does not see it that way, however. He sees Naipaul's attack on the importation of revolutionary language as an attack on the maturity, centrality and ability of Caribbean nation-states. Searle argues that Grenadians understood their revolutionary purpose well, and knew what the stakes were. He declines to suggest that there was ideological excess, and instead focuses on what he considers Naipaul's imperialist preferences, as 'one who has been adopted by the British ruling class and its fawning literati',[31] and on his willingness to belittle the Grenadians as unworthy of so much attention, or of such a big revolution. Searle is quite right to attack Naipaul for questioning the common Grenadian's understanding. It is a typical Naipaul trick to assign misunderstanding to others when perhaps it belongs with the writer. Naipaul often projects his existential dismay onto the population, particularly when questions of religion and tradition are to the fore, as in his studies of India and the Muslim World, *An Area of Darkness* (1964) and *Among the Believers* (1981). Searle writes in a worthy Caribbean tradition of trusting the people's understanding of politics and seeing that understanding in the cultural forms of the region, like calypso and village social organization, as other writers in this study have. But does this lack of respect for mass culture and faith in the Third World mean that Naipaul's earlier 'sparks of consciousness appeared to have turned to hatred, to self-mutilation, to solipsism and despair, to an abandonment of people and to a final contract with the forces of disgust and death'?[32]

Reading Naipaul as a Counter-revolutionary

Chris Searle is very good at pointing to the ignorance in Naipaul's summary of the Grenada revolution and its four-and-a-half-year life. Naipaul writes that 'for four and a half years the People's Revolutionary Government did nothing.'[33] This statement is absurd; the proof of Grenada's strides in literacy, public health and political participation is now easily documented. But in his long, hotly argued article, Searle not once reminds his readers what happened to the revolution before the invasion of marines and ignorant American journalists (days later). He does not dwell on the servile complicity of other Caribbean states, mentioning only Seaga (of Jamaica) and Adams (of Barbados) and ignoring Eugenia Charles of Dominica, who proudly stood beside the foreign conquerors at a news conference afterwards. And he does not once mention what happened to Maurice Bishop. This gap is filled by subsequent scholarship on the revolution. Maurice Bishop, together with several cabinet ministers, were imprisoned, freed by the people, and then killed by the army, days before the US marines arrived. There was no trial, and no evidence to convict them. Payne, Sutton and Thorndike recount the viciousness of army factions loyal to Bernard Coard, Bishop's ally turned rival, in their encounter with citizens loyal to Bishop. They write that

> on the 18th century battlements of the old slave fort, they had to choose between jumping over the edge – a 50 to 90 foot drop – or being machine-gunned ... one soldier counted 60 bodies outside the fort's walls alone. Bishop's body was unrecognisable as his head had been shattered; the others were mutilated by machine-gun fire.... The bodies of Bishop and his two colleagues were then taken away and burnt in a pit.[34]

What was Maurice Bishop's crime? He was accused of displaying bourgeois tendencies, and of selling out the country to the imperialists – the same thing, incidentally, that Naipaul is accused of by Searle. Historian of the Caribbean, Gordon Lewis, admitted that 'the real post-mortem had to deal with the fact that October 1983 was in large part a self-inflicted wound of the revolution itself.'[35] Chris Searle is not ready to accept that post-mortem.

The language of Bernard Coard and his hardline Leninist faction has drawn much attention from scholars. Despite Searle's claim that the revolution accommodated pictures of the Queen, and therefore was not a borrowed, doctrinaire movement, the centres of revolutionary power did not speak the vibrant creolized, popularized revolutionary slang. In fact, these centres saw devi-ation in the people's language. The minutes of the committee meetings, closely examined by Lewis, are full of the worst echoes of the Moscow show trials. Naipaul sensed this ominous use of the official language before the records were revealed (as opposed to the creolized terms like 'the revo'). As usual, he combined an uncanny insight with his aggravating contempt for common folk. But he did read the writing on the wall, and trembled. Maurice was denounced, in progressively more archaic Stalinist language, for his style of charismatic leadership (ironically this was Gairey's style too.) He and his friends were finally killed for this ideological deviation by Coard's faction and the army units that supported him, and those units machine-gunned the crowds who sought to save Bishop from this fate. Those are the sad facts of the Grenada revolution, facts never once mentioned in Searle's attack. The US invasion and the betrayal by some of the neighbouring states was ugly imperialist punishment, but it was the second ugly act of the revolution. Searle makes no mention of that fact in his denuncia-tion of Naipaul for bourgeois tendencies. Chris Searle's faith in the Grenadian people's understanding of their revolution, in the face of Naipaul's and America's cynical paternalism, saves Searle from seeing this nationalism in the Caribbean, and Naipaul's reading of it, as an alien or imposed ideological apparatus. But his faith in the intelligence of the Grenadians turns to a primordial utopianism that ignores the facts in the case and does injury to the nobility of the Grenadian revolutionary effort. And again, the Janus face of nationalism is frozen.

V.S. Naipaul's jaded imagination must take only sustenance from the reactions to his writings by critics like Searle and Cudjoe. But there is another kind of criticism levelled at Naipaul which does not question his right to imagine the nation. If from Searle and Cudjoe we learn something about the dangers of utopian Third World nationalism or crude ideological constructions of nationalism, in the criticisms of Timothy Brennan we can uncover an equally dubious tendency to divide Naipaul from his nation, not by impugning his intentions, but by circumscribing his imagination, and that of the people in his books.

Inventing the Nationless Cosmopolitan

A look at Timothy Brennan's book, *Salman Rushdie and the Third World*, might ultimately help us examine the nation of Trinidad and Tobago from yet another angle, but one that has been hinted at throughout this study: the place of Trinidadian culture and nationhood in global perspective, a perspective Naipaul's peripatetic imagination is quick to call up.[36] From many of the writers encountered here, the strength of Trinidadian national culture, in all its contested forms and invented traditions, has been very apparent. Writers like Samuel Selvon and Willi Chen have emphasized not only the confidence and vitality of Trinidad's carnival of identity but also its ability to translate, incorporate, transform and coopt influences as diverse as British cooking and American soul music. Trinidadian culture, emerging again and again from these invisible Trinidads, is repeatedly subjected to the semiotics of a global diaspora, and to the vagaries of a global mediascape and technoscape, as Arjun Appadurai would say. And yet, as evidenced by the steady output of novels, poems, plays and calypsos, Trinidadian culture, at home and abroad, is rich and healthy. V.S. Naipaul springs from this culture, a culture where neighbourhood parents might still envy the kid who gets an island scholarship to Oxford, but who also visit their children at school in Montreal, Washington DC, and Mona, Jamaica. For the working class and farmers, these same destinations might account for a couple of years of work, sometimes precariously on tourist visas, or even a semi-permanent relocation. It is this same culture wherein calypsos and soca music play non-stop from New Year's Day to carnival, but Jamaican dub music dominates the house parties and shakes the maxi-taxis along the Main Road. It is a culture where almost every kitchen from St James to Princess Town – Indian, African, Doogla, Syrian, Chinese – can produce a chop suey (usually including local products like yuca or christophene). After the recent coup attempt by a small Black Muslim group, one of the hottest calypsos, named after the leader of the coup, was 'Abu Bakr Take Over'. In the calypso, the singer turns on his television to see the fighting, and chimes 'I wonder if I watching MacGyver', an American adventure programme being rerun on Trinidad television and integrated into Trinidadian culture. It would be difficult to object to the terms 'cosmopolitan' or 'worldly' being applied to this Third World nation, nor to many others in today's world. Yet literary critic Timothy Brennan, like many other proponents of post-colonial literary theory, does deny the cosmopolitan, global nature of Trinidad and other Third World nationspaces. They assign the terms pejoratively to writers like Naipaul. For the rest of Trinidad's citizens they advocate a strict quarantine from worldly influence and a dependency-style protectionism for national culture for the real 'people'. As Brennan concludes his study: 'Discipline, organisation, people – these are words that the cosmopolitan sensibility refuses to take seriously.'[37] Brennan takes them seriously, but the people of Trinidad might prefer to make up their own minds.

Who is this cosmopolitan writer that Brennan has identified? His archetype is V.S. Naipaul. And it follows that Trinidad must be one of the post-colonial nation-states Brennan evokes, often in the abstract. In the chapter that lays the foundation for Brennan's distinction between cosmopolitan culture and national culture, he defines an international cosmopolitan literary figure by his or her

harsh questioning of radical decolonization theory; a dismissive or parodic attitude towards the project of national culture; a manipulation of imperial imagery and local legends as a means of politicizing current events; and a declaration of cultural hybridity – a hybridity claimed to offer certain advantages in negotiating the collisions of language, race and art in a world of disparate peoples comprising a single, if not exactly unified world.[38]

In addition to Rushdie, who is the textual focus of this book, Brennan names Mario Vargas Llosa, Isabel Allende, Carlos Fuentes, Gabriel García Márquez, Derek Walcott and Bharati

Mukherjee as among the most prominent cosmopolitan literary celebrities. But Naipaul's cosmopolitanism is taken by Brennan as both the model and the extreme. 'In a way, the obvious model is V.S. Naipaul, whose writing – too much commented on to be of use here – also departs from theirs [the other cosmopolitan writers] by largely abandoning any sympathy or acceptance of native culture', or attachment to a 'sentimental homeland', writes Brennan. 'In his early fiction – *A House for Mr Biswas*, *The Mystic Masseur* – Naipaul created an ambivalent mockery of East Indian Trinidad that became a general inspiration.' But, continues Brennan, 'the heavy weight he has since placed on the Western half of the cultural equation has cut him off from those who followed.'[39] There are a number of places to disagree with Brennan's formulation. Is Naipaul cut off and unsentimental about Trinidad? Does he have no sympathy for the nation? Why does the amount of comment on him disqualify him from detailed analysis yet allow him to be used as the 'obvious model'? And finally, what does Brennan mean by Western culture, by dividing the nation into half Western culture and half something unstated, by suggesting there are only two sides to culture and the nation, the Western and the Other? I have already discussed the way in which Naipaul has been wilfully read to drain his writing of any sympathy for the Third World nation or contempt for European colonial crimes. The question of Naipaul's attachment to a senti-mental homeland must be answered by a look at his most recent work, including *A Turn in the South* (1990) and *The Enigma of Arrival* (1988), in which Naipaul's prose is heavy with melancholy and memory of his Trinidadian youth and family. Arnold Rampersad's essay on this topic of his injured youth must occasion new thinking on Naipaul's attitude to Trinidad, and cause critics to examine the flippant way in which they often use Naipaul as the 'obvious model'.[40]

The South–South Cosmopolitan

For the purposes of this study, to make another reading of the text of Trinidadian national identity and to see the discourse on nationalism from yet another angle, I will concentrate on Brennan's great artificial divide between national and cosmopolitan culture, between people and intellectual, between Western bloc and Third World nation, between centre and periphery. I believe that Brennan's attempt to divide Naipaul from Trinidad is part of an anachronistic or even fanciful reading of the Third World nation in general, and certainly Trinidad in particular.

Brennan makes two mistakes when he tries to divide Trinidad and Naipaul, and to chastise Naipaul for his critical stance on nation-building in Trinidad and in the Third World. He speaks of cosmopolitan writers as a kind of stateless class, though to his credit he never calls them unified in imagination or politics, and consequently he writes at the level of a world system comprising Western World versus Third World, denying not only the specificity of Third World nations, but also the interaction between them. (For instance, the greatest threat to the national musical culture of calypso in Trinidad is Jamaican dub and American rap – can either of these forms be considered a First World intrusion?) And conversely, despite his global perspective, he makes the mistake of speaking of this world system as an impermeable and static structure in which the ideological boundaries of national culture versus cosmopolitan culture are clear, and presumably in which 'the people' always know the difference between valuable national culture and ersatz cosmopolitan culture, and would always choose the former. Trinidad's cosmopolitan national culture, capable of holding both V.S. Naipaul and David Rudder in its grasp, gives the lie to this romantic divide.

Or, to put these mistakes in other terms, Brennan uses a discredited model of dependency theory, linking it to a more recent model of post-colonial literary theory that should be qualified if not rejected. (Arun Mukherjee has recently challenged the totalizing tendency in post-colonial literary criticism, suspicious of the political and professional gains for critics who can link the white Canadian writing of Margaret Atwood to the Black Caribbean writing of Merle Hodge.[41]) To discuss the first failing, let us look at the theoretical foundation of Brennan's national culture/cosmopolitan culture dichotomy. Brennan begins with Antonio Gramsci, highlighting his writings on the internal colonization and national difference at the heart of Italy's North–South question. He notes in particular Gramsci's negative use of the term 'cosmopolitan', and his call for a national-popular literature. Brennan then calls upon Peruvian political activist Jose Carlos Mariategui, who saw a similar disregard for popular Andean Indian culture and an attempt by Peru's white minority to impose an internal cultural colonization on Peruvians by valorizing imported European culture. Next Brennan discusses the thought of Black British theorists A. Sivanandan and Paul Gilroy, discussed in Chapter 4. (Later in his book, Brennan's work on these two theorists and on the role of Rushdie in British nation-defining is very good, allowing for a cultural dynamism denied to much of the rest of the study, and to all of the Third World.) Brennan then moves on to Frantz Fanon and Amilcar Cabral. From Cabral he takes the idea of culture as 'a weapon of war' in the anti-colonial struggle and the famous insistence that the petty bourgeoisie must lead the struggle and commit suicide as a class in the process.[42] From Fanon, Brennan recalls the equally famous three phases of the colonial intellectual coming to revolutionary consciousness: the stage of assimilation, the stage of remembering, and the stage of fighting in which one veers toward the people.

At the end of his study Brennan concludes that, despite the good intentions of Rushdie (as opposed to the bad intentions of Naipaul, who according to the critic still has a 'nostalgia for the previous European status quo'[43]), he cannot write for the people but only translate to a Western public; and, although he shares with the theorists above a belief in the 'necessity of national struggle', he cannot bring himself to practise that belief.[44] Thus ultimately, despite trying to write a book about the schizophrenia of the migrant's life in Britain, he instead writes a book insensitive to the national cultures of Islam and gets condemned to death (a sentence Brennan does not explicitly denounce, incidentally).

Nationalism as Dependency Theory

Yet it is by no means clear how 'the necessity of the national struggle' or the theorists Brennan uses can be applied to the Caribbean, and therefore used to dismiss Naipaul (or take him as a model). What has happened in recent years is that the unity of the anti-colonial struggle, epitomized by these thinkers, has been preserved past its natural life into thirty years of post-colonialism by Brennan's use of dependency thinking – that Europe keeps post-colonial nations culturally underdeveloped, that the metropoles extract cosmopolitan literary figures from Third World nations and that they ignore or stifle what Barbara Harlow calls 'resistance literature', prohibiting national cultures, like national economies, from flourishing in the Third World. The problems with this cultural dependency theory are much the same as for its economic parent, which in its worst forms entailed a crude and static division of the globe into only two worthwhile categories – developed and underdeveloped. This vision, especially when applied to the cultural world, ignores Kwame Anthony Appiah's point that the contemporary Third World imagination does not care 'that the bicycle is the white man's invention: it is not there to be Other to the Yoruba Self; it is there because someone cared for its solidarity; it is there because it will take us further than our feet will take us; it is there because machines are now as African as novelists.'[45] National literatures have developed in the Third World despite the drain of cosmopolitans into the nether world of permanent exile. Trinidad has proven an obvious example. It is a literary Newly Industrialized Country. And often, cosmopolitan writers are indeed writing for their own nation, although for its literate classes. Mario Vargas Llosa's run for the presidency in Peru is a clear example of a cosmopolitan engaged in a national discourse. And finally, the flattening of Third World difference in national development and circumstance is a serious mistake. Trinidad is at once a Western nation, an immigrant nation, and a Third World nation. It has little in common in its cultural development structurally or ideologically with Pakistan or Iran. Brennan cites Samir Amin at the beginning of his book. Amin might be characterized as a leading proponent of a world systems theory of dependency. But one has only to look at an article such as Sheila Smith's devastating 'The Ideas of Samir Amin: Theory or Tautology' to recognize the serious handicap involved in using a global dependency theory for the basis of national economic development, never mind national cultural development. In her article, Smith concludes that 'Amin's proposition that only a radical and complete break with the world capitalist system will provide the necessary conditions for genuine development, can only be described as dangerous arrogance.'[46] There is some of that same arrogance in Brennan's assertion that the national writer, unlike the cosmopolitan writer, lives free of international contamination inside the struggle of a people.

Nor is it clear that, even if this path to national cultural development could be assured through some kind of severance of European culture, what would develop would be national in any sense. In the Caribbean, the national culture has always been international because the economy has always been international. James writes of the cosmopolitan sophistication of the Caribbean slave because of this international connection in the trade and technology of the sugar mills, not to mention the inter-ethnic contact of the slave trade and its indentured aftermath. There is no way to remove the international from the national in the Caribbean. Brennan, instead of using his theorists to make universal declarations, should have used them to make local ones. He could have found Frantz Fanon, in his study of the Caribbean, not Algeria, saying, 'The Martinican is a Frenchman, he wants to remain part of the French union ... I am a Frenchman. I am interested in French culture, French civilization, the French people.'[47] Fanon recognized the difference between Algeria and Martinique. Timothy Brennan cannot. His virulent critique and cooptation of Naipaulacity shows only the lack of concrete historical analysis endemic to the field of post-colonial literary theory today.[48] Neither Naipaul nor Trinidad appears willing to have outside critics sever their relationship, however. And the consequences for the discourse on nationalism in Trinidad are profound. If Brennan is wrong, and Naipaul is part of national culture in Trinidad, we are back at the beginning of this chapter, where in which it was noted that France has no trouble including Genet in its nation. Why must we suppose that the cosmopolitan nature of Caribbean culture cannot accommodate Naipaul? Indeed, what the negative criticism of Naipaul helps to show is that the carnival of identity that exists with such strength internally and diasporically also equips Trinidad and other Caribbean nations with the ability to include the cosmopolitan writers of the region like Derek Walcott and V.S. Naipaul, if not in the national discourse, then at least in the nation-space. It is telling that no less a pan-Caribbean cultural nationalist than Rex Nettleford (and fierce defender of the accomplishments of the Grenadian revolution) gave a recent speech at the Guyana Prize for Literature ceremonies in which he forgave Naipaul for his 'castrated metaphor' with which he claimed the Caribbean had no history and had produced nothing. Nettleford announced that it 'need not be seen as anything more than a rhetorical excess spat out at a society that admittedly denies too many of its own citizens a sense of place and purpose'. Nettleford added that 'Naipaul, for all his frustrations, is nonetheless a creation of that very society, and a brilliant one at that.'[49] Clearly, the people of the Caribbean would only be insulted by Brennan's heavy-handed attempt to save them from the cosmopolitan and help them with the national. What we learn from Naipaul's discourse on the nation is that Trinidad challenges Brennan's fearful European hegemony not with revolutionary discipline but with sophistication and historically produced confidence in the face of the foreign, the different, even the wicked of temper.

Notes

1. V.S. Naipaul, *The Mimic Men*, London: Penguin, 1969.

2. A good example of this allegorical and yet dispassionately apolitical view of Naipaul's work is Peggy Nightingale's *Journey Through Darkness: The writings of V.S. Naipaul*, St Lucia, Queensland: University of Queensland Press, 1987. Her statement that 'colonialism and imperialism robbed human nature of its dignity and human societies of their complexity' (p. 144) is both true and trite, and all too typical of the developed world's response to Naipaul.

3. At times, Naipaul appears to stretch this rejection of nationalism to all nations, but not often enough for Third World critics. See Victor Ramraj, 'V.S. Naipaul: the Irrelevance of Nationalism', *World Literature Written in English*, vol. 23, no. 1, 1984, pp. 187–96.

4. Helen Pyne-Timothy, 'Cultural Integration and the Use of Trinidad Creole', *Journal of Caribbean Studies*, vol 5, no. 2.

5. Eric Hobsbawm, *Nations and Nationalism Since 1780*, Cambridge: Cambridge University Press, 1990, and see in particular his last chapter.

6. C.L.R. James, *The Artist in the Caribbean*, Mona, Jamaica: Open Lecture Series, University of the West Indies, 1965, p. 30.

7. Gustavo Perez Firmat, *The Cuban Condition: Translation and Identity in Modern Cuban Literature*, Cambridge: Cambridge University Press, 1989.

8. A good example of the harmless criticism emanating from the

centres of literary power is Paul Theroux's *V.S. Naipaul: An Introduction to His Work*, London: Andre Deutsch, 1972, in which Theroux avoids any problems of nationalism and writerly responsibility by concluding that 'it is evidence of the uniqueness of his vision, but a demonstration of the odds against him, that no country can claim him' (p. 135).

9. Homi K. Bhabha, 'Introduction: Narrating the Nation', in Homi K. Bhabha, ed., *Nation and Narration*, London: Routledge, 1990, pp. 3–4.

10. Ibid. Particularly in his essay 'Dissemination', Bhabha's poetic invocation of the life of the exiled intellectual attempting to find a nation-space stands in sharp contrast to Timothy Brennan's dismissal, in the same volume and elsewhere, of exiled intellectuals as unworthy celebrities betraying the local cultures they left behind. It is into this unspoken conflict that I introduce Naipaul's texts.

11. John Thieme, 'Searching for a Centre: The Writings of V.S. Naipaul', *Third World Quarterly*, vol. 9, no. 4, p. 1362.

12. Gordon Rohlehr, 'The Ironic Approach', in Robert D. Hamner, ed., *Critical Perspectives on V. S. Naipaul*, Washington, DC: Three Continents Press, 1977, p. 182. Rohlehr, like many other critics, turns to *Biswas* to redeem Naipaul.

13. Arcadio Diaz Quinones, 'The Hispanic-Caribbean National Discourse: Antonio S. Pedreira and Ramiro Guerra y Sanchez', in *Intellectuals in the Caribbean*, University of Warwick, forthcoming.

14. The most sustained examination of the cooptation of popular nationalism by the lighter and better educated middle class in the Caribbean is in Ivar Oxaal's *Race and Class and the Dilemma of the Black Intellectual*, Cambridge, Mass.: Schenkman, 1982. Oxaal shows how Trinidad's urban petty bourgeoisie and foreign-educated Black (though often light-skinned) elites gradually marginalized the union leaders – both Black and East Indian – in the People's National Movement.

15. Manning Marable, *African and Caribbean Politics: From Kwame Nkrumah to Maurice Bishop*, London: Verso, 1987, p. 87.

16. Ibid., p. 95.

17. Manning points out the charismatic mythologizing qualities of Mobutu and others, but it is only fair to remember Benedict Anderson's observation of European nation-states that they also pretend to an immemorial history and future.

18. Timothy Brennan, *Salman Rushdie and the Third World*, New York: St Martin's Press, 1989. I will also look at two articles by Brennan, one in Bhabha, ed., *Nation and Narration*, entitled 'The National Longing for Form', and another entitled 'Cosmopolitans and Celebrities', in *Race and Class*, vol. 31, no. 1, 1989.

19. Selwyn Cudjoe, *V.S. Naipaul: a Materialist Reading*, Amherst, Mass.: University of Massachusetts Press, 1988.

20. Ibid., p. 166.

21. Ibid.

22. See, for instance, J. Stewart, 'Patronage and Control in Trinidad Carnival', in V. Turner and J. Bruner, eds., *The Anthropology of Experience*, Urbana: University of Illinois, 1986, pp. 289–316.

23. Ibid., p. 129.

24. Naipaul, *The Mimic Men*, p. 206.

25. Simon Malley, 'Ca Bascule', *Le Nouvel Afrique/Asie*, Paris, April 1991.

26. Ibid., p. 3. Malley has been friend and adviser to virtually every African independence leader, and his intellectual movement from anti-colonialist, to state socialist, to democratic socialist is indicative of the progressive pattern of political thought in the region and stands in contrast to Cudjoe's somewhat anachronistic stance.

27. Cudjoe, *Naipaul*, p. 158 (note).

28. Bill Warren, *Imperialism: Pioneer of Capitalism*, London: Verso, 1980, p. 185.

29. V.S. Naipaul, '"Heavy Manners in Grenada', *Sunday Times Magazine*, London, 12 February 1984.

30. Chris Searle, 'Naipaulacity: A Form of Cultural Imperialism', *Race and Class*, vol. 26, no. 2, 1984, p. 62.

31. Ibid., p. 46.

32. Ibid., p. 47.

33. Quoted from Naipaul, 'Heavy Manners in Grenada', in 'Naipaulacity', p. 53.

34. Anthony Payne, Paul Sutton and Tony Thorndike, *Grenada: Revolution and Invasion*, London: Croom Helm, 1984, p. 136.

35. Gordon Lewis, *Grenada: The Jewel Despoiled*, Baltimore: Johns Hopkins University Press, 1987, p. 161.

36. Brennan, *Salman Rushdie*.

37. Ibid., p. 166.

38. Ibid., p. 35.

39. Ibid., p. 35.

40. Arnold Rampersad, 'V.S. Naipaul', *Raritan*, vol. 10, no. 1, 1990.

41. Arun Mukherjee, 'Whose Post-Colonialism and Whose Postmodernism?', *World Literature Written in English*, vol. 30, no. 2, 1990, pp. 1–9.

42. Brennan, *Salman Rushdie*, pp. 46–57.

43. Ibid., p. 26

44. Ibid., p.166.

45. Kwame Anthony Appiah, 'Is the Post- in Postmodernism the Post- in Postcolonial?', *Critical Inquiry*, vol. 17, no. 2, 1991, p. 357.

46. Sheila Smith, 'The Ideas of Samir Amin: Theory or Tautology?', *The Journal of Development Studies*, vol. 17, no. 1, 1980, p. 20.

47. Frantz Fanon, *Black Skin, White Masks*, New York: Grove Press, 1967, p. 203.

48. For essay   /
theory, see Step   /:
Dangaroo, 198   fy
all post-coloni   .u-
sions of Post-Coloni..   .   ase
Study', *Ariel*, vol. 22, no. 3, pp. 44 ~ِ

49. Rex Nettleford, 'Communication With ᴏᴜ.   ᴊean
Artist and the Society', *Caribbean Affairs*, vol. 3, no. 2, 1990, p. ᴊɪ

CHAPTER 7

C.L.R. James and Egalitarian Nationalism in the Caribbean

I am sick to death that whenever they talk about the West Indian they say he is suffering; he's intelligent but he's looked upon as backward because he came from slavery... I am going to write a book in which I will show that the West Indian had more in him than that.[1]

The book C.L.R. James wrote was *The Black Jacobins*, first published in 1938, an acknowledged classic of revolutionary anti-colonial struggle and of the study of revolutions in general, and for many scholars the finest book ever written on the Caribbean.[2] But C.L.R. James gave this reason for writing his masterpiece not in the late 1930s, but rather in response to a question from an audience in North London in 1976. The questioner wanted to know why James, and George Padmore, childhood friend and a father of African emancipation, were so much more involved in the anti-colonial struggle and nation-building of Africa than that of the Caribbean. James holds out *The Black Jacobins* as early evidence of his dedication to the Caribbean struggle and adds that 'if they call me back to Trinidad tomorrow, I will go'. At first glance, the life and achievements of C.L.R. James might remind the reader of the careers of other great Caribbean men of this century, like Marcus Garvey, Frantz Fanon, Walter Rodney and George Padmore, men from the Caribbean whose influence has been felt around the world, but more around the world than in the Caribbean. At a speech in celebration of his seventieth birthday, however, James told his audience that the reason that *The Black Jacobins* continued to go into new editions nearly fifty years after it was written was that

> [it] still has a validity today, 1971, because I came originally from the kind of territory which produced Rene Maran, Marcus Garvey, George Padmore, Aime Cesaire and Frantz Fanon, and we were prepared not only to say what should be done in the Caribbean, but we were trained and developed in such a way that we were able to make tremendous discoveries about Western civilisation itself.[3]

C.L.R. James, like the other men from his territory in the Caribbean, did make tremendous discoveries about Western civilization, the full scope of which are only now being truly appreciated. The importance of his training and development in the Caribbean can hardly be doubted. His perspectives on Black America, on Africa, and on the European metropoles are full of both the wisdom and the distance of his West Indian upbringing. His superb autobiography, *Beyond a Boundary*,[4] is further proof of the importance of Caribbean cultural roots in his tremendous discoveries. Nonetheless, those tremendous discoveries, like those of Marcus Garvey or Frantz Fanon, were made outside of the Caribbean, and sadly, have had least effect in the territory that helped produce them. To consider C.L.R. James as Trinidad does is to consider the loyalty and devotion of a brilliant but often wayward son. When he returned in 1965 to form a Workers' and Farmers' Party and contest a general election, many looked upon him like a star come home, but many more whispered that he had been away too long now to understand Trinidad. Where does the truth lie? Did James take from the Caribbean and give elsewhere, or is his work, as he points out in *The Black Jacobins*, part of a half-century project of revolutionary nationalism in Trinidad and in the Caribbean?

It is heartening that the work of C.L.R. James is beginning to receive re-evaluation and to reach a widening audience, stretching for the first time in fifty years into leftist political discourse in the United States and Canada. However I want to look in this chapter at a still-neglected period in James's work: those essays and public lectures given in the late 1950s and early 1960s upon his return to his native Trinidad around the independence period. I want to argue that he was uniquely ready to think about nationalism in the Caribbean and to navigate the difficult relationship between Lenin's national question and the question of class in his new nation. Just as he had famously lectured Trotsky on the shortcomings of Trotsky's analysis of the race question in the United States – arguing that it could not be viewed narrowly as a question of nascent self-determination – he now faced the complexity of external colonial oppression and internal class difference in the Caribbean. He faced that complexity, and the difficulties of creating national consciousness that could not be coopted by a dominant class, in numerous lectures in union halls and public libraries throughout Trinidad, speaking directly to working people. In fact, I will argue that his nationalist project remains relevant today. The Caribbean has no coherent, collective analysis of the relationship between neo-colonial rhetoric and internal class oppression, comparable for instance, to the work in India, of the Subaltern Studies group.[5] And the Caribbean, rife with corruption, struggling unions, capital and intellectual flight, badly needs such a systematic analysis. James put down the roots of just such a specific Caribbean analysis of nationalism and class. He was peculiarly suited to do so.

C.L.R. James was born at the beginning of the century and lived virtually to its end, dying just before the collapse of the postwar order in Europe, but living to see and think about Polish Solidarity and the US Invasion of Grenada. He came from a town called Tunapuna along the main line of towns stretching east from Port of Spain under the green shadows of the Northern Range in Trinidad. His father was a schoolteacher and his mother and his aunts were active in the church. His biographer, Paul Buhle, describes his social status well when he notes that to be a schoolteacher in colonial Trinidad was to hold a position of little financial reward but much social esteem.[6] James describes much of his upbringing in *Beyond a Boundary*, but for now it is worth noting that the advantages of a schoolteacher for a father, and a well-read mother, helped James take the narrow and steep path out of colonial Tunapuna and become a teacher himself at Queen's Royal College in Port of Spain. There James quickly felt the constraints of the colonial (and island) world. Together with several other young intellectuals and writers, he started two journals, *The Beacon* and then *Trinidad*. Most of the rest of his circle were from the Port of Spain 'Coloured' middle class, like novelist Ralph De Boissiere, or from the Portuguese entrepreneurial class, like Alfred Mendes and Albert Gomes. Gomes would later become a prominent politician and would chide James when the latter returned to Trinidad, saying, 'You know what the difference is between all of you and me? You all went away; I stayed.' But in retelling the anecdote, James adds that

> I didn't tell him what I could have told him: you stayed not only because you had money but because your skin was white; there was a chance for you, but for us there wasn't – except to be a civil servant and hand papers, take them from the men downstairs and hand them to a man upstairs.[7]

(Years later, of course, in his mimic-man-like exile in London, Gomes would write of Englishmen approaching him on the street to tell him they had been to his native Pakistan – testimony to the fluidities and rigidities of the 'maze of colour', the title of his somewhat melancholic autobiography.) James left Trinidad and went to England at the invitation of Learie Constantine, the great Trinidadian cricketer, one of the earliest in a line of West Indian cricketers who would make the uneasy economic migration to English county cricket.

In the course of his peripatetic life James, would travel the furtive roads of radical politics throughout much of the world; he would help George Padmore and W.E.B. Du Bois set up pan-African conferences that would lead the way to decolonization in Africa; he would be sought out for advice by everyone from Kwame Nkrumah, to Eric Williams, to Stokely Carmichael. And he would move from the most violent anti-colonial atmospheres to the quiet of English county cricket with the naturalness that always belied those roots in a Caribbean territory. He would return to Trinidad in the late 1950s to help Eric Williams and his People's National Movement realize independence, and return again in 1964 to form a party to oppose his former pupil and the PNM. But by then he was a world-famous Marxist thinker and pan-Africanist. On both sojourns he threw himself into the work of making his homeland a better place by lecturing, writing and stirring up intellectual debate, believing that so much of what he had fought for in the worker's movements of America and Great

Britain, and in the decolonization of Africa, would be realized in the new Caribbean. As Anna Grimshaw put it, 'this is why James seized so readily the chance to be part of Trinidad's movement towards independence, for he conceived of it as much more than the replacement of colonial rule by a Caribbean government.'[8] But James was wrong, or rather he was overly optimistic. Eric Williams was no Toussaint L'Ouverture, and in post-colonial Trinidad the new boss was the same as the old boss, just darker and able to dig more convincingly into local dialect and culture to rabble-rouse. From 1956 onward, Eric Williams and his circle of privileged, educated and urban People's National Movement leaders developed an anti-colonial rhetoric that, as Ivar Oxaal has noted, demonized the European colonizer, implicated the reluctant nationalist Indian Trinidadian leadership, and disempowered both the African and Indian trade-union leadership, all in a totalizing drive of slave against slaveowner.[9] Trinidad's independence became the simple transfer of power from a British clerk class to an urban, Coloured clerk class. The new Trinidad James dreamed about put him under house arrest in 1965, claiming he was a danger to the established order.

An Alternative Nationalist Project

But it was also in this period of optimism about Trinidad's future that James would begin to build his intellectual nationalist project, finding its roots in his early work, just as he would find the roots of national independence in the Haitian revolution. His Trinidad never appeared. Too divided by the racial politics first of the colonial office and then of the PNM, and too timid in political nationalism to take on either the old imperialists or the new, Trinidad even rejected non-aligned status. Little changed. As one labour leader remarked, 'it has taken an expert on slavery to re-impose slavery on his people.'[10] (He was referring to Eric Williams, devoted pupil of James, who wrote the seminal study *Capitalism and Slavery*, the same Eric Williams who would betray James and the unions as prime minister.) In an immediate political sense, James failed to move Trinidad in the direction his heart hoped for. But he also had in mind another kind of nationalism, based on his new thinking about culture, the popular arts and mass political movement. He sought, in public talks and private memories, to kill off once and for all what had haunted him since the days of writing *The Black Jacobins*: the idea that the West Indies were without culture and history (and possibility) – what Naipaul called the Third World's Third World, where even ideas had to be imported. James was at the height of his intellectual and synthetic powers in the late 1950s and in the 1960s, and it can be argued that his writings on the Caribbean, far from being the record of a famous intellectual returned home in vain, are in fact an un-exploded shell of Caribbean history and thought, waiting for the 'development of a people' to strike it into a social explosion.

Indeed, C.L.R. James was lecturing to students in Washington, DC days before the 1970 revolution in Trinidad, and he predicted just such an explosion. When the explosion occurred, leaders and followers in the movement confirmed that they had found *The Black Jacobins* waiting there for them to uncover its force. The 1970 revolution combined much that James admired: spontaneous leaderships, public education campaigns, and, most important an attempt to reverse the privileged discourse of race over class. James wrote in an introduction to a labour history of Trinidad that

> Dr. Williams has written in public that one important thing that he has done is to keep the Indian and the African people apart. In reality, it is my belief, and I say it very plainly, that there is no salvation for the people in Trinidad unless those two sections of the population get together and work together.[11]

The key to that statement is the dynamic of 'working together'. The 1970 revolution featured a march by African Trinidadian students and workers into the sugar-growing lands of Caroni to demonstrate solidarity with the Indian Trinidadian farm labourer. James's statement might at first bring to mind the dominant discourse on nationalism in Trinidad – peoplehood before justice, and the same race-before-class rhetoric of Eric Williams. And, as we attempt to define the revolutionary nationalism of James, it is worth noting Richard Handler's cautionary words in his study on cultural nationalism in Quebec. Handler writes:

> nationalist discourse of whatever school shares features with that of other schools and even other places and times. Discourses (to personify

for the moment what is only the product of active speakers and inter-
preters) converse: ideologues and theorists imitate, borrow, and
compare among themselves.[12]

It is difficult even for James to speak outside of the discourse on
nationalism in the Caribbean. But in the context of the 1970 revolution, or the works of James, one can immediately see that nationalism for James, like Black Power, is a profoundly revolutionary
effort, requiring huge social upheaval and mass political change,
much more than mere decolonization, or the kind of cultural
nation-building of some West Indian intellectuals and politicians.

To understand the balance that James achieved between
nationalism and revolution, peoplehood and people's power, race
and class, is to understand not only the Jamesian project of revolutionary nationalism in the Caribbean, but also the failure and
disunity that has plagued Trinidad and the Caribbean since independence. In fact, just as he predicted the bright days of the 1970
revolution, he also, all too often, predicted the dark days of corrupt
leaderships, warring ethnicities and moral decay that have infested
the Caribbean.

Caribbean History Regained

At the heart of James's project was his conviction that if he gave
the people of the Caribbean the intellectual and spiritual inheritance that was theirs, they would do the rest. James spent years in
the revolutionary movements of the developed world insisting that
all the organization was finished, that the workers did not require
leadership, and that vanguardism led to totalitarianism. He was
often rebuffed and misunderstood because of this conviction, even
by the most libertarian of left groups. But his reading of Caribbean
history, and Caribbean developments of the recent decades, helped
him maintain a deep faith. He would recapture Caribbean history
and reconstruct the Caribbean man, and the children of this
Caribbean man would meet him 'at the rendezvous of victory'.
He set out to reveal the inevitable Caribbean-ness of every man
and woman from that territory, a common history and personality
that could never be left behind in travels to London or New York,

a common inheritance of power that would produce what he called 'an independent current of Western thought'[13] and build a revolutionary nationalism 'beginning with Cuba and ending with all three Guyanas'.[14]

By the time James first heard the call to return to Trinidad in the late 1950s, where he would edit the newspaper of the new People's National Movement, *The Nation*, and advise Eric Williams, he had once again taken up the nationalist project where he left it with the publication of *The Black Jacobins* twenty years before. But even before his brilliant account of Toussaint L'Ouverture and the San Domingo Revolution, he had begun his contribution to Caribbean nationalism with two important works written before he left Trinidad to join the great Trinidadian cricketer Learie Constantine in England. These two works were a novel called *Minty Alley*, and a political tract called *The Life of Captain Cipriani*.[15] Both reveal the later strategies and directions of his revolutionary nationalism, and both reveal the duplicity and weakness of those who have offered more partial nationalisms. And both forecast the Jamesian nationalist project of rethinking not only the 'habitus' of the Trinidadian man and woman, but also the epistemological break into revolutionary action.

'The Supreme Artist'

C.L.R. James has repeatedly defended and championed the Guyanese novelist and critic Wilson Harris and the Trinidadian novelist and essayist V.S. Naipaul. Both writers are at the front of the Caribbean literary renaissance, but both writers have also needed defending in the Caribbean. Naipaul's notorious comments from his travel essays in the West Indies, *The Middle Passage*, in which he suggested that nothing had ever been created in the West Indies and nothing ever would be, were the beginning of an argument that has lasted to this day. The argument has resurfaced with new poignancy in his recent works, particularly, as Arnold Rampersad notes, in *A Turn in the South* and *The Enigma of Arrival*.[16] After *The Middle Passage*, many West Indian critics and intellectuals announced that the young Naipaul, who had achieved worldwide acclaim for his novel *A House for Mr Biswas* and confirmed the literary surge of the Caribbean, was a Europhilic traitor and stopped reading him. But the change in tone and understanding that Rampersad detects in the recent works would come as no surprise to James, who – champion of the creative Caribbean – always maintained that Naipaul was misunderstood. This misunderstanding, according to James, comes from underestimating the Caribbean man, and fearing, unnecessarily therefore, the European side of Caribbean heritage. James explains this point in an essay on the man he considered the greatest social critic of the West Indies, calypsonian The Mighty Sparrow. Writing of Sparrow and poet Derek Walcott, James concludes that 'Behind him, and Mr. Walcott's analysis, there emerges a fact and direction that summarises the whole West Indian position as I see it, politics, economics, art, everything.' James is speaking of Walcott's famous poetic question of African/European heritage, 'where shall I turn divided to the bone?' James continues:

> We have to master a medium, whatever it is, that had developed in a foreign territory and on the basis seek and find out what is native, and build on that. It is obvious that our present race of politicians are too far gone ever to learn that. But there are signs that this truth is penetrating younger people.[17]

Guyanese novelist Wilson Harris gave the 1990 Smuts Memorial lecture series in Cambridge, England. He spoke about the dangers of 'the progressive realists' in Caribbean fiction. He would know of these dangers. He has been, for decades now, the suspicious target of 'progressive political' novelists and critics in the Caribbean and elsewhere in the Third World, who view his fantastical and mytho-philosophical texts with suspicion. His texts do not tell realistic stories of colonial exploitation and anti-colonial struggle. He fails to fit the programme of nationalists who seek to control the public discourse. His myth-making and Heideggerian liberty look dangerously spontaneous.

And yet James was careful always to include both Harris and Naipaul on any list of great Caribbean writers, always sure to explain that Naipaul's was a personal search and a personal 'area of darkness', not a Jamesonian national allegory. He repeats with great fondness the story of Naipaul writing to James to praise the first half of *Beyond a Boundary*, saying it was the first book that 'really explained us'. In short, he included Naipaul in his nationalist project, and saw the need for the Caribbean to do for all artists, 'what we can do. Let us create the conditions under which the artist can flourish. But to do that, we must have the consciousness that the nation which we are hoping to build, as much as it needs the pooling of resources and industrialisation and a higher productivity of labour, needs also the supreme artist.'[18] He thought that Naipaul's bitter abandonment of (and return to) Trinidad had much to do with ignorance in the middle class, and the lack of conditions of respect and attention for the artist in the Caribbean. Significantly, it is in an introduction to Wilson Harris's work that James reaffirms in 1965 that 'the finest study ever produced in the West Indies (or anywhere else I know) of a minority and the herculean obstacles in the way of its achieving a room in the national building [is] Naipaul's *A House for Mr Biswas*.'[19] It is significant both because he reconfirms that his interest in Naipaul is not just aesthetic but nationalistic, and also because he gathers Naipaul together with Lamming of Barbados, Vic Reid of Jamaica, and Harris, to say that 'the instinctive feelings and readiness of the West Indian populations for adventurous creation in all fields is proved by the literature these territories produce.'[20]

James concludes his introduction to Wilson Harris's lecture by saying that he hoped he had made 'Harris easier for West Indians to grasp. That is one trouble. Our novelists, as our cricketers, are recognised abroad for what they are, something new, creative and precious in the organisations and traditions of the West. But what they need is what Heidegger recognised in Hölderlin – a homecoming.'[21] He saw Harris and Naipaul, like himself and like Sparrow, as deeply West Indian men, whose achievements abroad should inspire not suspicion, but rather faith that those territories of the Caribbean continued to produce tremendous achievements. He later embraces Trinidadian novelists Michael Anthony and Earl Lovelace as truly national writers in the new sense of remaining local, but he never abandons Naipaul and Harris. In the construction of the Caribbean man, or what he calls 'The Making of the Caribbean People', every tremendous achievement should be counted. This defence and inclusion should be seen against James's pioneering novel of the 1930s, *Minty Alley*.

James as National Artist

Minty Alley is not a great novel, and the stiffness of the middle-class voyeur in the yards of Port of Spain suggests the stiffness of the schoolteacher's son from Tunapuna walking through the urban slums of Port of Spain for the first time. Alfred Mendes wrote a more interesting novel of black and white Portuguese tension and sexuality in this period, and Ralph De Boissiere probably wrote the most interesting, if uncontrolled, of the novels at the birth of Trinidadian literature.[22] Elsewhere in the Caribbean, Claude McKay had already achieved fame in the United States with his Jamaican novels, and the next twenty years would belong to the French Caribbean – to Aime Cesaire and the Haitian novelists.[23] But that does not diminish the importance of James's novel.

His early novel, together with several short stories, were an important attempt to legitimize the local language and culture, and reject a purely European sensibility. None of the novels written in Trinidad in the 1930s could compare to Aime Cesaire's *Return to My Native Land*[24] in announcing a powerfully new Caribbean and anti-European imagination – what Wilson Harris calls 'the native imagination'. But James asserted one thing with his early fiction. He would look at what was native and new in literature as a sign of the readiness of the West Indian people to burst forth in political creativity. Thus Naipaul and Harris, thirty years later, are defended not on facile ideological grounds but because they are Caribbean men, with Caribbean imaginations, and they stand for the capabilities of the West Indian, past and future. James once remarked that 'when I hear people arguing about Marxism versus the nationalist or racialist struggle, I am very confused.'[25] James is being coy in his remark, but he is also making a subtle and advanced point about revolution and the need to guard against new hegemonies springing from old, just as he would repeatedly warn the Caribbean peasant working class not to accept simply a change in the colour of leadership. He saw the trap of a single ideology, any version of Marxism or Black Power, that sought to curtail liberty in the name of revolution. His thoughts on the dangers of either a classless nationalism or a Europhilic vanguard-ism anticipated by twenty years the work of another innovative Marxist thinker, Ernesto Laclau. The oft-cited work of Laclau and co-author Chantal Mouffe insists that the struggle of the left must take place in what they term 'plural spaces' that are balanced by 'equivalence', on the one hand and 'autonomy' of struggle, on the other. Their thought has had a considerable degree of influence recently.[26] James anticipated this search for plural revolutionary spaces, not just in the Caribbean, but also in the United States in the 1940s and early 1950s, when he predicted that students, Blacks and women would lead a new American revolution.[27] James saw early in the Caribbean context the danger of excluding potential allies in the struggle, and perhaps something in his past rebelled against the notion of incorrect literature. He certainly understood, however, from his early attempts to liberate literature in Trinidad in the 1930s, that the works of Harris and Naipaul served the cause of liberation and pride in the Caribbean far more than they harmed the unity of approach and narrative. It is a political understanding he might have lacked were it not for the creative half of him, and it is an understanding – typical of James – that he reached far ahead of his time.

In a similar fashion, his *Life of Captain Cipriani* helped him connect the modern Caribbean man with his history, and helped him, forty years later, avoid a false racial consciousness, choosing Caribbean regional liberation instead.

> Cipriani was able to take the stand he did because the French Creoles had a long tradition of independent economic life and social differentiation.... But there was more to Cipriani.... That he was able to discover the tremendous qualities of the Caribbean population ... was due to the fact that history had presented him with political opportunities unfolding the capacities of a highly developed people. These soldiers were the descendants of Toussaint's army.[28]

This theme of the social outsider taking advantage of political upheaval to make tremendous discoveries is a steady one for James, who viewed the Caribbean man, always on the outside and yet often at the centre of historical cleavages, as the prime example of man transcending contemporary understanding to contribute something new. But the importance of his Cipriani work, and of his reaffirmation of it decades later, lies more in what it says about his sense of nationalism. Cipriani fought tirelessly for independence after the First World War, and he sought to make the emergent trade unions a vehicle for that nationalism. He had definite advantages – as a French Creole, he could say what Afro- or Indo-Caribbean men and women could not. But, as James notes, he was, despite his skin colour, a radical agent of revolution in Trinidad, far more so than the 'coloured' petty bourgeoisie which would take the nationalist symbol away from him and the other union leaders who followed him. Nonetheless, in the enthusiasm of Black nationalism in Trinidad in the late 1960s, and eventually inside trade-union culture, Cipriani was largely relegated to the position of sympathetic French Creole. A 1989 calypso by Sugar Aloes, called 'The Judge', suggested taking down the statue of Cipriani and putting up a statue of Eric Williams instead, and taking down the statue of Lord Harris and putting up one of McCandle Dagger, a leader of the Black Power movement in Trinidad. The calypso was widely popular, and, although Sugar Aloes is a well-known sympathizer of Williams's ousted PNM party, the song is telling. In the retelling of the anti-colonial nationalist struggle, there was little room for a French Creole hero (despite the fact that the trade-union college in Trinidad is named after Cipriani). But James rejected this version of events, both in the 1930s and in the 1960s. In fact, in a passage partly aimed at his own absence from the struggle, James says pointedly, speaking of Grantley Adams in Barbados and Cipriani in Trinidad, that

> in those revolutionary days, nowhere else did any member of the black middle class enter into politics. Today a whole lot of them are very noisy politicos, the way is very easy, you get a good salary, you can become a minister, and you can go to England and be entertained by royalty!

And then James adds, 'but, Cipriani and Grantley Adams started before World War II In those days there was nothing but work and danger.'[29]

From James's early works, even before *The Black Jacobins*, the roots of his revolutionary nationalism are already – as Cabral would say – plunged into the humus of Trinidad. And James had already begun to build what Benedict Anderson would consider a mass nationalism. His embrace of Cipriani and of the vagaries of literary discourse anticipate the rejection of official, state national-ism, as it stretches from Eric Williams to Sugar Aloes. He sought a nationalism that would inspire all the peoples of the Caribbean, not a nationalism that would become simply the tool of Black and Coloured middle-class politicos being entertained by English royalty. And, ever aware of the need to recapture the creativity and talents suppressed by racism, he nonetheless saw the dangers of a nationalism predicated solely on race, fearing with typical prescience that racialist nationalism could obscure the aspirations of mass participation and creativity, exchanging white oppressors for Black. But most of all, his early writing predicts his thunderous argument for the tremendous achievements, and consequent potential, of the Caribbean woman and man. By 1966, he could effortlessly end lectures with such operatic climaxes as this:

> Here I shall give a list of names, a list without which it is impossible to write of the history and literature of Western civilization. No account of Western civilization could leave out the names of Toussaint L'Ouverture, Alexander Hamilton, Alexander Dumas (the father), Leconte Delisle, Jose Maria de Heredia, Marcus Garvey, Rene Maran, Saint-John Perse, Aime Cesaire, George Padmore, Frantz Fanon, and allow me to include one contemporary, a Cuban writer, Alejo Carpentier.

But James is not finished there; after mentioning the literary surge of the English-speaking Caribbean he adds: 'I end this list by a name acknowledged by critics all over the world as an unprecedented, unimaginable practitioner of his particular art – I refer, of course, to Garfield Sobers.'[30] Such a remarkable passage was typical of James's talks to audiences in the Caribbean, Britain, Canada and the United States in the 1960s and 1970s. In the body of those talks we see the perfection of a revolutionary nationalism that defies his political failures in Trinidad, as it challenges the hegemonic discourse both of the egalitarian nationalism which sought to defeat him and the imperialism that feared him.

The Nationalist Project Begun

A look at James's public lectures and essays in the post-independence period reveals that, as a creative thinker on nationalism and peoplehood, James has no peer in the Caribbean. His revolutionary excitement is most often expressed through a new kind of literary criticism which takes as its purpose the location of worthy creative achievements not just in individual writers and revolutionaries, but in Caribbean society as a whole. James insisted, therefore, that Toussaint L'Ouverture defeated the most sophisticated European army of its day, not just because he and his brilliance sprang from the ordinary slave community, but because that brilliance continued to be reflected in each slave who battled with him. Similarly, the novels of George Lamming indicate the reinvention of colonialism not only by a superb modernist novelist, but in the constant telling and retelling by every Caribbean woman and man. For James each nationalist and literary figure was sustained not by his exceptionalism but by the very inevitability of his springing from the people. His lectures can be seen as an evolving set of creative efforts to imagine a nation and a people. Imagining a people, and not just a nation, is what gave James his popular nationalism. He believed in the genius of the people, just as he feared the official nationalism that sought to manipulate that genius. It was a genius he found not only in contemporary novelists and cricketers, but also in their enslaved ancestors; and it is with their history, as told by James, that an analysis of his revolutionary nationalism should start.

James was adamant about this popular history, and casually stood Caribbean history on its head to prove it. It was a brave victory for the Caribbean people and a bold look at the history of slavery. Since *The Black Jacobins*, James had been interested in the idea that it was the African slaves that ended slavery in the New World, through ceaseless rebellion, revolution (in Haiti), and civil war (in the United States). James once claimed that he had given his student, Dr Eric Williams, the idea for his seminal book, *Capitalism and Slavery*.[31] Williams's book changed the scholarship on slavery forever, but his contention that slavery was ended not because of new enlightened attitudes but because it had become economically unworkable for the imperial powers seems too deterministic for James. James preferred an explanation of mass genius – from Haiti to Brazil to Alabama, the slaves themselves threatened slavery. James goes further in his exploration of slave life and culture in the plantation economies of the Caribbean. 'The Negroes who came from Africa brought themselves', announced James.[32] And elsewhere, again, 'he [the negro] brought with him the content of his mind, his memory. He thought in the logic and the language of his people.'[33] With words like these James drew his sword against the common myth that the slave was stripped of all culture and content by the Middle Passage.[34] Nor, according to James, was the slave, once in the Caribbean, rootless (and this historical point has particular relevance for his modern nationalism.) 'A new community was formed; it took its form in the slave quarters of the plantations and the black sections of the cities', James insisted. 'It gave them an independent basis for life ... and even if they were sold down the river they would find themselves on new plantations. Here, people who shared a common destiny would help them find a life in the new environment.'[35] James has found the history of community in the Caribbean, challenging the notion of permanent fragmentation and drift caused by the institution of slavery and the colonial economy.

But he has only begun the process of giving back to the people what was theirs.

> I want to put it as sharply as possible. The slaves ran the plantations; those tremendous plantations, the great source of wealth of so many English aristocrats and merchants, the merchant princes who cut such a figure in English society (and French too, but we are speaking of English society). Those plantations were run by slaves.[36]

And for this reason, nationalism after independence means trusting the people who have always run the Caribbean economies with the means of production.

> The first point I believe a West Indian political grouping has to take care of in the West Indies is the transfer of the land from the large landowners to a peasant population – a peasant population such as exists in Denmark and Holland, of a highly developed cultural and scientific outlook.[37]

James has his eye not only on the historian, both metropolitan and local, but on contemporary politicians who refuse to trust the West Indian peasant. And James goes further, discovering account after account by Europeans of the skills and values of the slave labourers, their absolute mastery and indispensability. He concludes that they made not only the plantation economy, but capitalism, possible in the Caribbean. The skills and know-how of the slaves, their remarkable abilities to adapt to climate, language and technology, meant that the slaves themselves were the great assets of the plantation economy. In short, James reverses the master–slave relationship, using not literature but historical fact, or at least historical sources, revealing that the slaves were in fact masters of the economy. Armed with this knowledge, we should view neither the San Domingo revolution nor the Grenadian revolution with surprise or scepticism.

This reversal of the master–slave relationship, and this revelation of the cultural and technological completeness of the Caribbean masses, have dangerous consequences for official nationalism in the Caribbean, as James intended them to have. It is a call for democratic nationalism, not a transfer of power and flags. James has as his target what John Sender and Sheila Smith have identified in post-colonial Africa, noting that

> the failure to identify the forces which really exist and are operative, in particular the denial of the existence of a working class, and the absence of an analysis of rural class structures, has resulted in the ideological dominance of a classless nationalism, albeit expressed in the language of socialism.[38]

James wants no part of this classless nationalism, either in Africa or in the Caribbean. His nationalist project seeks to recognize the technical potential of the working class in the Caribbean, and as early as 1962, in his devastating essay on the West Indian middle class, he already saw the perversion of classless nationalism.

> When you try to tell the middle classes of today – why not place responsibility for the economy on the people? – their reply is the same as that of the old slave owners: You will ruin the economy, and further what can you expect from people like these? The ordinary people of the West Indies who have borne the burden for centuries are very tired of it. They do not want to substitute new masters for old.[39]

James was walking a thin line in these lectures. He wanted to give the Caribbean people the tremendous achievements that were theirs; he wanted them to know the wickedness of colonialism and the genius of their response. But he also worried about this knowledge falling into the wrong hands, being used by a cynical middle class in a toothless nationalist manipulation of the masses.

The Artist as Product of the People

James's revolutionary strategy therefore tried to bind race and class in a popular nationalism, taking from both what was necessary but also using each to keep the other in check. Most of his talks, and his autobiographical work from early in this period, *Beyond a Boundary*, maintain a keen awareness of class while insisting on the tremendous achievements of Caribbean individuals, but individuals who have risen from a sea of popular imagination and ability. He challenged, throughout the 1960s and the 1970s, national leaders and intellectual elites who fell back into classless nationalism, whether in Ghana or Trinidad, Chile or Guyana. His commitment to the genius of the descendants of slaves even brought him into conflict with so-called socialist experiments in the Caribbean, and their intellectual support systems. James admired Michael Manley's conviction in Jamaica, but his belief in the technological and managerial capabilities of the working Caribbean men and women would seem to question the dependency theories of the New World Group of economists who influenced Manley. And his emphasis on local class structures would surely shift some of the blame from multinationals to local elites of all colours.[40] And yet, James had kind words for Manley's effort. He was a product of the Caribbean.

James was particularly careful to guard against an elitist chauvinism or filiopiety in the frequent references to cultural and literary figures in his lectures and papers. Two of his best and earliest available talks, 'The Artist in the Caribbean' (1959) and 'The Mighty Sparrow' (1961), stressed the vital resource of popular imagination in the careers of great Caribbean men and women. And he placed as much faith in the calypso as in the traditional poem. James has less to say about carnival. But other intellectual heirs to James have taken up the call to cultural nationalism by privileging the popular arts, including carnival. Edward Brathwaite, an important founding figure of the Caribbean Artists Movement in London, and then of the influential Carifesta arts celebration in the Caribbean, noted that, 'this kind of cultural awareness/possibility: multi-ethnic, multi-cultural requires a model more flexible than priest or politician, philosopher or the schools can cater for.'[41] More recently, Rex Nettleford has renewed his tireless call for an end to the idea of cultural dependency and inferiority. In his article 'The Caribbean: The Cultural Imperative and the Fight against Folksy Exoticist Tastes', Nettleford echoes these independence-era lectures that James gave in the Caribbean. He lists the numerous great artists produced throughout the island, and the list has stretched since James first made it. He numbers the popular festivals, dialects, dances, religions and sports among the strengths of national culture. He also cautions that

> the nation-builders – the politicians rather than the elitist planning bureaucrats – have been wise to pay such native 'outpourings' from the Caribbean people the attention they have since received in response to the signals from the mass of the population who have always had something to say about their own destiny.[42]

James would have been pleased with that 'always.'

The Nation as Product of the People

It should be clear by now, to use a Jamesian rhetorical phrase, that James used history to level nationalism. (In a similar vein, one is aware of James's lifelong struggle to reclaim Lenin as a great leveller and true egalitarian facing both the administrative hierarchies of Trotsky and the productive hierarchies of Stalin.) Highlighting the ordinary genius of the slave, and linking great Caribbean figures to the social and cultural ferment from which they sprang, he gave back that interior, egalitarian history, that history from the bottom up, that was missing from Caribbean state nationalism. His cricket writing is a fitting place to end this look at his nationalist project. For James, the entire Caribbean, has already, intact, a people and a history. He would not have agreed with the position put forward by Brackette Williams in the article 'A Class Act: Anthropology and the Race to Nation Across Ethnic Terrain'. Williams states the classic case of a plural society held in check by an ethnically distinct minority elite, when he states that

> to clarify both the material and ideological impact of the race/class/ nation conflation on political relations among members of the same objective class, we must recognize that for those outside this conflation its construction results in a national process aimed at homogenizing

heterogeneity fashioned around assimilating elements of heterogeneity through appropriations that devalue and deny their link to marginalized others' contributions to the patrimony (be these immigrant groups or home-grown minorities), thereby establishing what Gramsci refers to as a transformist hegemony.[43]

James would perhaps have struck a note of optimistic defiance in the face of this determinist analysis. He would have said that there is a fully imagined nation, beneath the putative nation Brackette Williams is studying, made of more than residual cultures, in Raymond Williams's phrase, or informal organizations, to use Abner Cohen's phrase. His cricket writing indicates that this imagined nation exists in the habitus of the Caribbean people, but also in the creativity that makes and remakes habitable texts of identity, that breaks and rebuilds that habitus.

'What I want to challenge', states James, in the manner that he would often begin a lecture on history to a trade union, 'is the belief invariably expressed about his innings that [Learie] Constantine brought to this Test the carefree and impudent manner in which he played Saturday afternoon league cricket.... There was no air of gaiety or impudence in the innings that he played or in thousands that he scored. There were times when he would amaze spectators by the audacity, even the daring of his strokes but it was all very seriously and systematically done.'[44] What James is challenging is a crypto-racist description of Trinidad's greatest cricketer as a carefree colonial. But it is what he substitutes – or, more importantly, quotes Constantine as substituting – for this misreading of the interior history of the Caribbean man that crystallizes the Jamesian nationalist project and rejects the static models of plural competition (the academic equivalent of official nationalism in post-colonial politics) in the nation-space. James notes that Constantine wrote frequently and eloquently on the game, among other topics, and quotes:

> Conditions are such in the West Indies that we shall never be able to play cricket in the style that it is played by so many Englishmen and not a few Australians, and it is my firm belief that we can learn the atmosphere of Test cricket, get together as a side in order to pull our full weight and yet as a side preserve that naturalness and ease which distinguish our game.[45]

Here is Constantine, attributing his genius to a common cultural style of his people, recognizing and naming that style for himself, proving again the soundness of the Jamesian nationalist project.

Notes

1. C.L.R. James, 'George Padmore: Black Marxist Revolutionary – A Memoir', in *At the Rendezvous of Victory*, London: Allison & Busby, 1984, p. 263.

2. C.L.R. James, *The Black Jacobins*, New York: Vantage Books, 1963.

3. C.L.R. James, 'The Old World and the New', in *At The Rendezvous of Victory*, p. 211.

4. C.L.R. James, *Beyond a Boundary*, New York: Pantheon, 1983.

5. For a kind of manifesto of the work of the Subaltern Studies group, see Ranajit Guha, 'On Some Aspects of the Historiography of Colonial India', in *Subaltern Studies I*, Oxford: Oxford University Press, 1982, pp. 1–7.

6. Paul Buhle, *C.L.R. James: The Artist as Revolutionary*, London: Verso, 1988, pp. 15–23.

7. C.L.R. James, 'Discovering Literature in Trinidad: The 1930s', in *Spheres of Existence*, London: Allison & Busby, 1980, p. 239.

8. Anna Grimshaw, 'Popular Democracy and the Creative Imagination: The Writings of C.L.R. James, 1950–1963', *Third Text*, no. 10, Spring 1990, p. 22.

9. Ivar Oxaal, *Black Intellectuals and the Dilemmas of Race and Class in Trinidad*, Cambridge, Mass.: Schenkman,1982.

10. Ron Ramdin, *From Chattel Slave to Wage Earner: A History of Trade Unionism in Trinidad and Tobago*, London: Martin Brian and O'Keefe, 1982, p. 252.

11. C.L.R. James, Introduction to Ramdin, *From Chattel Slave to Wage Earner*, p. 14.

12. Richard Handler, *Nationalism and the Politics of Culture in Quebec*, Madison: University of Wisconsin Press, 1988, p. 26.

13. Mike Phillips, 'The Caribbean Mind' (interview), *Time Out*, 11–17 July 1990, p. 15.

14. C.L.R. James, *80th Birthday Lectures*, London: Race Today Publications, 1984, p. 19.

15. C.L.R. James, *Minty Alley* (1936) and *The Life of Captain Cipriani*, (1932), published as *The Case for West Indian Self-Government*, London: Hogarth, 1933.

16. Arnold Rampersad, 'V.S. Naipaul', *Raritan*, vol. 10, no. 1, 1990.

17. C.L.R. James, 'The Mighty Sparrow', in *The Future in the Present*,

London: Allison & Busby, 1977, p. 201.

18. C.L.R. James, 'The Artist in the Caribbean', in ibid., p. 190.

19. C.L.R. James, 'On Wilson Harris', in *Spheres of Existence*, p. 172.

20. Ibid., p. 171

21. Ibid., p. 172.

22. An excellent reference and bibliographical source about early Trinidadian writing is Reinhold Sander, *The Trinidad Awakening*, New York: Greenwood Press, 1988. However, the tension of ethnicization and creolization among the Portuguese Trinidadians is more evident in books like Charles Reis's amateur history of the Portuguese clubs of Port of Spain, *Associacao Portugueza Primeiro de Dezembro*, Port of Spain, Trinidad: Charles Reis, 1945. The minutes of the meetings are often dominated by tension between true Madeirans of the older generation together with newly arrived relatives and creolized Portuguese who 'mixed with Creole women' and want to use the club to throw fêtes.

23. The best single study of Caribbean fiction and society is J. Michael Dash, *Literature and Ideology in Haiti, 1915–1961*, Brunswick, N. J.: Barnes & Noble, 1981; but see also Fred Case, *The Crisis of Identity: Studies in the Guadeloupean and Martiniquan Novel*, Sherbrooke, Quebec: Naaman, 1985.

24. Aime Cesaire, *Return to My Native Land*, Paris: Presence Africaine, 1968.

25. C.L.R. James, 'Towards the Seventh: The Pan-African Congress', in *At the Rendezvous of Victory*, p. 242.

26. Ernesto Laclau and Chantal Mouffe, *Hegemony and Socialist Strategy*, London: Verso, 1985, pp. 176–93.

27. See two Jamesian scholars, Anna Grimshaw and Keith Hart, writing on this prescience in 'Clairvoyance from Stateside', *Times Higher Educational Supplement*, 24 March 1989, p. 17, which accompanied an unpublished excerpt from a C.L.R. James manuscript on the United States.

28. C.L.R. James, 'The Making of the Caribbean People', in *Spheres of Existence*, p. 188.

29. Ibid., p. 189.

30. Ibid., p. 190.

31. Eric Williams, *Capitalism and Slavery*, London: Andre Deutsch, 1964; and *From Columbus to Castro*, London: Andre Deutsch, 1970.

32. James, 'The Making of the Caribbean People', p. 174.

33. James, 'The Atlantic Slave Trade', in *The Future in the Present*, p. 243.

34. It is worth noting, at the risk of repetition, that James's contention that African slaves did have a world-view and a culture despite the hardships of enslavement predates the important work on slave culture in the United States by scholars like Eugene Genovese and Leon Litwack. See, for instance, E. Genovese, *Roll, Jordan, Roll: The World the Slaves Made*, New York: Pantheon Books, 1974; and L. Litwack, *Been in the Storm So Long: The*

Aftermath of Slavery, New York: Knopf, 1979.

35. James, 'The Atlantic Slave Trade', p. 244.

36. Ibid., p. 181.

37. C.L.R. James, 'A National Purpose for Caribbean Peoples', in *At the Rendezvous of Victory*, p. 152.

38. John Sender and Sheila Smith, *The Development of Capitalism in Africa*, London: Methuen, 1986, p. 130.

39. C.L.R. James, 'The West Indian Middle Class', in *Spheres of Existence*, p. 140.

40. Anthony Payne, 'Dependency Theory and the Commonwealth Caribbean', in A. Payne and P. Sutton, eds., *Dependency Under Challenge*, Manchester: Manchester University Press, 1984, pp. 2–10.

41. Edward Brathwaite, 'Doing It Our Way', *New Community*, vol. 3, no. 4, p. 346.

42. Rex Nettleford, 'The Caribbean: The Cultural Imperative and the Fight against Folksy Exoticist Tastes', *Caribbean Affairs*, vol. 2, no. 2, 1990, p. 28.

43. Brackette F. Williams, 'A Class Act: Anthropology and the Race to Nation Across Ethnic Terrain', *Annual Review of Anthropology*, no. 18, 1989, p. 435.

44. C.L.R. James, 'Learie Constantine', in *Spheres of Existence*, p. 254.

45. Ibid.

CONCLUSION

Mud Mas: Playing Identity

In a section on the history of the non-Latin Caribbean, *The Cambridge Encyclopedia of Latin America and the Caribbean* contains this entry: 'Caribbean peoples faced problems of identity, which related chiefly to colour and ethnicity, a sense of place and nationality.' The entry continues solemnly: 'the West Indian's sense of uncertain racial identity is compounded by an ambivalence about his belonging to the West Indies.'[1] Samuel Selvon finds both advantage and disadvantage in this state of being. 'I think the mixture of identities helps give the Trinidadian a wider outlook on life and the world,' Selvon once said, 'which is very useful, except that, perhaps, suddenly he turns around and says, it's all well and good to appreciate what the world is like and what people are like but who the hell am I, and where do I fit into it, have I got roots, am I an Indian, am I a Negro, what am I, what is a Trinidadian?'[2]

Or, as C.L.R. James put it, 'so there we are, all tangled up together, the old barriers breaking down and the new ones not yet established, a time of transition, always and inescapably turbulent.'[3] But James is not bothered by this turbulence. It is part of building what he called 'a national community'. In a personal letter he tells a story from his youth in Port of Spain, about his landlady. Driven by her brother's drinking, gambling and pimping, she rises finally to speak to him. James describes the uncharacteristic speech to the brother as pure poetry. He recalls that he, a literate young man, was wonderstruck by her eloquence. And he notes that this single outburst of poetry from his landlady is the very same poetry as that sustained day after day by the great poets of civilization.[4] If James could perceive the poetry of great civilizations in his landlady, it is little wonder he kept his faith in a national community for Trinidad and the Caribbean.

I have kept a similar faith in this national community throughout this study, and the more riotous with identity the community becomes in the imagination of its people, the more wondrous it becomes to me. I have called this conclusion 'mud mas'. Mud mas is played on jouvert morning, really the middle of the night before Carnival Monday. The carnival celebrants march the street covered in mud, oil and only a few clothes, and carrying signs mocking politics or recalling mythological figures of the Carnival. Covered in mud and oil, who is who, from what class, race and religion, nobody can guess. Even the gusto of the gyrations of the celebrants cannot hint at class or race. The celebrants are quick to point out that sometimes the most raucous dancers come from money up on the hill. Among the play of metaphors I have picked up and discarded wandering through the imaginations of the Trinidadian nation, the image of the mud mas stays with me as the most enduring.

The writers considered in this book pick up, discard and return to their share of metaphors and images of the nation. Earl Lovelace and Michael Anthony appear to search for truly habitable images of their nation, even if their search is disruptive of the more dogmatic political nationalism they are asked to serve. Valerie Belgrave is perhaps the most earnest in searching out metaphors for the history of her nation. But she turns up more questions about gender and skin colour than she finds habitable texts of identity, especially for Trinidadian women. The burden is on scholars to pick up the contradictions she accidentally unearths. Elsewhere, Vera Kutzinski in *Sugar's Secrets: Race and the Erotics of Cuban Nationalism* has made the effort to excavate these earthworks in that nation. Trinidad and the Eastern Caribbean are without a good sociological study of images of women in the arts and culture.

Willi Chen comes closest in many ways to liberating the nation of Trinidad. We also gain an insight into the likely direction of future research when we ask why it is that he comes closer than other writers. He is not only a short-story writer, but also a playwright, mas-maker, visual artist, and part of an informal collective of Port of Spain artists. This is surely the direction for future studies in both culture and nationalism in Trinidad. The lively arts, as they were once called and could certainly be called again in the Caribbean, contain much that is new and vibrant in the region. Dance, mas-making, theatre, calypso, rapso spoken poetry – these are vastly under-studied and immensely rich and cross-cutting expressive forms in the Caribbean.

Aside the from the lively arts, the other area of study most desperately in need of attention is the culture of the Caribbean diasporas. The enthusiastic reviews of Paul Gilroy's most recent book, *The Black Atlantic*, are testament to the dearth of good scholarship in this area.[5] Samuel Selvon – whose recent death diminished Caribbean literature greatly – and Neil Bissoondath imagined a people who carried a nation with them. But the nation they carried forward and the nation they brought back are two different nations. The Trinidadian in Toronto who returns each February to play mas in his favourite band leaves a Toronto she has changed forever, and returns to a Trinidad she changes with every visit. Beyond even the sociological study of the culture of the diasporas is the need to insist on the diasporas as viable units of study in development economics and political sociology. Scholars of the Caribbean can follow labour and migration scholars into the diasporas, especially scholars like Robin Cohen, whose work in *The New Helots* could be developed in the direction of understanding how people from the Caribbean act and react in New York politics or in the music business in Toronto and London.

Of all the writers in this book, Naipaul offers the most direct challenge to Cultural Studies itself. As I have tried to show in this study, he has made himself a target of those active in building projects of cultural resistance in the Third World. He has similarly turned away from traditional nationalists of the Third World and their project of the classless, anti-colonial, or anti-post-colonial, nation. I believe the complexity of his imagination has also revealed a fatal flaw in so-called post-colonial theory. As rootless and un-attached as the multinationals they claim to critique, post-colonial theorists lack the concrete local analysis necessary to praise or criticize a writer like Naipaul.

Contemporary theorists of nationalism like Hobsbawm, Gellner and Nairn could not be said to lack concrete analysis, but I believe this book has diagnosed a certain Eurocentrism in their perspective. They might reply that they are studying European nationalism. Yet the very high quality of their work on Europe makes the glaring absence of more studies of nationalism in Third World, New World nations more apparent.[6] Inevitably New World nations, especially those without indigenous populations, require a more overt imagining. I suspect that Trinidad's subversion of this more overt imagining is not unusual among nations of this type.

However the modernization, development, industrialization, are also imagined before they are realized. Tom Nairn, writing recently in the *London Review of Books* on Ireland's peace process, asked: 'if Shakespeare is yours by right, what use is Van Morrison?' Nairn concludes that Van Morrison is in fact absolutely necessary. He insists that images of ancestral voices are also images of a future, a modernizing future. He says that 'nostalgia is not only for the past, it looks for horizons yet to see, for revelations in the order of the world.' The Irish Protestants will need Van Morrison and have to let go partly of Shakespeare if a 'civic nationalism' or a 'parochial universalism' that looks to the future is to be born.[7] Nationalism as capitalist modernization and as nostalgic imagining are not separate in Nairn's analysis. They are perhaps not separate finally in Trinidad either. This study has focused on the imagination. The next must focus on the economics of nationalism in the Caribbean and its diaspora. This will be nationalism of visas, wired money, British Rail pensions, drugs, music and tourism – the modernizing nationalism.

With writers, I can perhaps go no further into nationalism in Trinidad, and no further into a sociology of culture. Ultimately this may simply be because of C.L.R. James's advice to the American writer Ntozake Shange. 'Write what you have to say,' he wrote to her, 'and maybe what you write about your day-to-day, everyday, commonplace, ordinary life will be some of the same problems that the people of the world are fighting out.'[8] As James would be the first to acknowledge, this writing might shed some light on a problem like Third World, New World nationalism, or it might not. Or, like the writers of James's Trinidad, this writing might simply spread out across the land like the mud mas celebrants on a jouvert morning.

Notes

1. *The Cambridge Encyclopedia of Latin America and the Caribbean*, edited by S. Collier, H. Blakemore, and T.E. Skidmore, Cambridge: Cambridge University Press, 1985, p. 292.

2. Peter Nazareth, 'Interview with Samuel Selvon', *World Literature Written in English*, vol. 18, no. 2, 1979, p. 427.

3. C.L.R. James, *Beyond a Boundary*, New York: Pantheon, 1983, p. 243.

4. Selwyn Cudjoe, ed., 'Selected Letters of C.L.R. James', *The C.L.R. James Journal*, vol. 3, no. 1, 1992, p. 99.

5. Paul Gilroy, *The Black Atlantic: Modernity and Double Consciousness*, Cambridge, Mass.: Harvard University Press, 1993.

6. One noteworthy exception to this is Thomas Hylland Eriksen's *Us and Them in Modern Societies: Ethnicity and Nationalism in Mauritius, Trinidad and Beyond*, Oslo: Scandinavian University Press, 1992. However, this book is better for its critique of the concept of the 'plural society' than it is for an alternative theory of the nation in Third World, New World nation-states.

7. Tom Nairn, 'On the Threshold', *London Review of Books*, vol. 17, no. 6, 23 March 1995, pp. 9–11.

8. C.L.R. James, "Three Black Women Writers', in *The C.L.R. James Reader*, edited by Anna Grimshaw, Oxford: Basil Blackwell, 1992, p. 417.

References

Adam, I., and Tiffin, H., eds., *Past the Last Post*, Hemel Hempstead: Harvester Wheatsheaf, 1991.

Ahmad, A., 'Reply to Jameson' *Social Text*, vol. 3, no. 17, 1986, pp. 3–25.

Anderson, B., *Imagined Communities: Reflections on the Origins and Spread of Nationalism*, London: Verso, 1983.

Anthony, M., *Glimpses of Trinidad and Tobago*, Port of Spain: Columbus Publishers, 1974.

——— *Green Days By the River*, London: Heinemann, 1973.

——— *Parade of Carnivals of Trinidad: 1839–1989*, Port of Spain, Trinidad: Circle Press, 1989.

Appadurai, A., 'Disjuncture and Difference in the Global Cultural Economy', *Public Culture*, vol. 2, no. 2, 1990.

Appiah, K.A., 'Is the Post- in Postmodernism the Post- in Postcolonial?' *Critical Inquiry*, vol. 17, no. 2, 1991, pp. 336–57.

Ashcroft, B., Griffiths, G., and Tiffin, H., *The Empire Writes Back*, London: Routledge, 1989.

Banton, M. *Racial and Ethnic Competition*, Cambridge: Cambridge University Press, 1983.

Barth, F., *Ethnic Groups and Boundaries: The Social Organization of Cultural Difference*, London: Allen & Unwin, 1969.

Belgrave, V., *Ti Marie*, Oxford: Heinemann, 1988.

Bentley, G.C., 'Ethnicity and Practice', *Comparative Studies in Society and History*, vol. 29, no. 1, 1987, pp. 24–55.

——— 'A Reply to Yelvington', *Comparative Studies in Society and History*, vol. 33, no. 1, 1991, pp. 169–75.

Bhabha, H.K., 'Introduction: Narrating the Nation', and 'Dissemination: Time, Narrative, and the Margins of the Modern Nation', in H.K. Bhabha, ed., *Nation and Narration*, London: Routledge, 1990, pp. 1–7 and 291–322.

Birbalsingh, F., ed., *Indenture and Exile: The Indo-Caribbean Experience*, Toronto: TSAR, 1989.
——— *Passion and Exile: Essays in Caribbean Literature*, London: Hansib, 1988.
——— 'Samuel Selvon and the West Indian Literary Renaissance', *Ariel*, vol. 8, no. 3, 1977, pp. 3–22.
Bissoondath, N., *A Casual Brutality*, Toronto: Macmillan, 1988.
——— *Digging Up the Mountains*, Toronto: Macmillan, 1985.
Boal, A., *Theatre of the Oppressed*, London: Pluto, 1979.
Bourdieu, P., *Outline of a Theory of Practice*, Cambridge: Cambridge University Press, 1977.
Bourne, J., 'Cheerleaders and Ombudsmen: The Sociology of Race Relations in Britain', *Race and Class*, vol. 21, no. 4, 1980, pp. 331–52.
Brathwaite, E., 'Carifesta: Doing It Our Way', *New Community*, vol. 3, no. 4, 1974, pp. 343–8.
Brathwaite, L., *Social Stratification in Trinidad: A Preliminary Analysis*, Kingston, Jamaica: University of the West Indies Press, 1975.
Brennan, T., 'Cosmopolitans and Celebrities', *Race and Class*, vol. 31, no. 1, 1989, pp. 1–19.
——— 'The National Longing for Form', in H.K. Bhabha, ed., *Nation and Narration*, London: Routledge, 1990, pp. 44–70.
Breton, R., ed., *Ethnic Indentity and Equality*, Toronto: University of Toronto Press, 1990.
Brereton, B., *A History of Modern Trinidad: 1783–1962*, London: Heinemann, 1981.
——— *Race Relations in Colonial Trinidad: 1870–1900*, Cambridge: Cambridge University Press, 1979.
Breuilly, J., *Nationalism and the State*, Manchester: Manchester University Press, 1982.
Brown, S., Morris, M., and Rohlehr, G., eds., *Voice Print: An Anthology of Oral and Related Poetry from the Caribbean*, Harlow: Longman, 1989.
Buhle, P., *C.L.R. James: The Artist as Revolutionary*, London: Verso, 1988.
Calvino, I., *Invisible Cities*, New York: Harcourt Brace Jovanovich, 1972.
Cambridge Encyclopedia of Latin America and the Caribbean, edited by S. Collier, H. Blakemore and T. Skidmore, Cambridge: Cambridge University Press, 1985.
Campbell, M., *The Witness and the Other World: Exotic European Travel Writing: 400–1600*, Ithaca, N.Y.: Cornell University Press, 1988.
Carby, H., 'The Quicksand of Representation', in Henry Louis Gates, ed., *Reading Black, Reading Feminist: A Critical Anthology*, New York: Meridian, 1990, pp. 76–90.
Case, F.I., *The Crisis of Identity: Studies in the Guadeloupean and Martiniquan Novel*, Sherbrooke, Quebec: Naaman, 1985.
Cashmore, E., and Troyna, B., 'Growing Up in Babylon', in Cashmore

and Troyna, eds., *Black Youth in Crisis*, London: Allen & Unwin, 1982.

Cesaire, A., *Return to My Native Land*, Paris: Presence Africaine, 1968.

Chang, V.L., 'Elements of the Mock Heroic in West Indian Fiction', in E. Smilovitz and R. Knowles, eds., *Critical Issues in West Indian Literature*, Parkersburg, Ind.: Caribbean Books, 1984.

Chatterjee, P. *Nationalist Thought and the Colonial World: A Derivative Discourse*, Tokyo: United Nations University and Zed Books, 1986.

Chen, W., *King of the Carnival*, London: Hansib Publishing, 1988.

Chin, D.S., *The Philosophy of Nation-building*, Port of Spain, Trinidad: Horsham's Printing, 1990.

Clarke, A., 'A Stranger in a Strange Land', *Globe and Mail* (Toronto), 15 August 1990, p. 30.

Clarke, C., 'Pluralism and Plural Societies: Caribbean Perspectives', in C. Clarke, D. Ley and C. Peach, *Geography and Ethnic Pluralism*, London, George Allen & Unwin, 1984, pp. 51–86.

—— ed., *Society and Politics in the Caribbean*, London, Macmillan, 1991.

Cohen, A., 'Drama and Politics in the Development of a London Carnival', *Man*, vol. 15, no. 1, 1980, pp. 65–87.

—— 'A Polyethnic London Carnival as Contested Cultural Performance' *Ethnic and Racial Studies*, vol. 5, no. 1, 1982, pp. 23–41.

Cohen, P., and Bains, H.S., eds., *Multi-Racist Britain*, London: Macmillan, 1988.

Cohen, R., *The New Helots: Migrants in the International Division of Labour*, Aldershot: Gower, 1987.

Connerton, P., *How Societies Remember*, Cambridge: Cambridge University Press, 1989.

Cross, M., 'Colonialism and Ethnicity: A Theory and Comparative Case Study', *Ethnic and Racial Studies*, vol. 1, no. 1, pp. 37–59.

—— *Urbanization and Urban Growth in the Caribbean*, Cambridge: Cambridge University Press, 1979.

Cudjoe, S., ed., *Caribbean Women Writers*, Wellesley, Mass.: Calaloux Publications, 1990.

—— *Resistance and Caribbean Literature*, Athens, Ohio: University of Ohio Press, 1980.

—— ed., 'Selected Letters of C.L.R. James', *The C.L.R. James Journal*, vol. 3, no. 1, 1992, pp. 85–104.

—— *V.S. Naipaul: A Materialist Reading*, Amherst, Mass.: University of Massachusetts Press, 1988.

Dabydeen, D., *Coolie Odyssey*, London: Hasib/Dangaroo, 1988.

Dabydeen, D., and Samaroo, B., eds., *India in the Caribbean*, London: Hansib, 1987.

Dabydeen, D., and Wilson-Tagoe, N., 'Selected Themes in West Indian Literature: An Annnotated Bibliography', *Third World Quarterly*, vol. 9, no. 3, 1987, pp. 921–60.

Dance, D.C., ed., *Fifty Caribbean Writers*, New York: Greenwood Press, 1986.

Dash, J.M., *Literature and Ideology in Haiti*, Brunswick, N.J.: Barnes & Noble, 1981.

Dathorne, O.R., *Dark Ancestors*, Baton Rouge: Louisiana State University Press, 1981.

Deleuze, G., and Guattari, F., 'Kafka: Toward a Minor Literature', *New Literary History*, vol. 16, no. 3, 1985, pp. 591–608.

Derrida, J., *Acts of Literature*, edited by D. Attridge, New York: Routledge, 1992.

Douglass, W.O., 'A Critique of Recent Trends in the Analysis of Ethnonationalism', *Ethnic and Racial Studies*, vol. 11, no. 2, 1988, pp. 192–206.

Durix, J.P., 'Review of *Critical Perspectives on Sam Selvon*', *Commonwealth*, vol. 13, no. 2, 1989, pp. 125–6.

Eriksen, T.H., 'The Cultural Contexts of Ethnic Differences', *Man*, vol. 26, no. 2, pp. 127–44.

Espinet, R., *Creation Fire: A CAFRA Anthology of Caribbean Women's Poetry*, Toronto: Sister Vision, 1990.

Fabre, M., 'Samuel Selvon' in B. King, ed., *West Indian Literature*, London: Macmillan, 1979.

Fanon, F., *The Wretched of the Earth*, Harmondsworth: Penguin, 1970.

Fardon, R., 'African Ethnogenesis: Limits to the Comparability of Ethnic Phenomenon', in L. Holy, ed., *Comparative Anthropology*, Oxford: Blackwell, 1987, pp. 140–66.

Figueroa, J., 'The Relevance of West Indian Literature', in C. Brock, *The Caribbean in Europe*, London: Frank Cass, 1986, pp. 220–30.

Firmat, G.P., *The Cuban Condition: Translation and Identity in Modern Cuban Literature*, Cambridge: Cambridge University Press, 1989.

Fischer, M., 'Ethnicity and the Postmodern Arts of Memory', in J. Clifford and G. Marcus, eds., *Writing Culture: The Poetics and Politics of Ethnography*, Berkeley: University of California Press, 1986, pp. 194–234.

Foner, N., 'The Jamaicans: Cultural and Social Change among Migrants in Britain', in J. Watson, *Between Two Cultures: Migrants and Minorities in Britain*, Oxford: Basil Blackwell, 1977, pp. 120–50.

Foucault, M., 'The Order of Discourse', in Robert Young, ed., *Untying the Text*, Boston and London: Routledge & Kegan Paul, 1981, pp. 55–68.

Froude, J.A., *The English in the West Indies*, London: Longman, Green, 1888.

Gellner, E., *Nations and Nationalism*, Oxford: Basil Blackwell, 1983.

Genovese, E., *Roll, Jordan, Roll: The World the Slaves Made*, New York: Pantheon Books, 1974.

Giddens, A., *A Contemporary Critique of Historical Materialism*, Berkeley: University of California Press, 1981.

Gilbert, S., and Gubar, S., 'Forward into the Past: The Complex Female Affiliation Complex', J. McGann, ed., *Historical Studies and Literary Criticism*, Madison, Wis: University of Wisconsin Press, 1985, pp. 240–65.

Glazier, S., *Marchin' the Pilgrims Home: Leadership and Decision-Making in an Afro-Caribbean Faith*, London: Greenwood Press, 1983.

Gomes, A., 'I am an Immigrant', in A. Salkey, ed., *Caribbean Essays*, London: Evans Brothers, 1973, pp. 3–59.

Gramsci, A., *Selections from the Prison Notebooks of Antonio Gramsci*, trans. Q. Hoare and G.N. Smith, New York: International, 1971.

Griffiths, G., and Tiffin, H., eds., *The Empire Writes Back: Theory and Practice in Post-colonial Literature*, London: Routledge, 1989.

Grimshaw, A., 'Popular Democracy and the Creative Imagination: the Writings of C.L.R. James, 1950–1963', *Third Text*, no. 10, 1990, pp. 22–30.

Grimshaw, A. and Hart, K., 'Clairvoyance from Stateside', *Times Higher Educational Supplement*, 24 March 1989, p. 17.

Gundara, J., 'Lessons from History for the Black Resistance in Britain', in J. Tierney, ed., *Race, Migration, and Schooling*, London: Holt, 1982, pp. 44–57.

Hall, S., 'Pluralism, Race, and Class in Caribbean Society', in J. Rex, ed., *Race and Class in Post-Colonial Society*, Paris: UNESCO, 1975, pp. 150–81.

Hamner, R., 'The Measure of the Yard Novel: From Mendes to Lovelace', *Commonwealth*, vol. 9, no. 1, pp. 98–106.

Handler, R., *Nationalism and the Politics of Culture in Quebec*, Madison, Wis.: University of Wisconsin Press, 1988.

Hannerz, U., *Cultural Complexity: Studies in the Social Organization of Meaning*, New York: Columbia, 1992.

Harney, R.F., '"So Great A Heritage As Ours"', *Daedalus*, vol. 117, no. 4, pp. 51–97.

Harney, S., 'Men Goh Have Respect for All O' We', *World Literature Written in English*, vol. 30, no. 2, 1990, pp. 110–19.

Harney, S., 'Ethnos and the Beat Poets', *Journal of American Studies*, vol. 25, no. 3, 1991, pp. 363–80.

Heath, J., ed., *Profiles in Canadian Literature No. 4*, Toronto: Dundurn, 1982.

Henry, P., 'Decolonization and Cultural Underdevelopment in the Commonwealth Caribbean', in P. Henry and C. Stone, eds., *The Newer Caribbean: Decolonization, Democracy, and Development*, Philadelphia: ISHI, 1983, pp. 92–120.

Hesse, J., ed., *Voices of Change: Immigrant Writers Speak Out*, Vancouver: Pulp Press, 1990.

Hill, E., *Trinidad Carnival: Mandate for a National Theatre*, Austin: University of Texas Press, 1972.

Hobsbawm, E., *Nations and Nationalism since 1780*, Cambridge: Cambridge University Press, 1990.

Hobsbawm, E., and Ranger, T., eds., *The Invention of Tradition*, Cambridge: Cambridge University Press, 1986.

Horowitz, D., *Ethnic Groups in Conflict*, Berkeley: University of California Press, 1985.

Hutcheon, L., and Richmond, M., eds., *Other Solitudes: Multicultural Fictions*, Toronto: Oxford University Press, 1990.

Itwaru, A., *Invention of Canada: Literary Texts and the Immigrant Imaginary*, Toronto: TSAR, 1990.

Jacobs, W.R., ed., *Butler Versus the King: Riots and Sedition in 1937*, Port of Spain, Trinidad: Key Caribbean, 1976.

James, C.L.R., *The Artist in the Caribbean*, Mona, Jamaica: University of the West Indies Open Lecture Series, 1965.

—— *At the Rendezvous of Victory*, London: Allison & Busby, 1984.

—— *Beyond a Boundary*, London: Pantheon, 1983.

—— *The Black Jacobins*, New York: Vantage Books, 1963.

—— *The Case for West Indian Self-Government (The Life of Captain Cipriani)*, London, Hogarth, 1933.

—— *80th Birthday Lectures*, London: Race Today Publications, 1984.

—— *The Future in the Present*, London: Allison & Busby, 1977.

—— *Minty Alley* (c. 1936), London: New Beacon Books, 1975.

—— *Spheres of Existence*, London: Allison & Busby, 1980.

James, L., ed., *The Islands In Between: Essays on West Indian Literature*, London: Oxford University Press, 1968.

Jameson, F., 'Third World Literature in the Era of Multinational Capitalism', *Social Text*, vol. 15, no. 1, 1986, pp. 65–88.

John, E., *A Time... and A Season: 8 Caribbean Plays*, St Augustine, Trinidad: University of the West Indies, 1976.

Kaufman, M., *Jamaica under Manley: Dilemmas of Socialism and Democracy*, London: Zed Books, 1985.

Khan, I., *The Jumbie Bird*, London: Longman, 1985.

King, B., *The New Literatures in English: Cultural Nationalism in a Changing World*, London: Macmillan, 1980.

Kureishi, H., 'A Casual Brutality', (book review), *New Statesman & Society*, vol. 1, 16 September 1988, p. 42.

Laclau, E., and Mouffe, C., *Hegemony and Socialist Strategy*, London: Verso, 1985.

La Guerre, J., *Calcutta to Caroni: The East Indians of Trinidad*, Port of Spain, Trinidad and New York: Longman Caribbean, 1974.

—— *The Politics of Communalism*, Port of Spain, Trinidad: Pan Caribbean Publications, 1982.

—— 'Under the Rainbow: Social Stratification in Trinidad' (unpublished paper).

Lecker, R., 'The Canonization of Canadian Literature: An Inquiry into Value', in *Critical Inquiry*, vol. 16, no. 1, 1990, pp. 1–24.

Lehmann, D., *Democracy and Development in Latin America: Economics, Politics, and Religion in the Post-war Period*, Cambridge: Polity Press, 1990.

Lewis, G., *Grenada: The Jewel Despoiled*, Baltimore: Johns Hopkins University Press, 1987.

Lieber, M., *Street Liming: Afro-American Culture in Urban Trinidad*, Boston, Mass.: G.K. Hall, 1981.

Littlewood, R., and Lipsedge, M., *Aliens and Alienists: Ethnic Minorities and Psychiatry*, London, Unwin & Hyman, 1989.

Litwack, L., *Been in the Storm So Long: The Aftermath of Slavery*, New York: Knopf, 1979.

Lloyd, D., *Nationalism and Minor Literature: James Clarence Mangan and the Emergence of Irish Cultural Nationalism*, Berkeley: University of California Press, 1987.

Lovelace, E., *The Dragon Can't Dance*, London: Longman, 1979.

Lowenthal, D., *West Indian Societies*, London: Oxford University Press, 1972.

McBurnie, B., 'West Indian Dance', in Andrew Salkey, ed., *Caribbean Essays*, London: Evans Brothers, 1973, pp. 95–9.

Mackay, C., *Harlem*, New York: E.P. Dutton, 1940.

McWatt, M., ed., *West Indian Literature in its Social Context*, Mona, Jamaica: University of the West Indies, 1985.

Magid, A., 'Imperial Administration and Urban Nationalism in British Trinidad', *Canadian Review of Studies in Nationalism*, vol. 27, no. 1–2, 1990, pp. 95–105.

Magocsi, P.R., 'The Ukrainian National Revival: A New Analytical Framework', *Canadian Review of Studies in Nationalism*, vol. 26, no. 1–2, 1989, pp. 45–62.

Mahabir, N., and Mahraj, A., 'Hosay as Theatre', *The Toronto South Asian Review*, vol. 5, no. 1, 1986, pp. 118–21.

Malley, S., 'Ca Bascule', *Afrique/Asie* (Paris), April 1991, p. 10.

Marable, M., *African and Caribbean Politics: From Kwame Nkrumah to Maurice Bishop*, London: Verso, 1987.

Marquez, R., 'Nation, Nationalism, and Ideology', in F. Knight and C. Palmer, *The Modern Caribbean*, Chapel Hill, N.C.: University of North Carolina Press, pp. 293–340.

Maughan-Brown, D., *Land, Freedom and Fiction: History and Ideology in Kenya*, London: Zed Books, 1985.

Mendes, J., *Cote Ci Cote La: A Dictionary of Trinidadian English*, Port of Spain, Trinidad: College Press, 1986.

Miller, D., 'Absolute Freedom in Trinidad', *Man*, vol. 26, no. 2, 1991, pp. 323–41.

Millete, J., *Society and Politics in Colonial Trinidad*, London: Zed Books, 1985.

Moore, S.F., 'The Production of Cultural Pluralism as a Process', *Public Culture*, vol. 1, no. 2, 1989, pp. 26–48.

Mordecai, P., and Wilson, B., eds., *Her True-True Name*, London: Heinemann, 1989.

Morris, M., ed., *Contemporary Caribbean Short Stories*, London: Faber & Faber, 1990.

———— 'Introduction', in S. Selvon, *Moses Ascending*, London: Heinemann, 1984.

Mukherjee, A., 'The Exclusions of Post-Colonial Theory and Mulk Raj Anand's *Untouchable*: A Case Study', *Ariel*, vol. 22, no. 3, pp. 44–65.

———— *Towards An Aesthetic of Opposition*, Stratford, Ontario: Williams & Wallace, 1988.

———— 'Whose Postcolonialism and Whose Postmodernism?', in *World Literature Written in English*, vol. 30, no. 2, 1990, pp. 1–9.

Mullard, C., *Race, Power, and Resistance*, London: Routledge & Kegan Paul, 1985.

Munro, I., and Sander, R., 'The Return of a West Indian Writer' (interview with Michael Anthony), *Bim*, vol. 14, no. 56, 1973, pp. 212–18.

Naipaul, V.S., 'Heavy Manners in Grenada', *Sunday Times Magazine*, 12 February 1984.

———— *The Loss of El Dorado*, London: Andre Deutsch, 1969.

———— *The Middle Passage*, New York: Macmillan, 1963.

———— *The Mimic Men*, Harmondsworth: Penguin Books, 1969.

Nairn, T., *The Break-Up of Britain*, London: New Left Books, 1977.

Nasta, S., ed., *Critical Perspectives on Sam Selvon*, Washington, DC: Three Continents Press, 1988.

———— 'Sam Selvon Interviewed', *Wasafiri*, vol. 1, no. 2, 1985, pp. 5–7.

Nazareth, P., 'Interview with Samuel Selvon', *World Literature Written in English*, vol. 18, no. 2, 1979, pp. 420–36.

Nettleford, R., 'The Caribbean: The Cultural Imperative and the Fight against Folksy Exoticist Tastes', *Caribbean Affairs*, vol. 2, no. 2, 1990, pp. 29–44.

———— 'Communicating With Ourselves: The Caribbean Artist and the Society', *Caribbean Affairs*, vol. 3, no. 2, 1990, pp. 33–42.

Nightingale, P., *Journey Through Darkness: The Writings of V.S. Naipaul*, St. Lucia, Queensland: University of Queensland Press, 1987.

Niven, A., 'My Sympathies Enlarged', *Commonwealth*, no. 2, 1976, pp. 45–62.

Owusu, K., *The Struggle for the Black Arts in Britain: What Can We Consider Better than Freedom*, London: Comedia, 1986.

Oxaal, I., *Black Intellectuals and the Dilemmas of Race and Class in Trinidad*, Cambridge, Mass.: Schenkman, 1982.

Patterson, O., *Slavery and Social Death*, Cambridge, Mass.: Harvard University Press, 1982.

Payne, A., 'Dependency Theory and the Commonwealth Caribbean', in A. Payne and P. Sutton, eds., *Dependency Under Challenge*, Manchester: Manchester University Press, 1984, pp. 2–10.

Payne A., Sutton, P., and Thorndike, T., eds., *Grenada: Revolution and Invasion*, London: Croom Helm, 1984.

Phillips, M., 'The Caribbean Mind' (interview with C.L.R. James), *Time Out*, 11–17 July 1990, p. 15.

Pryce, K., *Endless Pressure: A Study of Lifestyles in Bristol*, Bristol: Bristol Classical Press, 1986.

Pyne-Timothy, H., 'Cultural Integration and the Use of Trinidad Creole', in *Journal of Caribbean Studies*, vol. 5, no. 2, pp. 2–10.

Questal, V., 'Views of Earl Lovelace', *Caribbean Contact*, vol. 5, no. 3, 1977, pp. 15–16.

Quinones, A.D., 'The Hispanic-Caribbean National Discourse: Antonio S. Pedreira and Ramiro Guerra y Sanchez', in *Intellectuals in the Caribbean*, Centre for Caribbean Studies, University of Warwick, forthcoming.

Ramchand, K., 'An Approach to Earl Lovelace's Novel through an Examination of Indian–African Relations in *The Dragon Can't Dance*', *Wasafiri*, vol. 1, no. 2, pp. 40–54.

——— 'Physician, Heal Thyself', *Third World Quarterly*, vol. 11, no. 2, 1989, pp. 176–8.

——— 'Song of Innocence, Song of Experience: Samuel Selvon's *Lonely Londoners* as a Literary Work', *World Literature Written in English*, vol. 21, no. 3, 1982, pp. 643–54.

——— *The West Indian Novel and Its Background*, London: Faber & Faber, 1970.

Ramdin, R., *From Chattel Slave to Wage Earner: A History of Trade Unionism in Trinidad and Tobago*, London: Martin Brian and O'Keefe, 1982.

——— *The Making of the Black Working Class in Britain*, Aldershot: Gower, 1987.

Rampersad, A., 'V.S. Naipaul', *Raritan*, vol. 10, no. 1, 1990, pp. 24–47.

Ramraj, V., 'V.S. Naipaul: The Irrelevance of Nationalism', *World Literature Written in English*, vol. 23, no. 1, 1984, pp. 187–96.

Reddock, R., 'Women and Slavery in the Caribbean: A Feminist Perspective', *Latin American Perspectives*, vol. 44, no. 12, 1985, pp. 63–80.

Reis, Charles, *Associacao Portugueza Primeiro de Dezembro*, Port of Spain, Trinidad: Charles Reis, 1945.

Rex, J., and Mason, D., eds., *Theories of Race and Ethnic Relations*, Cambridge: Cambridge University Press, 1986.

——— Tomlinson, S., *Colonial Immigrants in a British City*, London: Routledge & Kegan Paul, 1979.

Reyes, A., 'Carnival: Ritual Dance of the Past and Present in Earl Lovelace's *The Dragon Can't Dance*', *World Literature Written in English*, vol. 24, no. 1, 1984, pp. 107–20.

Rohlehr, G., 'Images of Men and Women in the 1930s Calypsos', in P. Mohammed and C. Shepard, eds., *Gender in Caribbean Development*, St Augustine, Trinidad: University of the West Indies, 1988.

——— 'The Ironic Approach', in R.D. Hamner, ed., *Critical Perspectives on V.S. Naipaul*, Washington, DC: Three Continents Press, 1977.

Ryan, S., *Race and Nationalism in Trinidad and Tobago*, Toronto: University of Toronto Press, 1972.

Sander, R., 'C.L.R. James and the Haitian Revolution', *World Literature Written in English*, vol. 26, no. 2, 1986, pp. 277–90.

——— 'Interview with C.L.R. James', in R. Sander and I. Munro, eds., *Kas-Kas: Interviews with Three Caribbean Writers*, Austin: University of Texas Press, 1972.

——— *The Trinidad Awakening: West Indian Literature of the 1930s*, New York: Greenwood Press, 1988.

Searle, C., 'Naipaulacity: A Form of Cultural Imperialism', *Race and Class*, vol. 26, no. 2, 1984, pp. 45–62.

Selvon, S., *A Brighter Sun*, Harlow: Longman Caribbean, 1979.

——— *The Lonely Londoners*, Harlow: Longman Caribbean, 1985.

——— *Moses Ascending*, London: Heinemann Caribbean, 1984.

——— *Moses Migrating*, Harlow, Longman Caribbean, 1983.

——— 'Three into One Can't Go', in D. Dabydeen and B. Samaroo, eds., *India in the Caribbean*, London: Hansib, 1987, pp. 13–24.

——— *Ways of Sunlight*, Harlow: Longman, 1957.

Sender, J., and Smith, S., *The Development of Capitalism in Africa*, London: Methuen, 1986.

Seton-Watson, H., *Nations and States: An Enquiry into the Origins of Nations and the Politics of Nationalism*, Boulder, Colo.: Westview Press, 1977.

Shaw, T.A., 'To Be or Not To Be Chinese', *Ethnic Groups*, vol. 6, no. 1, 1985, pp. 155–85.

Sherlock, P.M., *West Indian Nations: A New History*, New York: St. Martin's Press, 1973.

Simmons, A., 'New Wave Immigrants', in Shiva Halli et al., eds., *Ethnic Demography* Ottawa: Carleton University Press, 1990.

Sivanandan, A., *A Different Hunger*, London: Pluto, 1982.

Slemon, S., and Tiffin, H., eds., *After Europe*, Sydney: Dangaroo Press, 1989.

Smart, I., *Central American Writers of West Indian Origin: A New Hispanic Literature*, Washington, DC: Three Continents Press, 1985.

Smith, A.D., 'The Myth of the Modern Nation and the Myth of Nations', *Ethnic and Racial Studies*, vol. 11, no. 2, 1988, pp. 1–26.

——— 'The Origins of Nations', *Ethnic and Racial Studies*, vol. 12, no. 3, 1989, pp. 341–67.

——— *State and Nation in the Third World*, Brighton: Harvester, 1983.

Smith, M.G., *Plural Society in the British West Indies*, Berkeley: University of California Press, 1965.

——— *Stratification in Grenada*, Berkeley: University of California Press, 1965.

Smith, S., 'The Ideas of Samir Amin: Theory or Tautology?', *Journal of Development Studies*, vol. 17, no. 1, 1980, pp. 1–28.

Smyer, R., 'Enchantment and Violence in the Fiction of Michael Anthony', *World Literature Written in English*, vol. 21, no. 1, pp. 148–59.

Spivak, G.C., *The Post-Colonial Critic: Interviews, Strategies, Dialogues*, New York: Routledge, 1990.

Stewart, J., 'Patronage and Control in Trinidad Carnival', in V. Turner and J. Bruner, eds., *The Anthropology of Experience*, Urbana, Ill.: University of Illinois Press, 1986, pp. 289–316.

Sutton, C., and Makiesky, S., 'Migration and West Indian Racial and Ethnic Consciousness', in H. Safa and B. DuToit, *Migration and Development*, The Hague: Mouton Publishers, 1976, pp. 150–69.

Theroux, P., *V.S. Naipaul: An Introduction to His Work*, London: Andre Deutsch, 1972.

Thieme, J., 'Searching for a Centre: the writing of V.S. Naipaul', *Third World Quarterly*, vol. 9, no. 4, pp. 1352–65.

Thomas, C., *The Poor and the Powerless: Economic Policy and Change in the Caribbean*, London: Latin American Bureau 1988.

Thomas, J.J., *Froudacity: West Indian Fables Explained*, London: New Beacon Books, 1969.

Thomas-Hope, E., 'Caribbean Diaspora, the Inheritance of Slavery: Migration from the Commonwealth Caribbean', in C. Brock, ed., *The Caribbean in Europe*, London: Frank Cass, 1986, pp. 15–35.

Thorpe, M., 'Samuel Selvon's Return', in E. Smilovitz and R. Knowles, eds., *Critical Issues in West Indian Literature*, Parkersbury, Iowa: Caribbean Books, 1984.

Thorpe, M., 'Turned Inside Out: South Asian Writing in Canada', *Ariel*, vol. 22, no. 1, pp. 33–55.

Tinker, Hugh, ed., *East Indians in the Caribbean*, Millwood, N.Y.: Kraus, 1982.

Trinidad Express (Port of Spain, Trinidad), 8–18 November 1989.

Trinidad Guardian (Port of Spain, Trinidad), 23 November 1989, and 23 March 1990.

Trinidad Sunday Express (Port of Spain, Trinidad), 5 November 1989.

Turbide, D., 'A Novelist's Stunning Debut', *Maclean's Magazine*, vol. 101, 1 October 1988, pp. 63–4.

Warner, K., *The Trinidad Calypso*, London: Heinemann, 1982.

Warner-Lewis, M., 'Rebels, Tyrants, and Saviours: Leadership and Power Relations in Lovelace's Fiction', *The Journal of West Indian Literature*, vol. 2, no. 1, 1987, pp. 76–89.

Warren, B., *Imperialism: Pioneer of Capitalism*, London: Verso, 1980.

Williams, B., 'A Class Act: Anthropology and the Race to Nation Across Ethnic Terrain', *Annual Review of Anthropology*, no. 18, 1989, pp. 401–44.

Williams, E., *Capitalism and Slavery*, London: Andre Deutsch, 1964.

——— *From Columbus to Castro*, London: Andre Deutsch, 1970.

——— *Inward Hunger: Education of a Prime Minister*, London: Andre Deutsch, 1969.

Yelvington, K., 'A Comment on Bentley', *Comparative Studies in Society and History*, vol. 33, no. 1, 1991, pp. 158–68.

——— 'Vote Dem Out', *Caribbean Review*, vol. 15, no. 4, 1987, pp. 8–12, 28–33.

Index